Westfield Memorial Library
Westfield, New Jersey

HELLBOY™
IN HELL

THE DESCENT

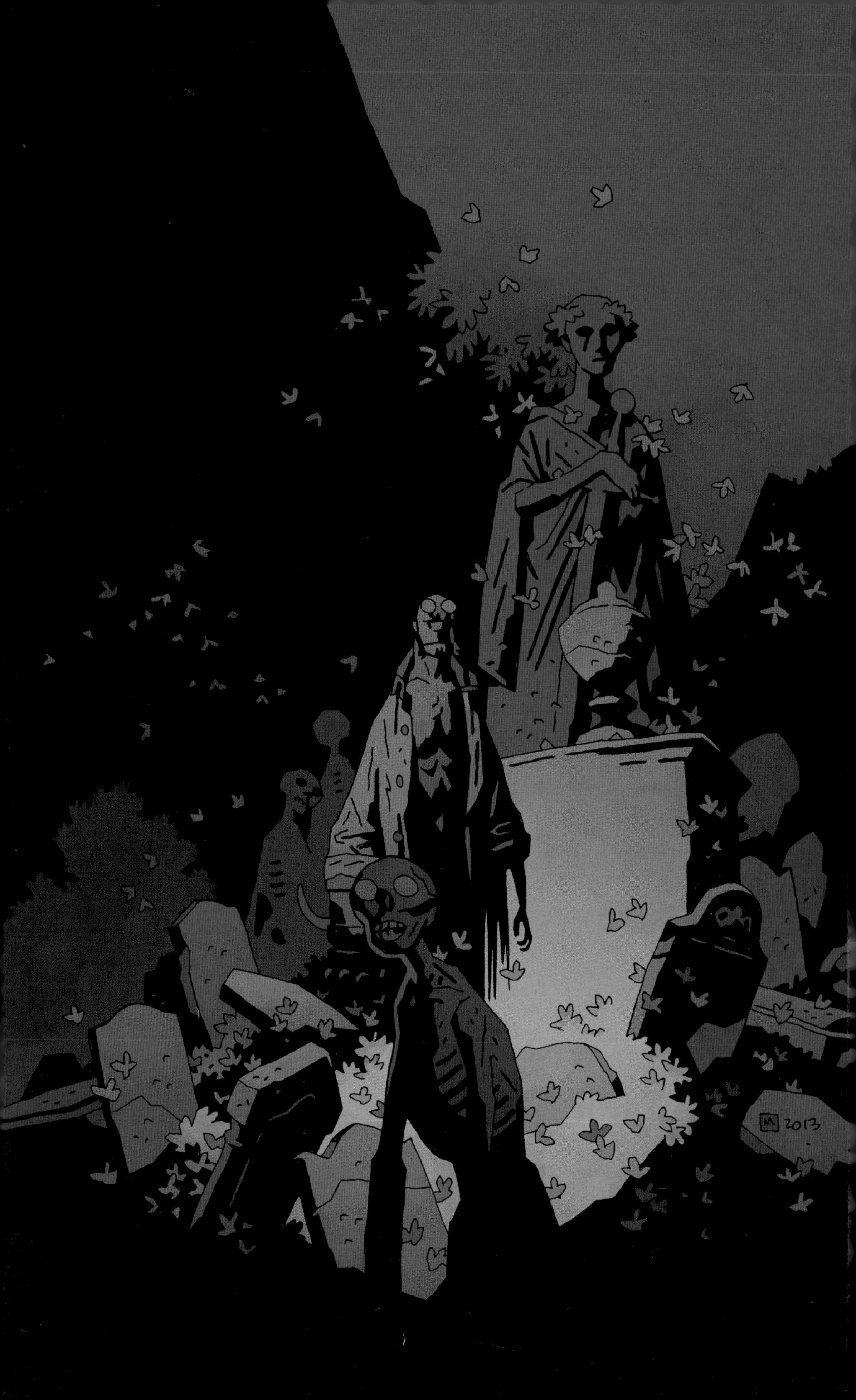
M 2013

Westfield Memorial Library
Westfield, New Jersey

HELLBOY IN HELL

THE DESCENT

Story and art by
MIKE MIGNOLA

Colored by
DAVE STEWART

Lettered by
CLEM ROBINS

✠

Cover art by
MIKE MIGNOLA & DAVE STEWART

Edited by
SCOTT ALLIE

Associate Editor
DANIEL CHABON

Collection designed by
MIKE MIGNOLA & CARY GRAZZINI

Publisher
MIKE RICHARDSON

DARK HORSE BOOKS

Neil Hankerson ✷ *Executive Vice President*
Tom Weddle ✷ *Chief Financial Officer*
Randy Stradley ✷ *Vice President of Publishing*
Michael Martens ✷ *Vice President of Book Trade Sales*
Anita Nelson ✷ *Vice President of Business Affairs*
Scott Allie ✷ *Editor in Chief*
Matt Parkinson ✷ *Vice President of Marketing*
David Scroggy ✷ *Vice President of Product Development*
Dale LaFountain ✷ *Vice President of Information Technology*
Darlene Vogel ✷ *Senior Director of Print, Design, and Production*
Ken Lizzi ✷ *General Counsel*
Davey Estrada ✷ *Editorial Director*
Chris Warner ✷ *Senior Books Editor*
Diana Schutz ✷ *Executive Editor*
Cary Grazzini ✷ *Director of Print and Development*
Lia Ribacchi ✷ *Art Director*
Cara Niece ✷ *Director of Scheduling*
Tim Wiesch ✷ *Director of International Licensing*
Mark Bernardi ✷ *Director of Digital Publishing*

Published by
Dark Horse Books
A division of Dark Horse Comics, Inc.
10956 SE Main Street
Milwaukie, OR 97222

First edition
May 2014
ISBN 978-1-61655-444-6

HELLBOY™ IN HELL VOLUME 1: THE DESCENT trademark and copyright
© 2012, 2013, 2014 Mike Mignola. Hellboy™ and all other prominently featured characters are
trademarks of Mike Mignola. Dark Horse Books® and the Dark Horse logo are registered trademarks
of Dark Horse Comics, Inc. No portion of this publication may be reproduced or transmitted, in any form
or by any means, without the express written permission of Dark Horse Comics, Inc. Names, characters,
places, and incidents featured in this publication either are the product of the author's imagination
or are used fictitiously. Any resemblance to actual persons (living or dead), events,
institutions, or locales, without satiric intent, is coincidental.

This volume collects *Hellboy in Hell* #1–#5, originally published by Dark Horse Comics.

1 3 5 7 9 10 8 6 4 2

Printed in China

HELLBOY
A Brief History

On December 23, 1944, Hellboy appeared in a fireball in the ruins of a church near East Bromwich, England. In 1952 he was granted honorary human status by a special act of the United Nations and began working as a field agent for the Bureau for Paranormal Research and Defense. He quit the B.P.R.D. in 2001 and traveled to Africa, where he was abducted by mermaids. After several years lost at sea, he returned to England, fought some giants, fell in love, and learned that he was a direct descendant of King Arthur and therefore the rightful King of all Britain.

Shortly thereafter he fought a dragon and was killed.

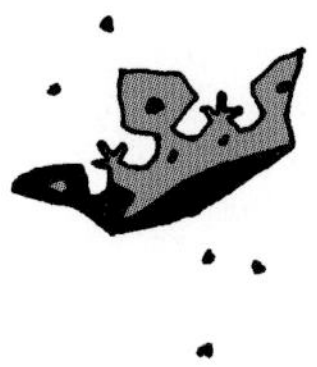

Chapter One

The Descent

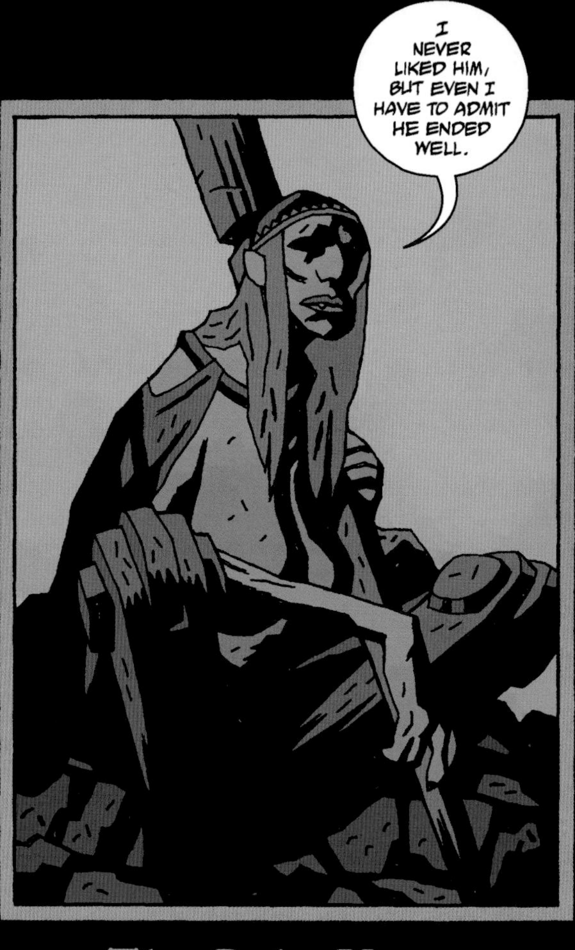
I NEVER LIKED HIM, BUT EVEN I HAVE TO ADMIT HE ENDED WELL.

The Baba Yaga

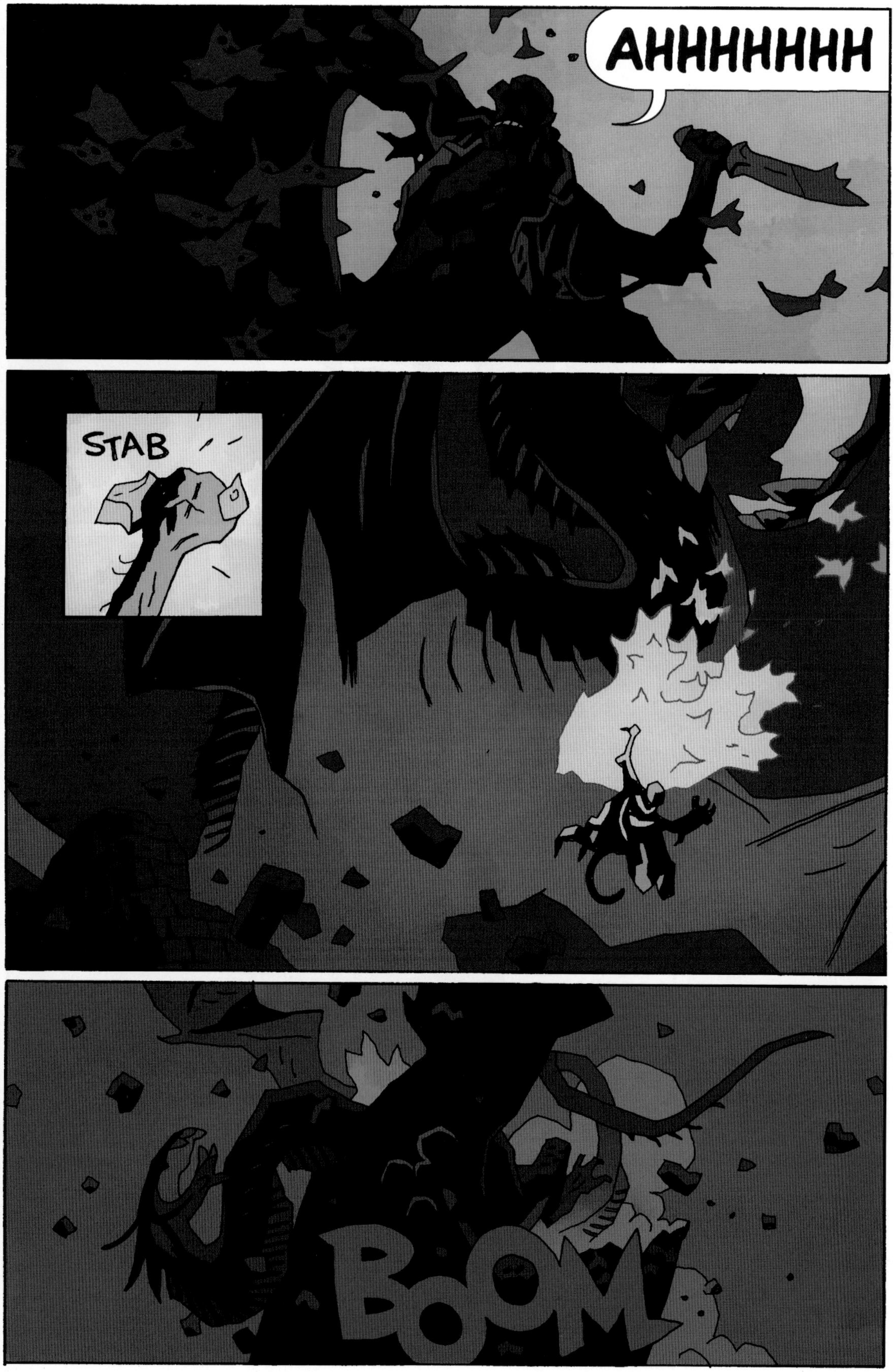
AHHHHHHH
STAB
BOOM

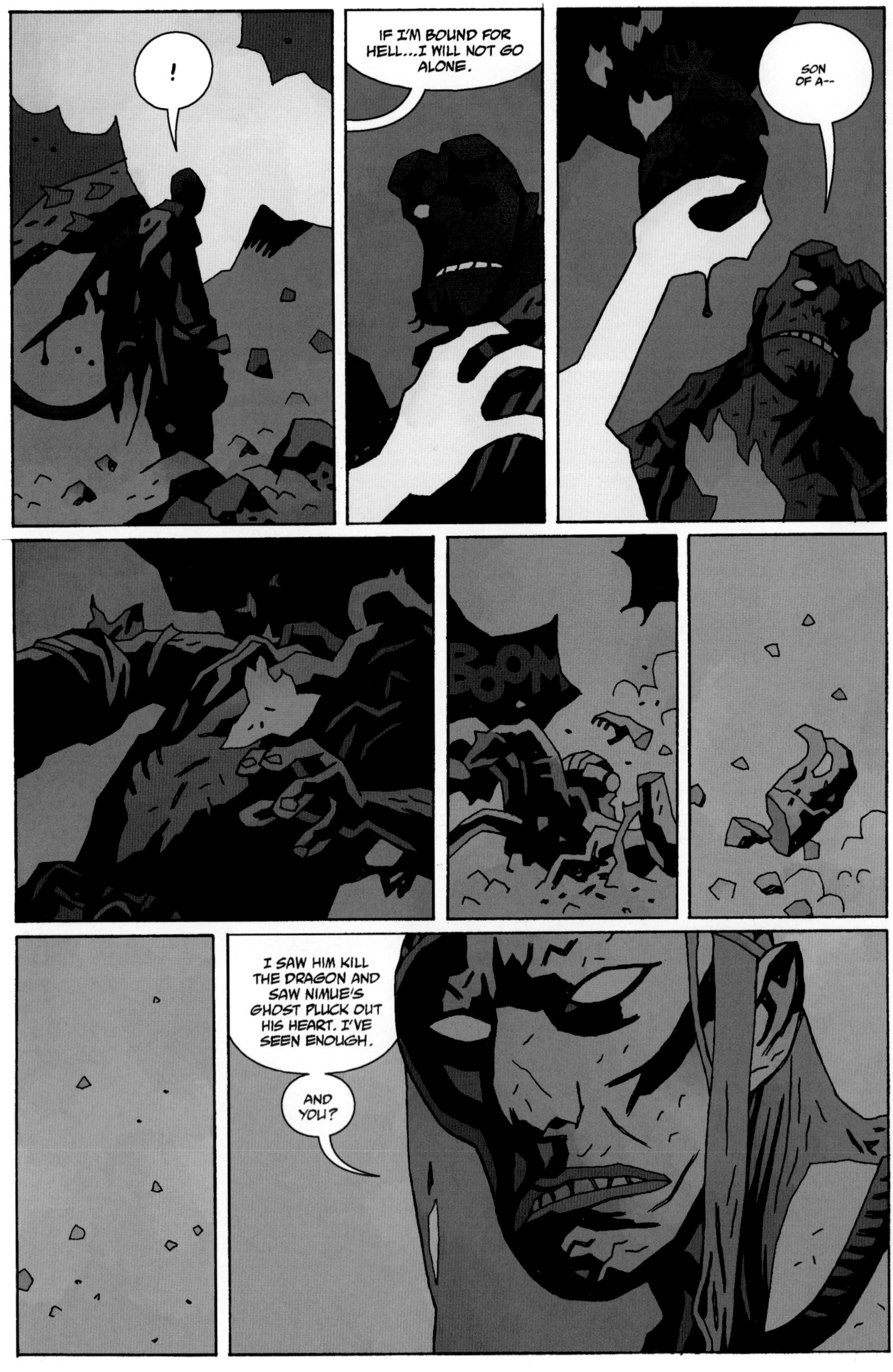
!
IF I'M BOUND FOR HELL...I WILL NOT GO ALONE.
SON OF A--
BOOM
I SAW HIM KILL THE DRAGON AND SAW NIMUE'S GHOST PLUCK OUT HIS HEART. I'VE SEEN ENOUGH.
AND YOU?

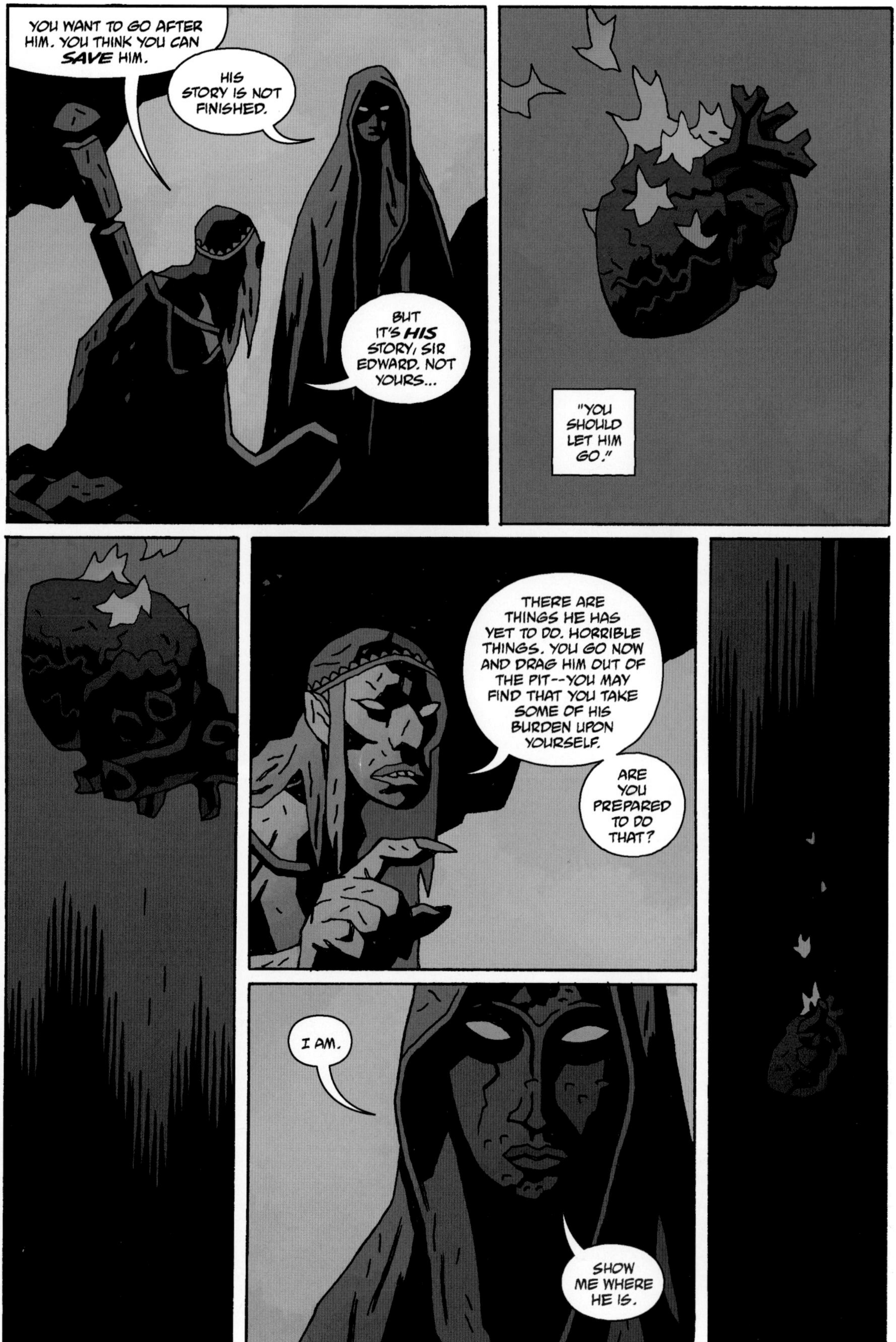

YOU WANT TO GO AFTER HIM. YOU THINK YOU CAN *SAVE* HIM.
HIS STORY IS NOT FINISHED.
BUT IT'S *HIS* STORY, SIR EDWARD. NOT YOURS...
"YOU SHOULD LET HIM GO."
THERE ARE THINGS HE HAS YET TO DO. HORRIBLE THINGS. YOU GO NOW AND DRAG HIM OUT OF THE PIT--YOU MAY FIND THAT YOU TAKE SOME OF HIS BURDEN UPON YOURSELF.
ARE YOU PREPARED TO DO THAT?
I AM.
SHOW ME WHERE HE IS.

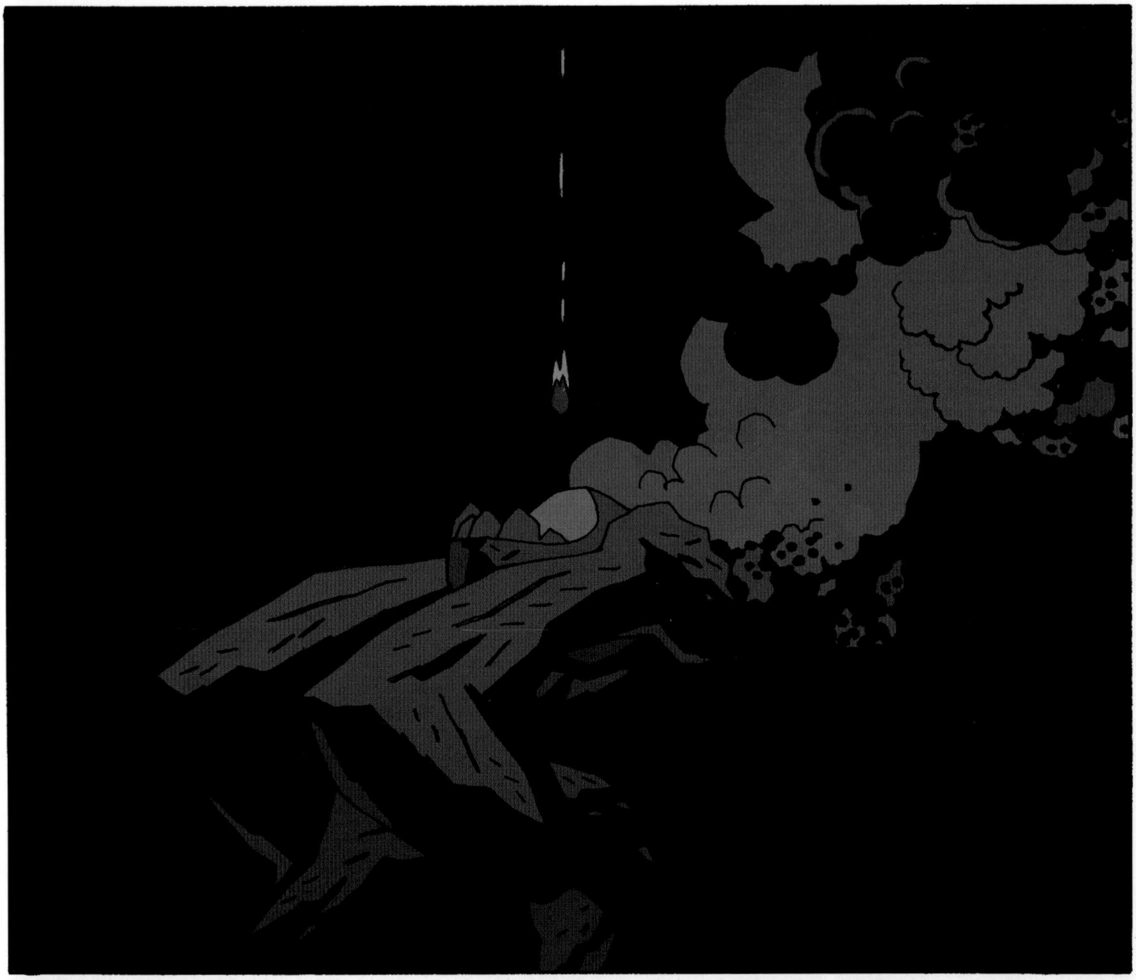

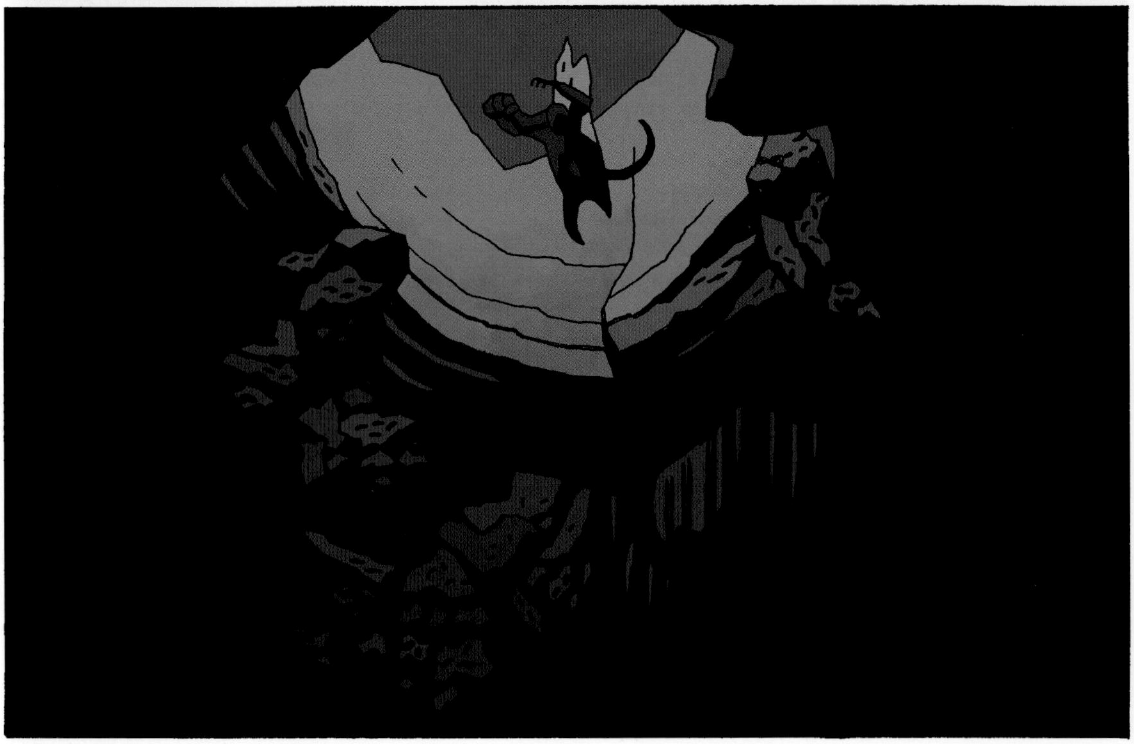

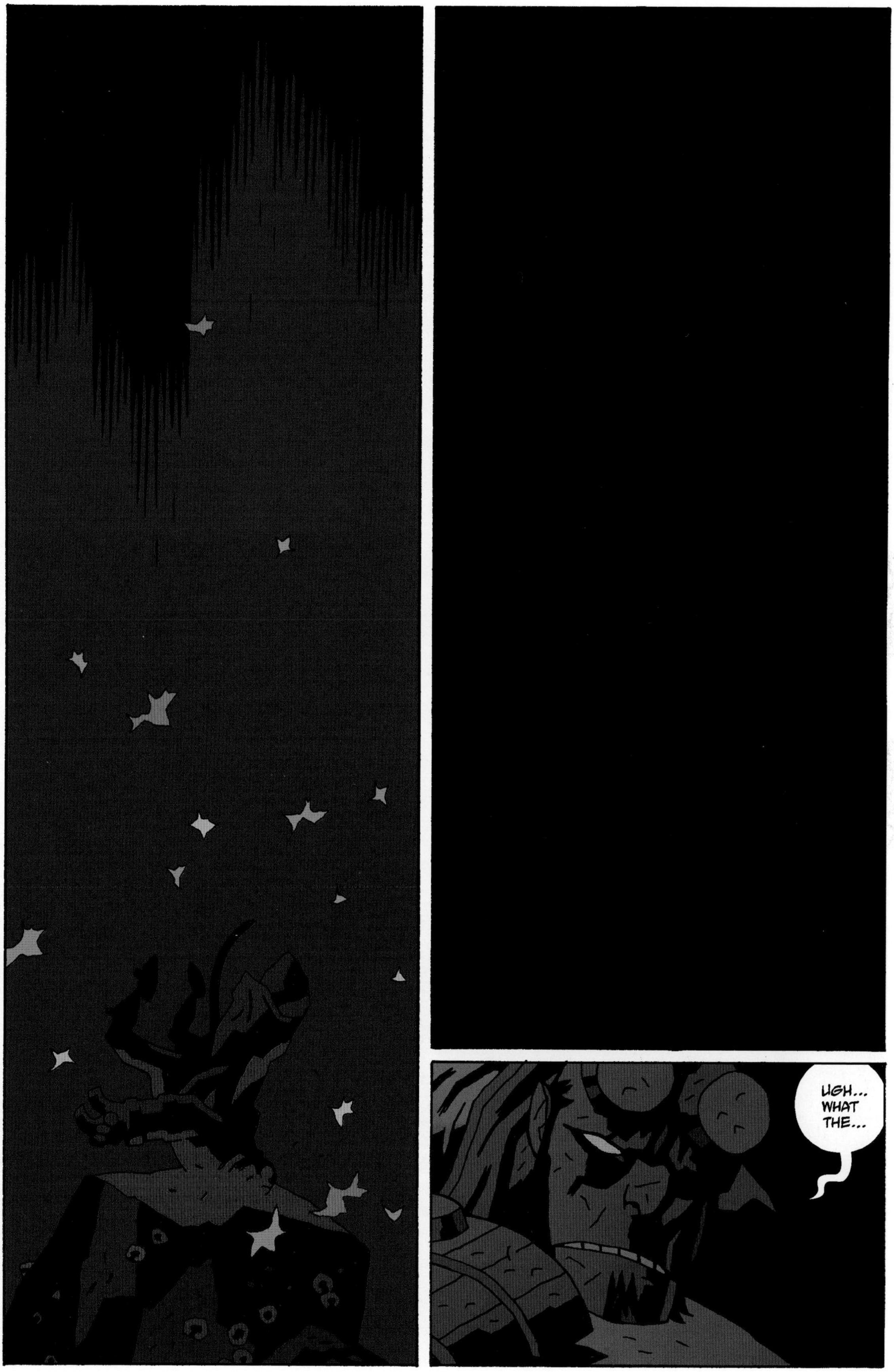
UGH... WHAT THE...

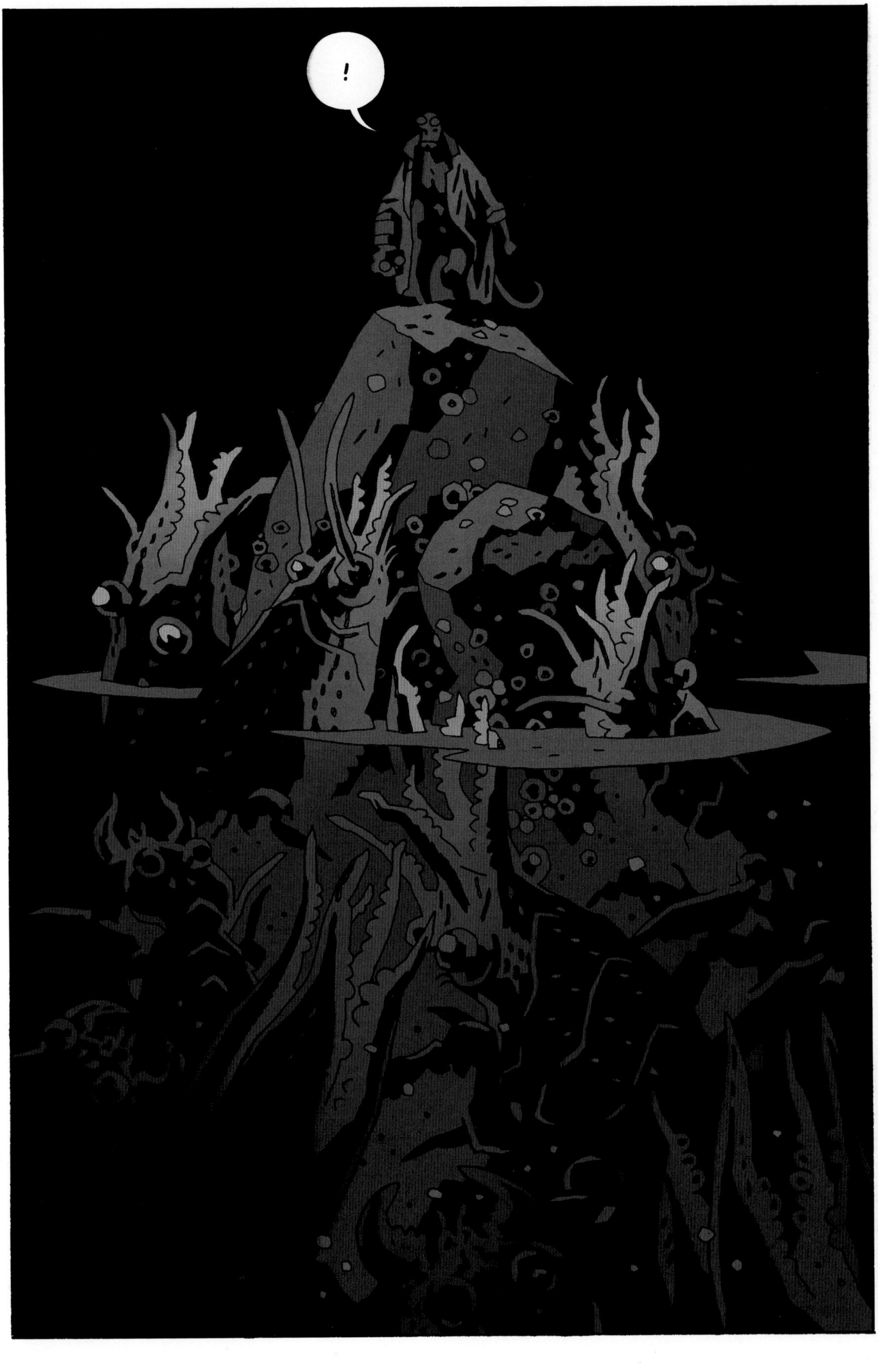
!

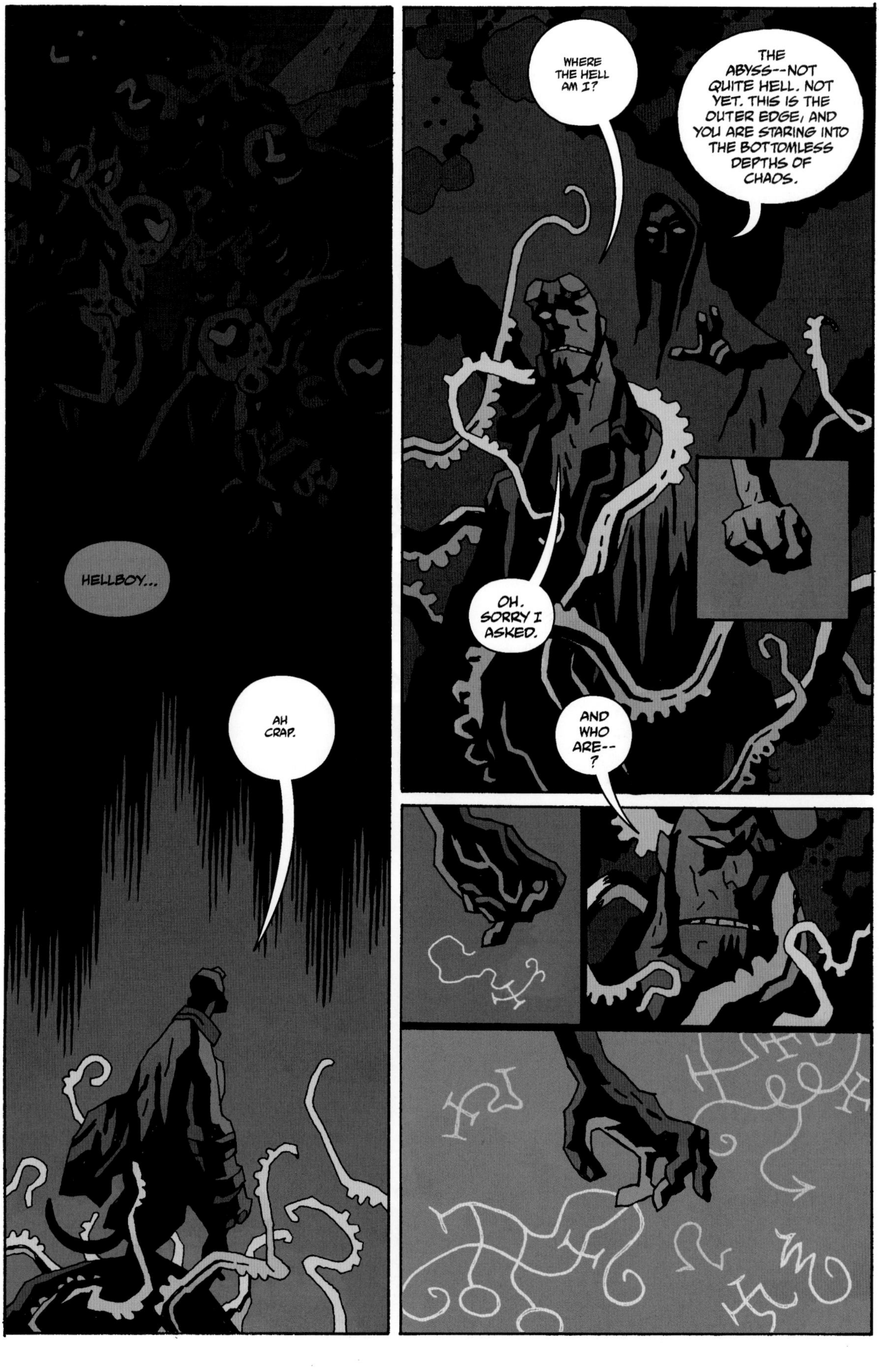
HELLBOY...
AH CRAP.
WHERE THE HELL AM I?
THE ABYSS--NOT QUITE HELL. NOT YET. THIS IS THE OUTER EDGE, AND YOU ARE STARING INTO THE BOTTOMLESS DEPTHS OF CHAOS.
OH. SORRY I ASKED.
AND WHO ARE-- ?

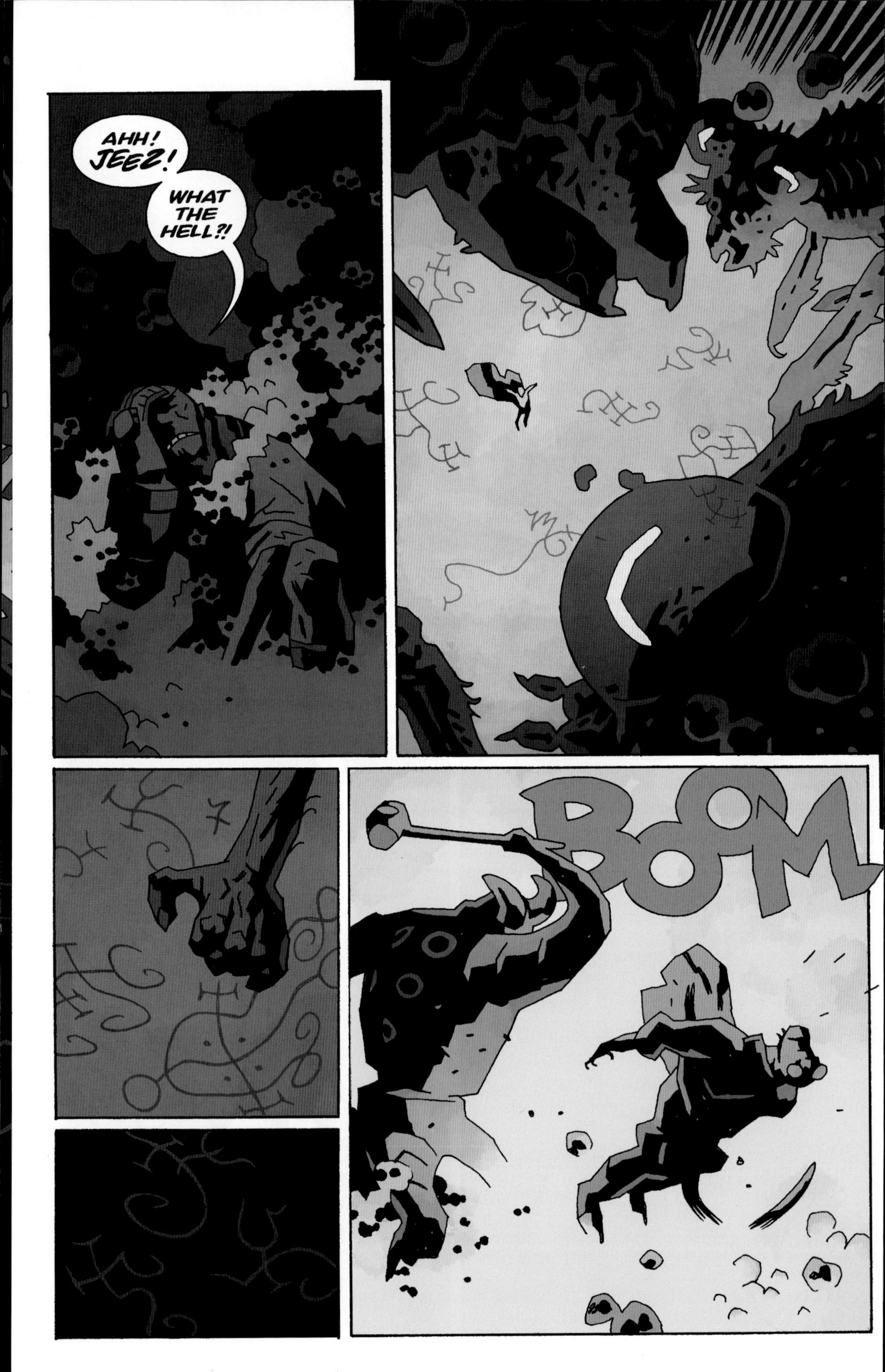
AHH! JEEZ!
WHAT THE HELL?!
BOOM

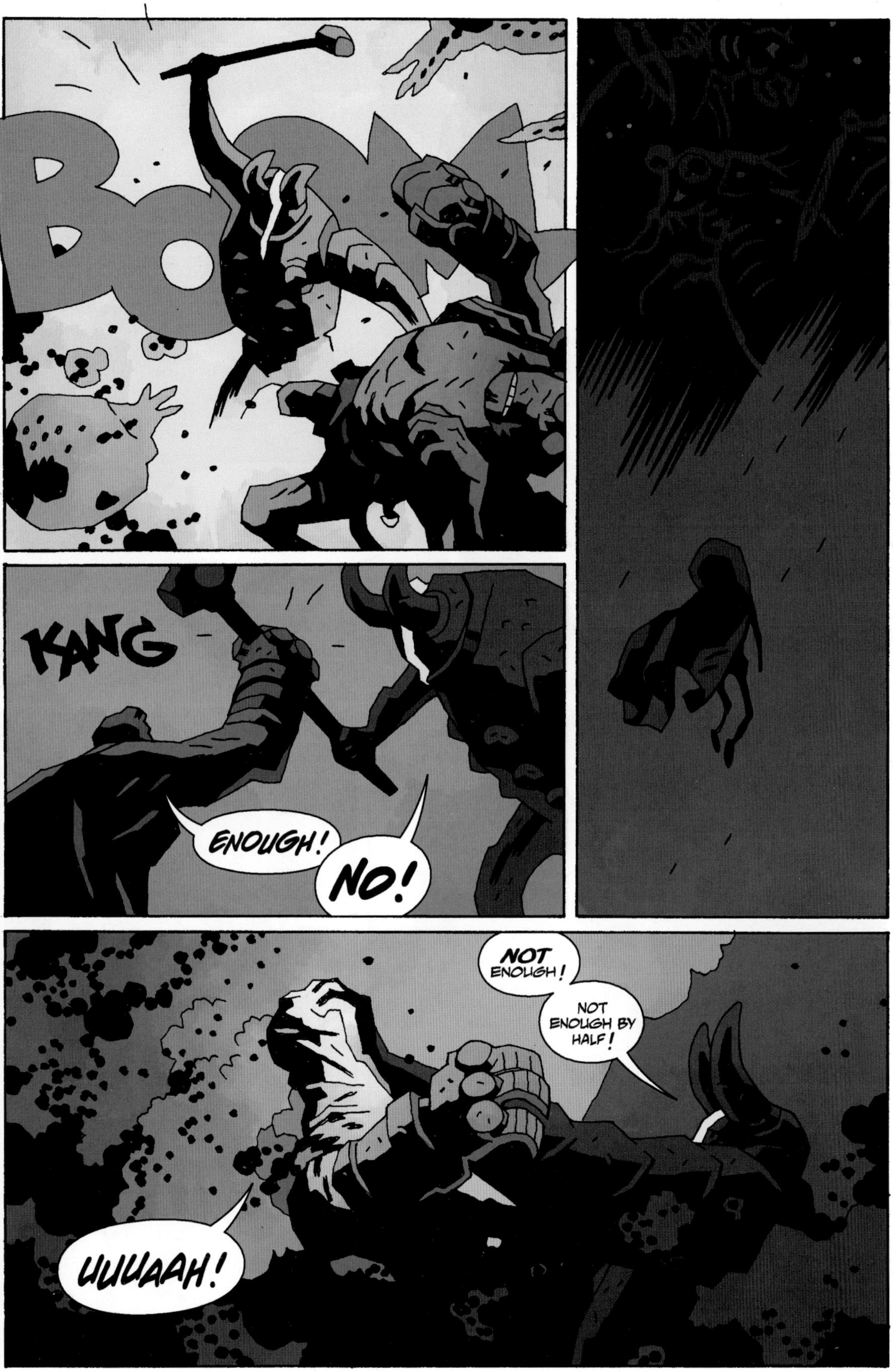
BOOM
KANG
ENOUGH!
NO!
NOT ENOUGH!
NOT ENOUGH BY HALF!
UUUAAH!

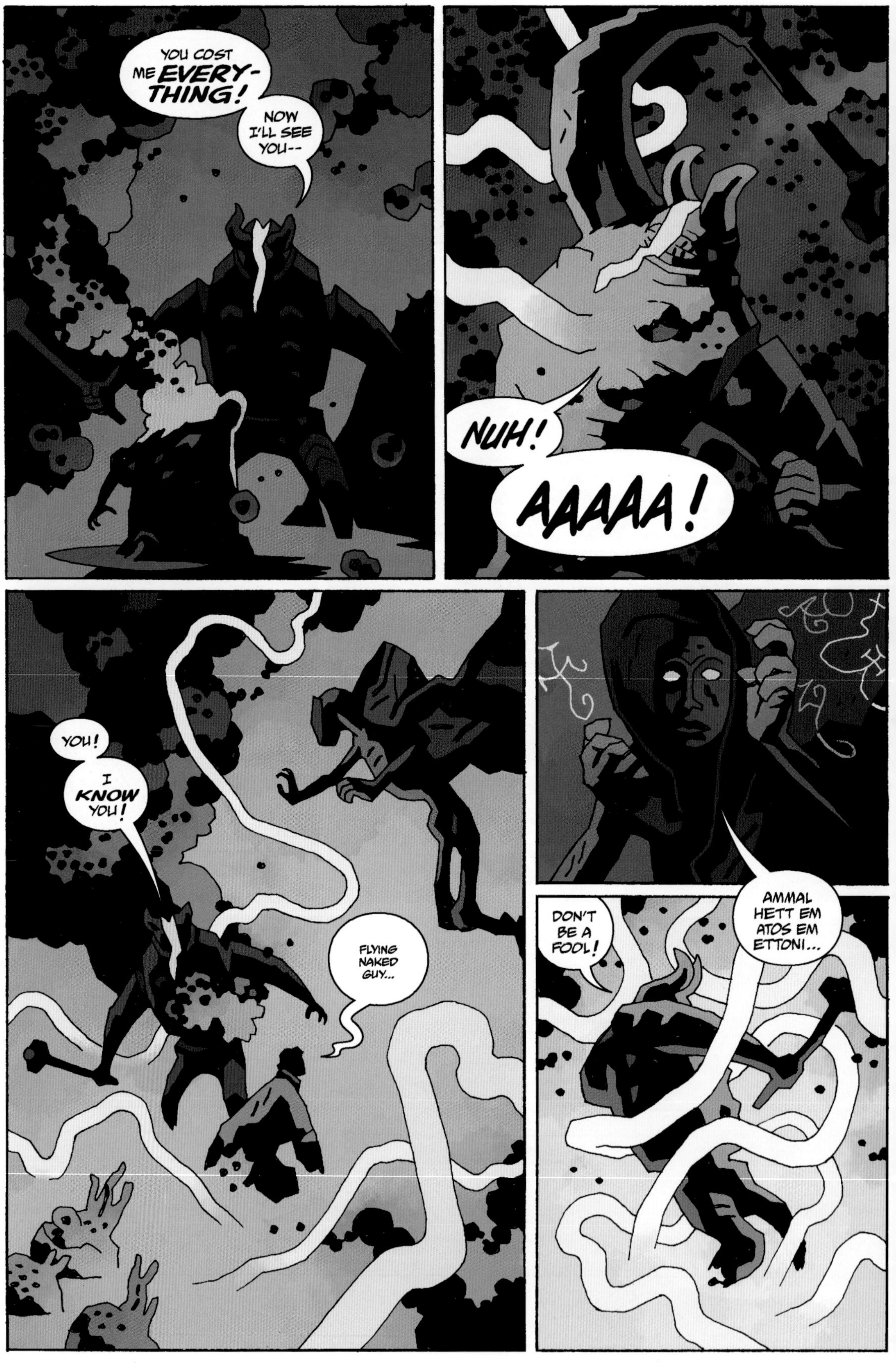
YOU COST ME EVERY-THING!
NOW I'LL SEE YOU--
NUH!
AAAAA!
YOU!
I KNOW YOU!
FLYING NAKED GUY...
AMMAL HETT EM ATOS EM ETTONI...
DON'T BE A FOOL!

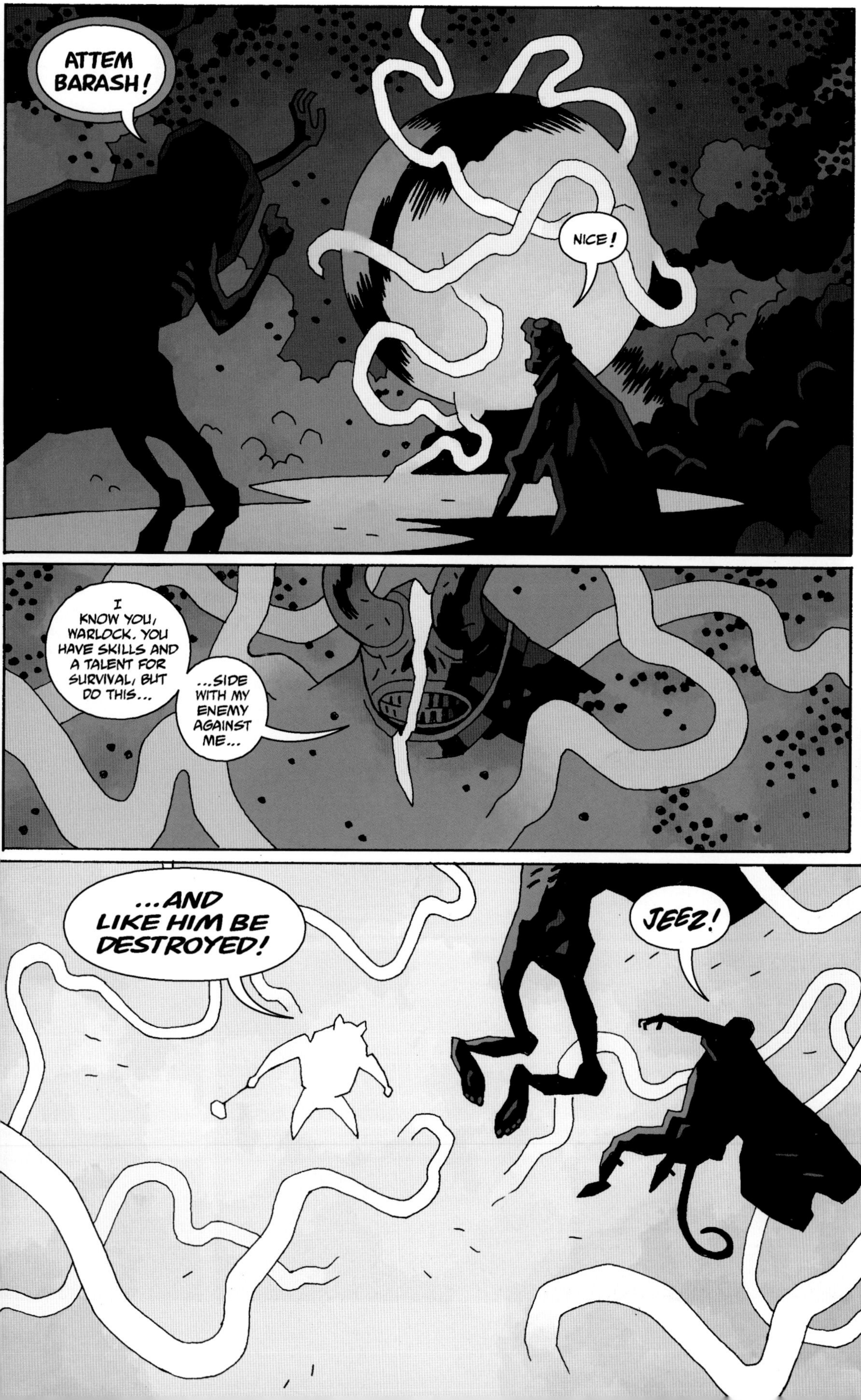
ATTEM BARASH!
NICE!
I KNOW YOU, WARLOCK. YOU HAVE SKILLS AND A TALENT FOR SURVIVAL, BUT DO THIS...
...SIDE WITH MY ENEMY AGAINST ME...
...AND LIKE HIM BE DESTROYED!
JEEZ!

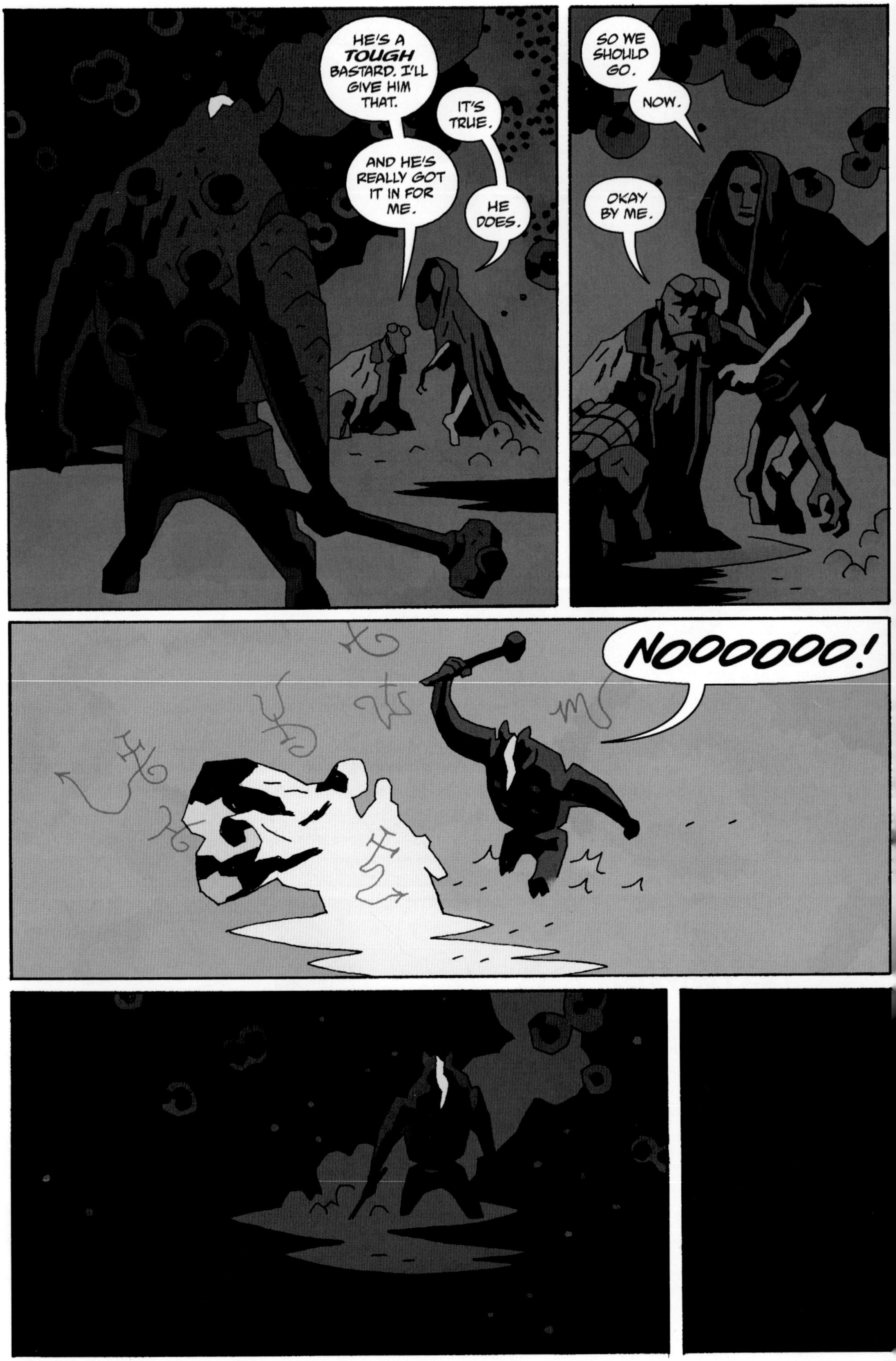
HE'S A TOUGH BASTARD. I'LL GIVE HIM THAT.
IT'S TRUE.
AND HE'S REALLY GOT IT IN FOR ME.
HE DOES.
SO WE SHOULD GO.
NOW.
OKAY BY ME.
NOOOOOO!

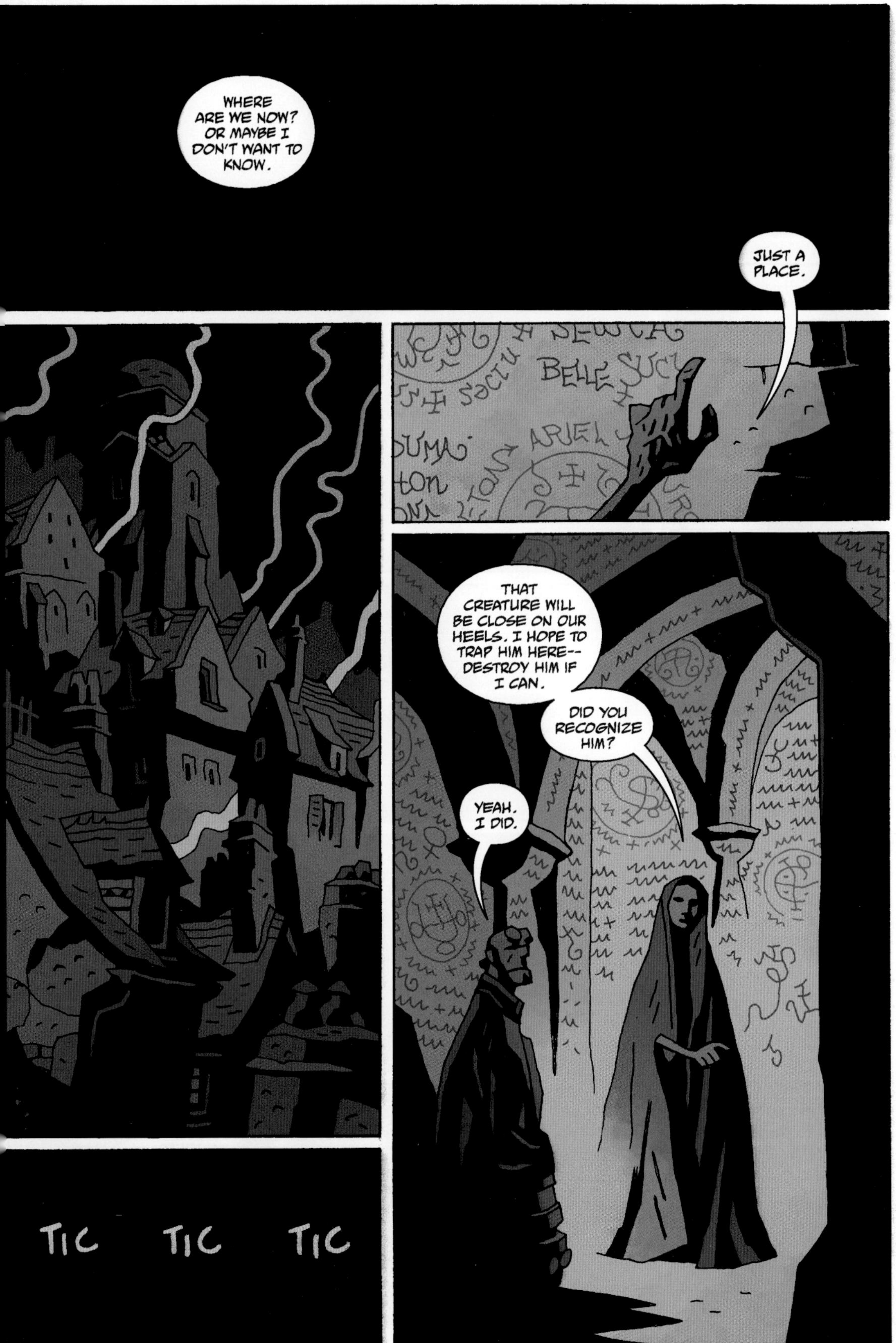
WHERE ARE WE NOW? OR MAYBE I DON'T WANT TO KNOW.
JUST A PLACE.
THAT CREATURE WILL BE CLOSE ON OUR HEELS. I HOPE TO TRAP HIM HERE-- DESTROY HIM IF I CAN.
DID YOU RECOGNIZE HIM?
YEAH. I DID.
TIC TIC TIC

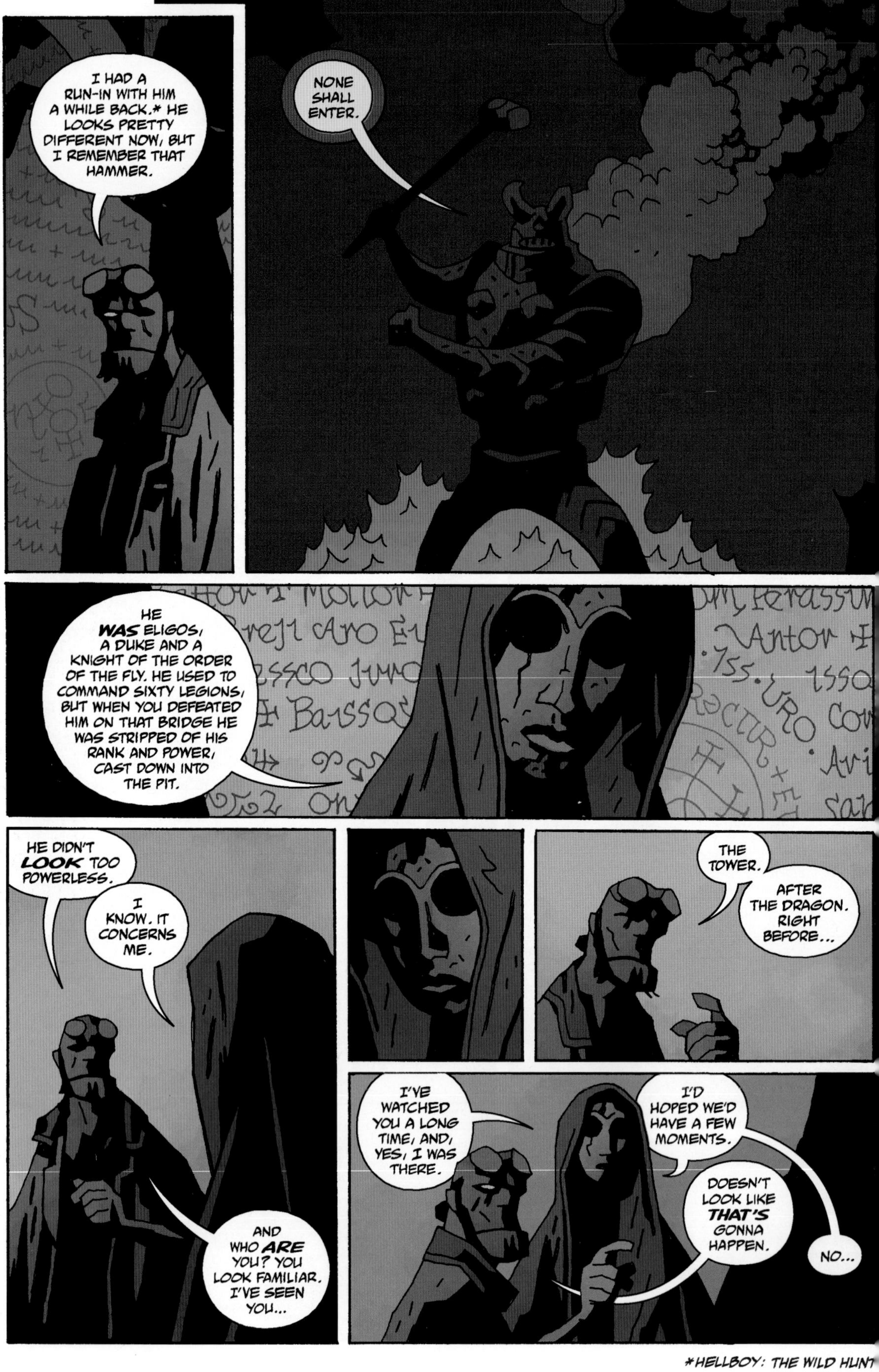
I HAD A RUN-IN WITH HIM A WHILE BACK.* HE LOOKS PRETTY DIFFERENT NOW, BUT I REMEMBER THAT HAMMER.
NONE SHALL ENTER.
HE WAS ELIGOS, A DUKE AND A KNIGHT OF THE ORDER OF THE FLY. HE USED TO COMMAND SIXTY LEGIONS, BUT WHEN YOU DEFEATED HIM ON THAT BRIDGE HE WAS STRIPPED OF HIS RANK AND POWER, CAST DOWN INTO THE PIT.
HE DIDN'T LOOK TOO POWERLESS.
I KNOW. IT CONCERNS ME.
AND WHO ARE YOU? YOU LOOK FAMILIAR. I'VE SEEN YOU...
THE TOWER.
AFTER THE DRAGON. RIGHT BEFORE...
I'VE WATCHED YOU A LONG TIME, AND, YES, I WAS THERE.
I'D HOPED WE'D HAVE A FEW MOMENTS.
DOESN'T LOOK LIKE THAT'S GONNA HAPPEN.
NO...

*HELLBOY: THE WILD HUNT

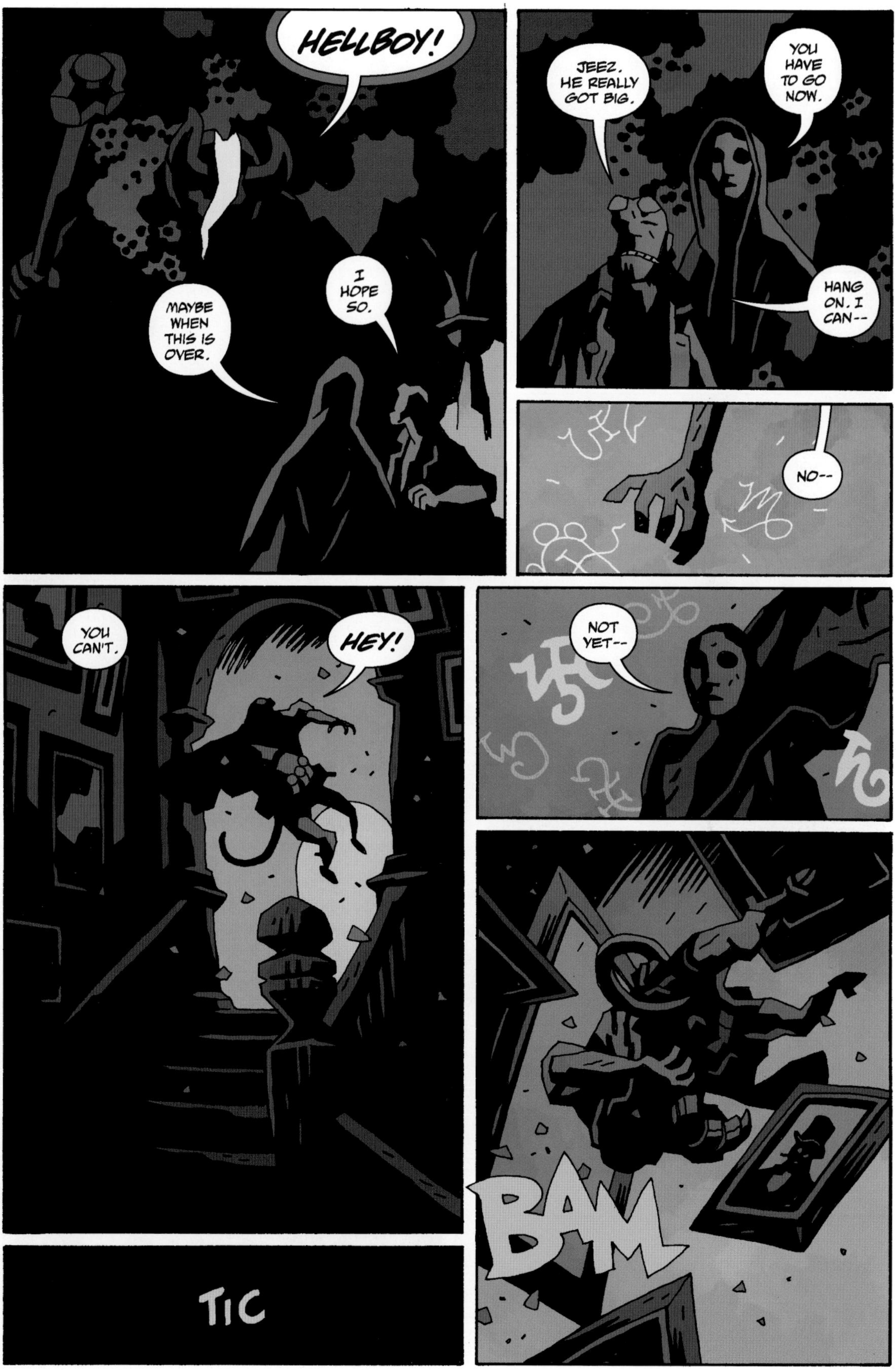
HELLBOY!
MAYBE WHEN THIS IS OVER.
I HOPE SO.
JEEZ. HE REALLY GOT BIG.
YOU HAVE TO GO NOW.
HANG ON. I CAN--
NO--
YOU CAN'T.
HEY!
NOT YET--
BAM
TIC

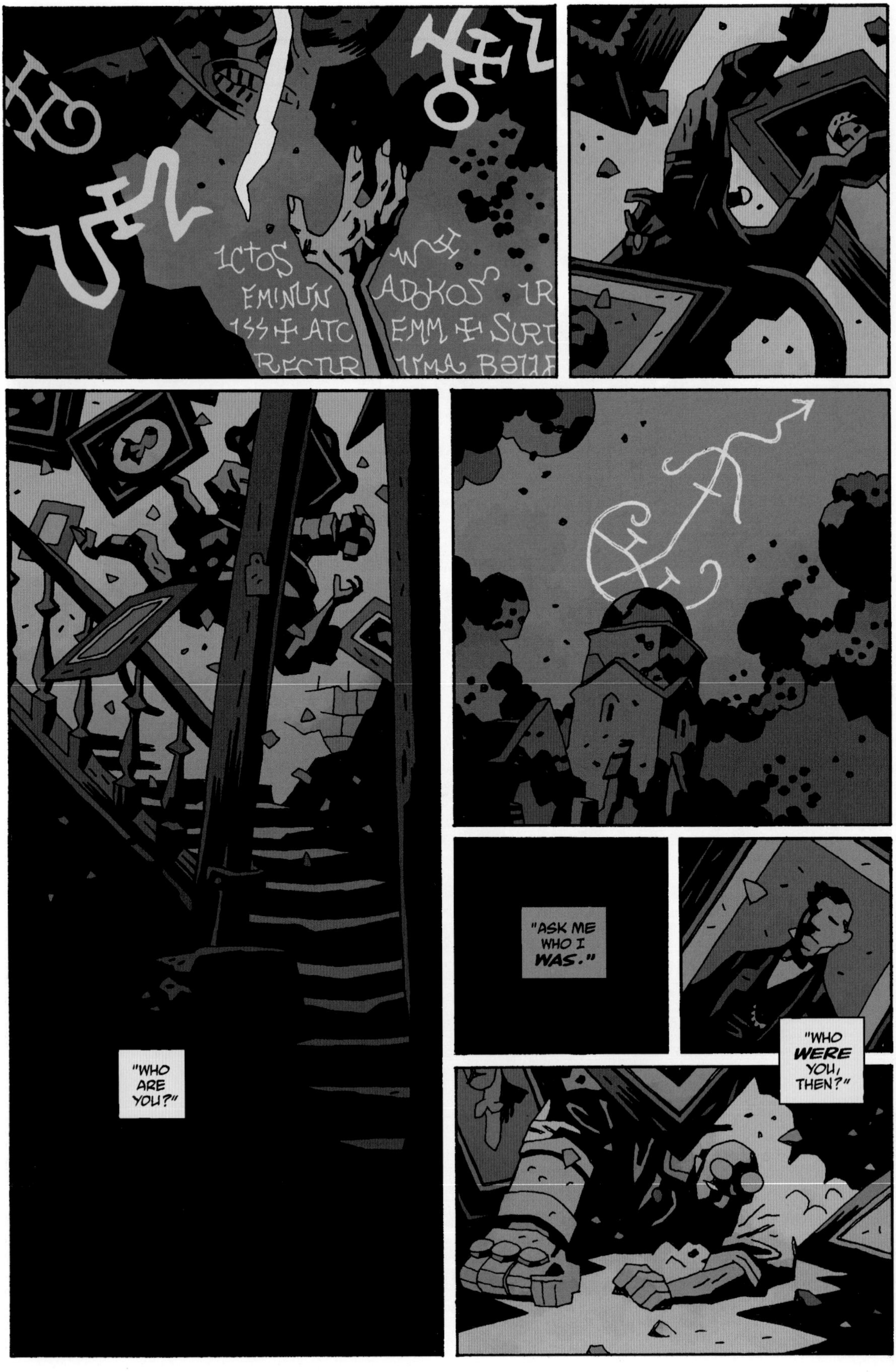
"WHO ARE YOU?"
"ASK ME WHO I *WAS*."
"WHO *WERE* YOU, THEN?"

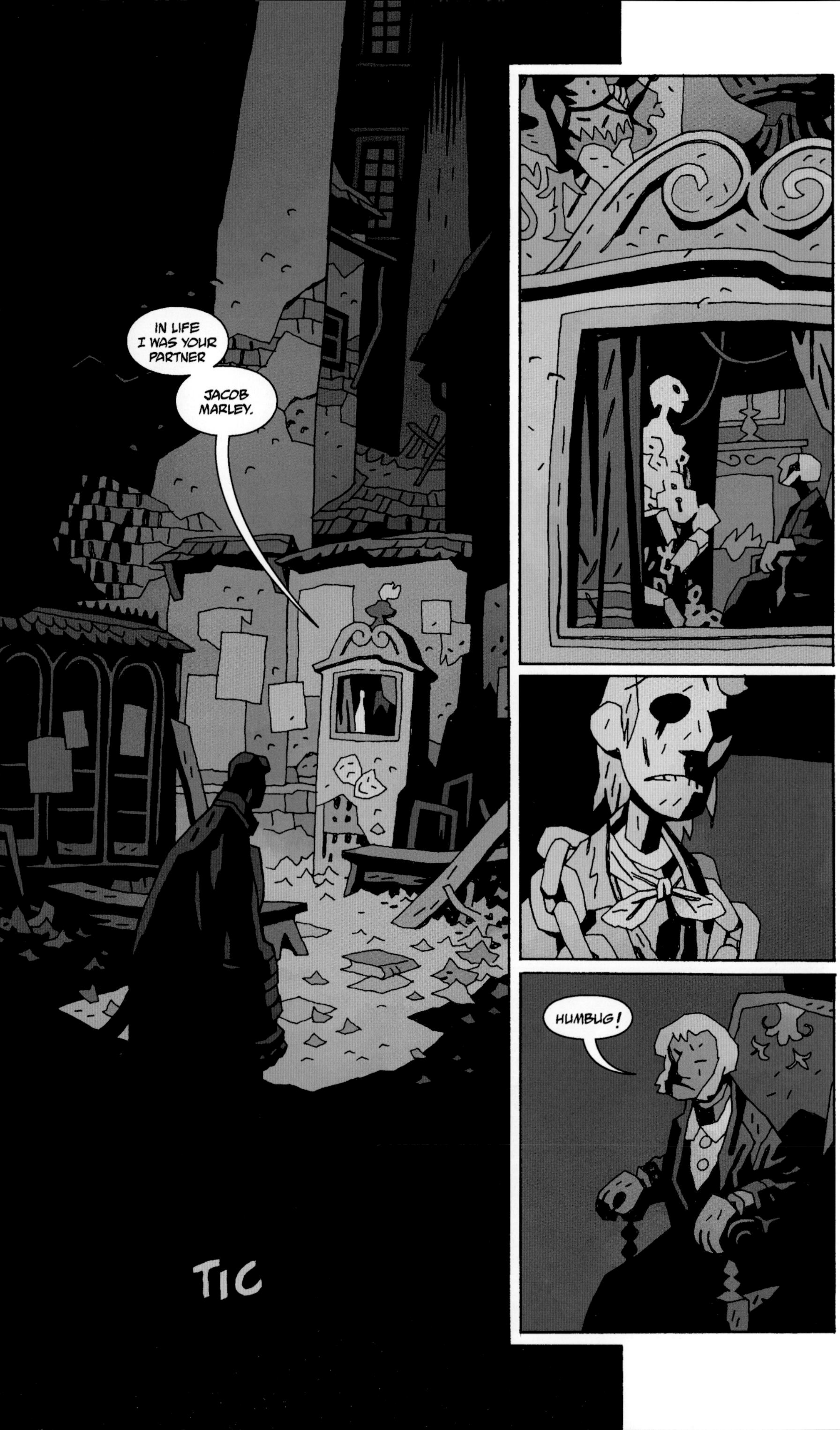
IN LIFE I WAS YOUR PARTNER
JACOB MARLEY.
TIC
HUMBUG!

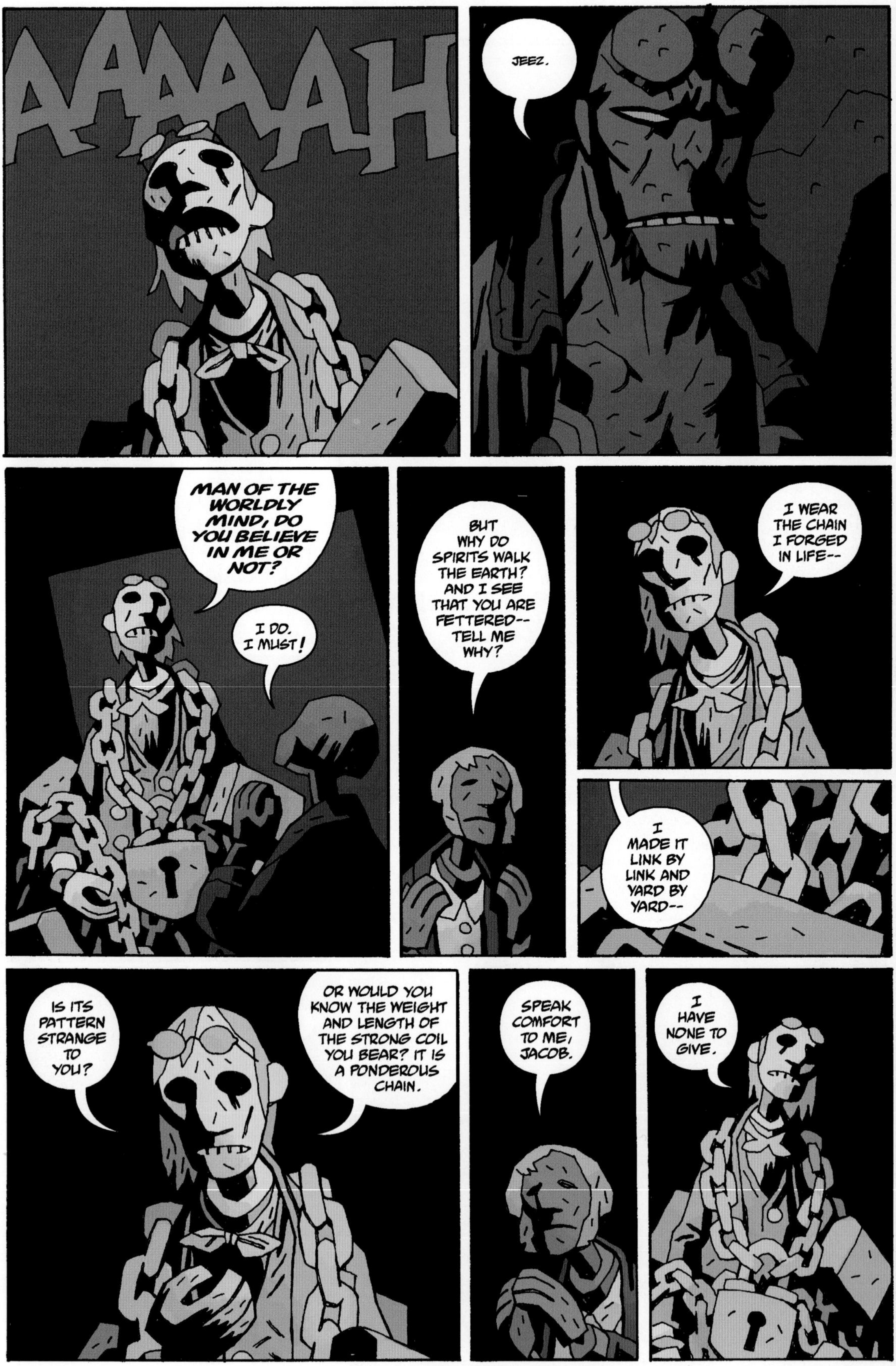
AAAAAH
JEEZ.
MAN OF THE WORLDLY MIND, DO YOU BELIEVE IN ME OR NOT?
I DO. I MUST!
BUT WHY DO SPIRITS WALK THE EARTH? AND I SEE THAT YOU ARE FETTERED-- TELL ME WHY?
I WEAR THE CHAIN I FORGED IN LIFE--
I MADE IT LINK BY LINK AND YARD BY YARD--
IS ITS PATTERN STRANGE TO YOU?
OR WOULD YOU KNOW THE WEIGHT AND LENGTH OF THE STRONG COIL YOU BEAR? IT IS A PONDEROUS CHAIN.
SPEAK COMFORT TO ME, JACOB.
I HAVE NONE TO GIVE.

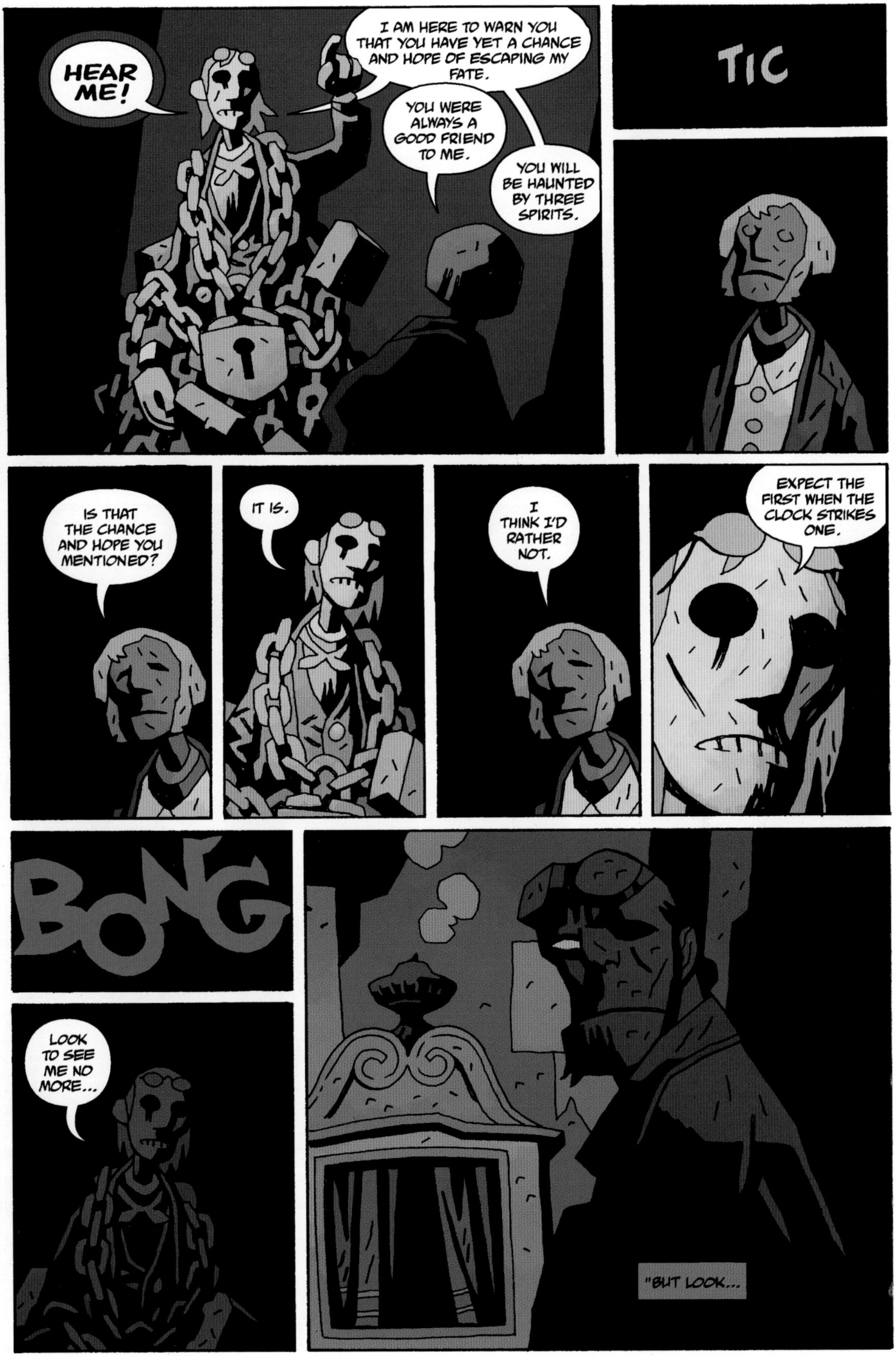
HEAR ME!
I AM HERE TO WARN YOU THAT YOU HAVE YET A CHANCE AND HOPE OF ESCAPING MY FATE.
YOU WERE ALWAYS A GOOD FRIEND TO ME.
YOU WILL BE HAUNTED BY THREE SPIRITS.
TIC
IS THAT THE CHANCE AND HOPE YOU MENTIONED?
IT IS.
I THINK I'D RATHER NOT.
EXPECT THE FIRST WHEN THE CLOCK STRIKES ONE.
BONG
LOOK TO SEE ME NO MORE...
"BUT LOOK...

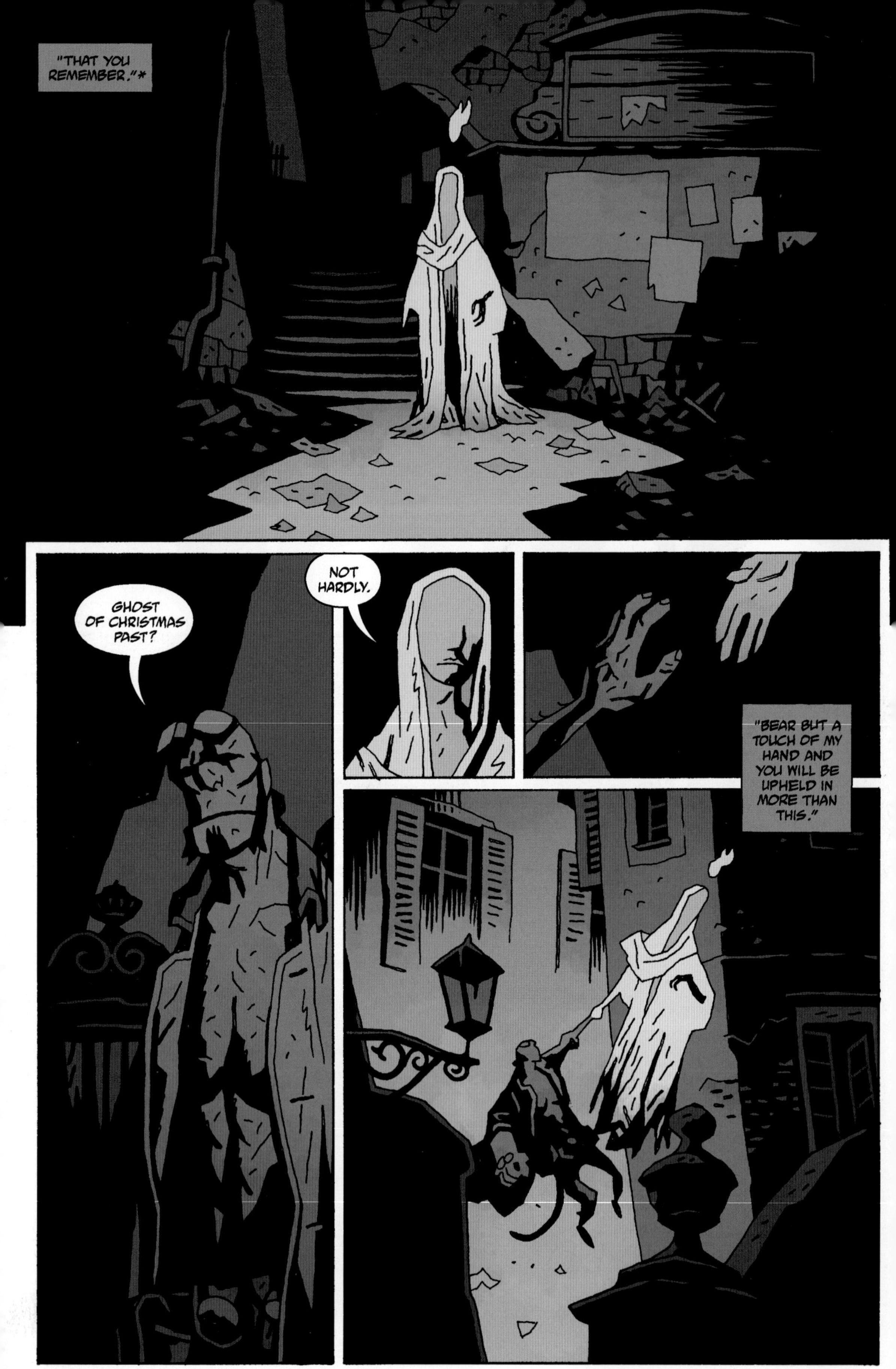
"THAT YOU REMEMBER."*
GHOST OF CHRISTMAS PAST?
NOT HARDLY.
"BEAR BUT A TOUCH OF MY HAND AND YOU WILL BE UPHELD IN MORE THAN THIS."

*PUPPET SHOW FREELY ADAPTED FROM
A CHRISTMAS CAROL BY CHARLES DICKENS

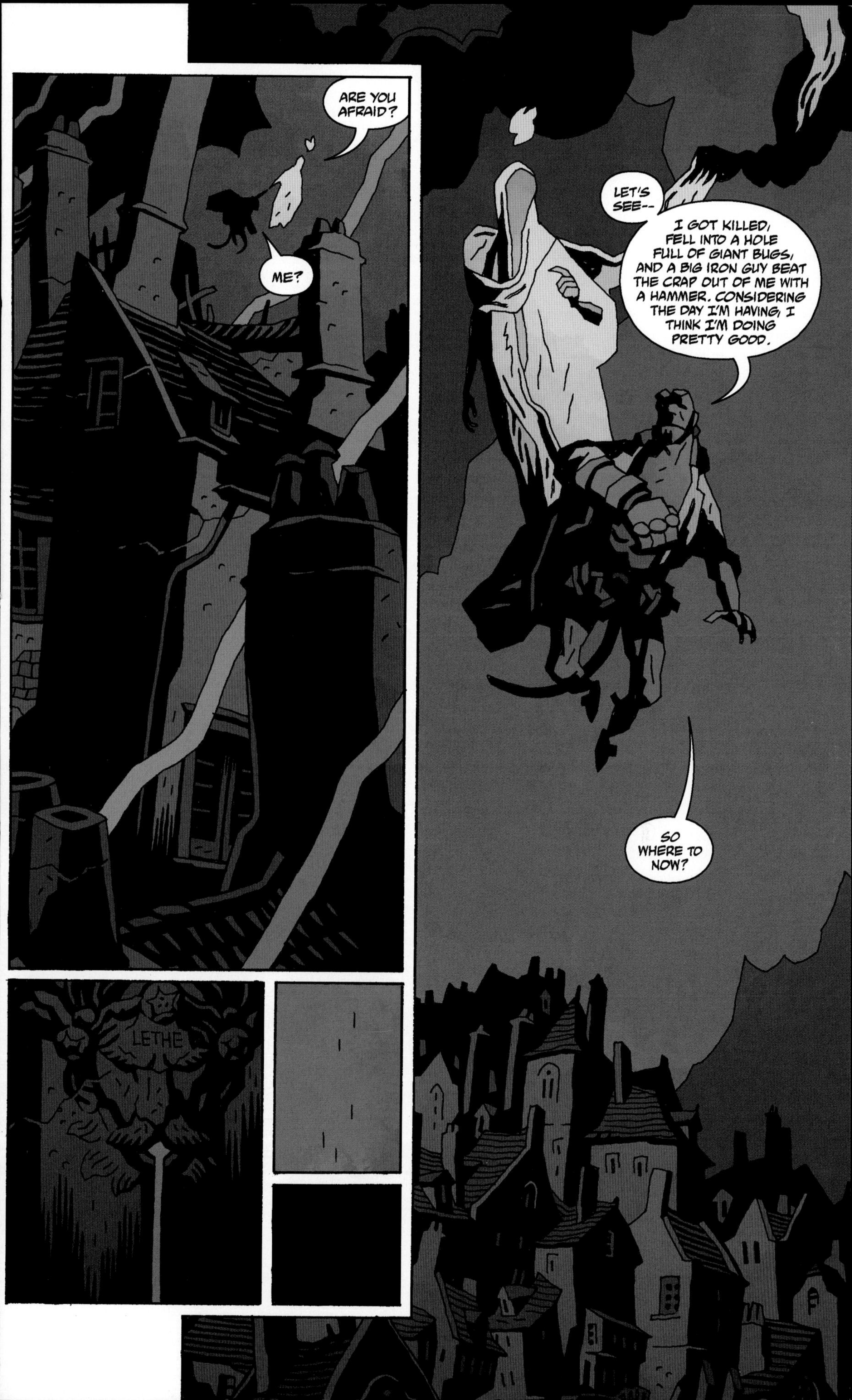

ARE YOU AFRAID?
ME?
LET'S SEE--
I GOT KILLED, FELL INTO A HOLE FULL OF GIANT BUGS, AND A BIG IRON GUY BEAT THE CRAP OUT OF ME WITH A HAMMER. CONSIDERING THE DAY I'M HAVING, I THINK I'M DOING PRETTY GOOD.
SO WHERE TO NOW?
LETHE

CHAPTER TWO

PANDEMONIUM

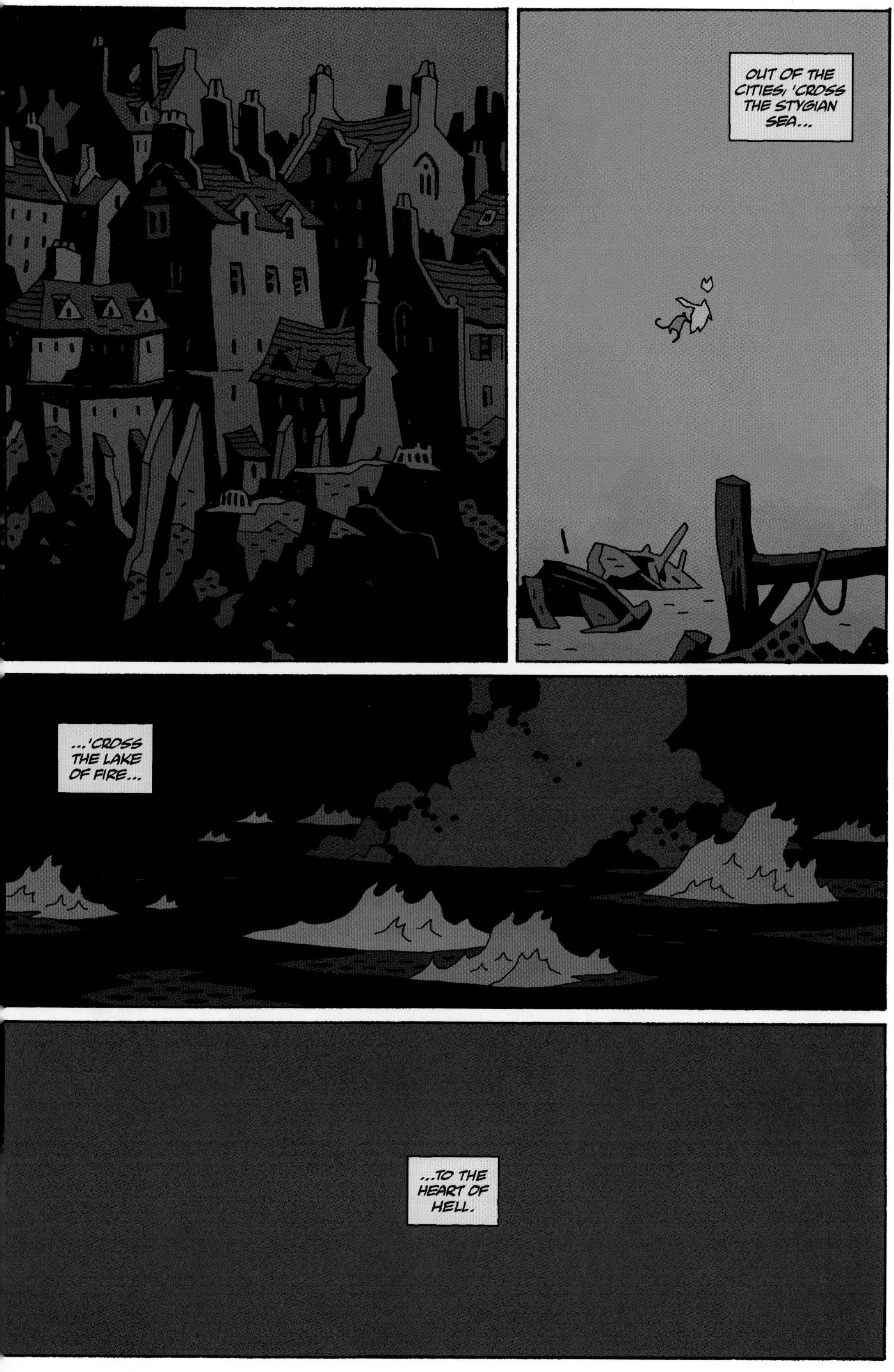
OUT OF THE CITIES, 'CROSS THE STYGIAN SEA...
...'CROSS THE LAKE OF FIRE...
...TO THE HEART OF HELL.

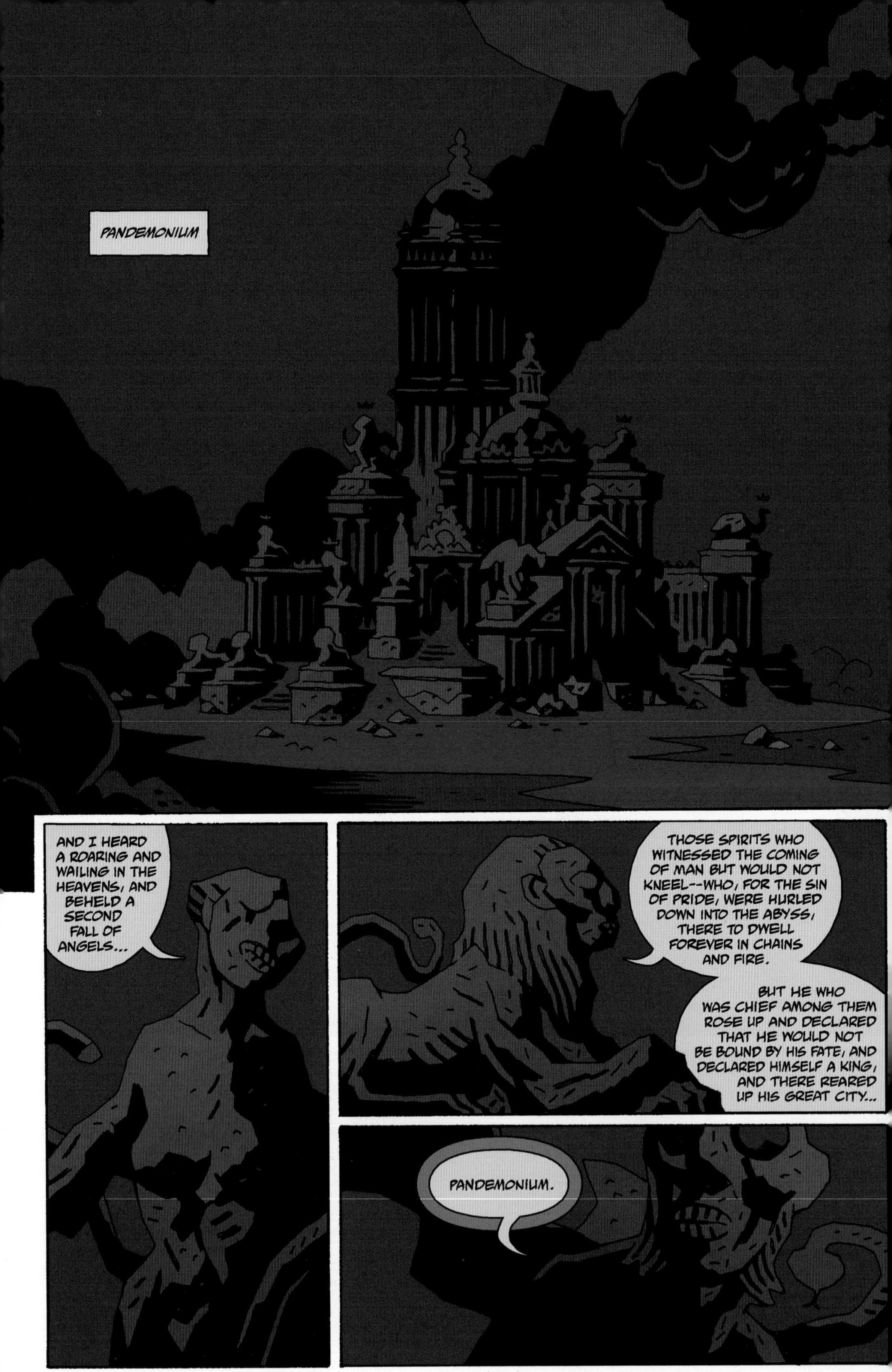
PANDEMONIUM
AND I HEARD A ROARING AND WAILING IN THE HEAVENS, AND BEHELD A SECOND FALL OF ANGELS...
THOSE SPIRITS WHO WITNESSED THE COMING OF MAN BUT WOULD NOT KNEEL--WHO, FOR THE SIN OF PRIDE, WERE HURLED DOWN INTO THE ABYSS, THERE TO DWELL FOREVER IN CHAINS AND FIRE.
BUT HE WHO WAS CHIEF AMONG THEM ROSE UP AND DECLARED THAT HE WOULD NOT BE BOUND BY HIS FATE, AND DECLARED HIMSELF A KING, AND THERE REARED UP HIS GREAT CITY...
PANDEMONIUM.

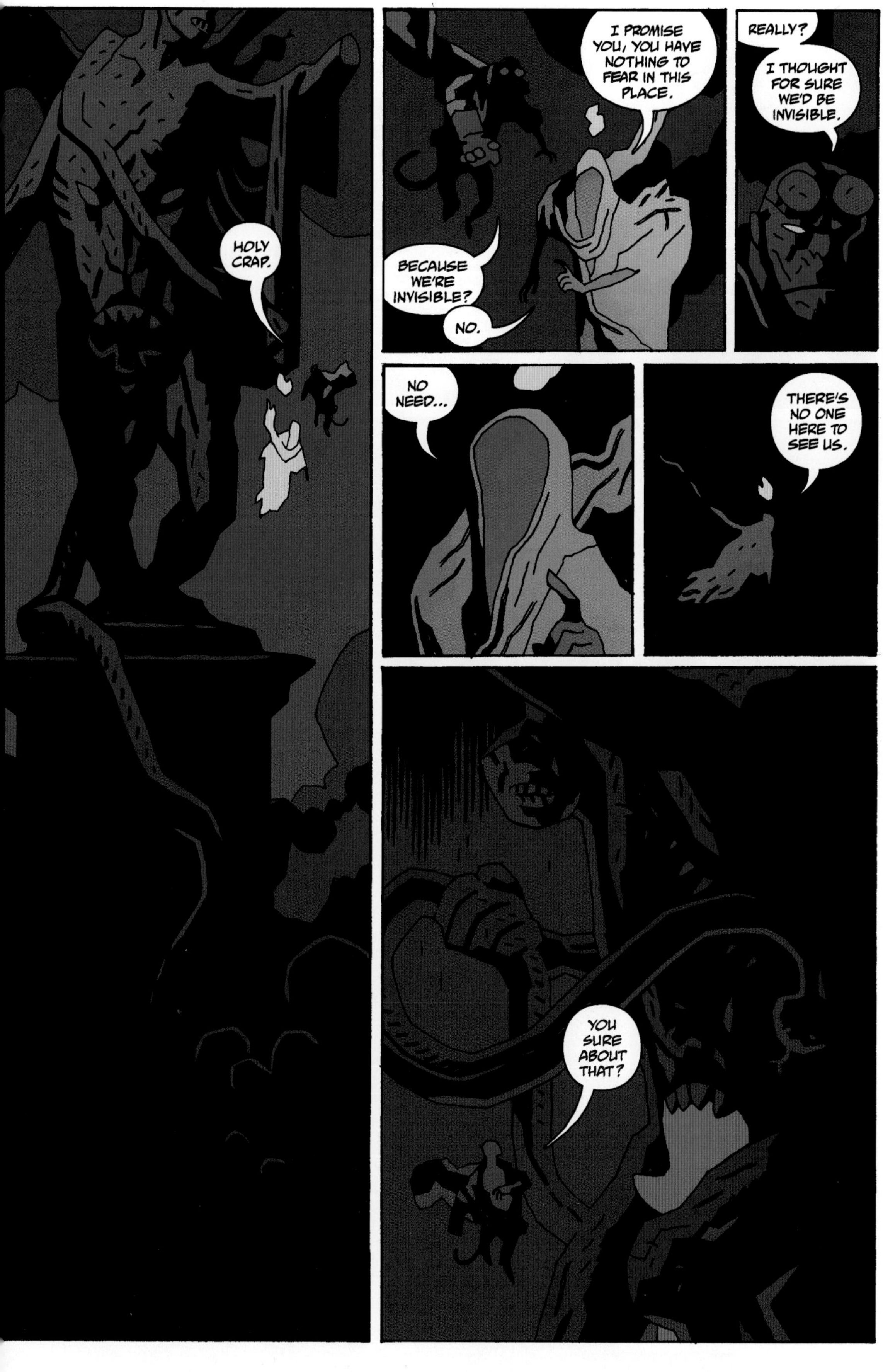
HOLY CRAP.
I PROMISE YOU, YOU HAVE NOTHING TO FEAR IN THIS PLACE.
BECAUSE WE'RE INVISIBLE?
NO.
REALLY?
I THOUGHT FOR SURE WE'D BE INVISIBLE.
NO NEED...
THERE'S NO ONE HERE TO SEE US.
YOU SURE ABOUT THAT?

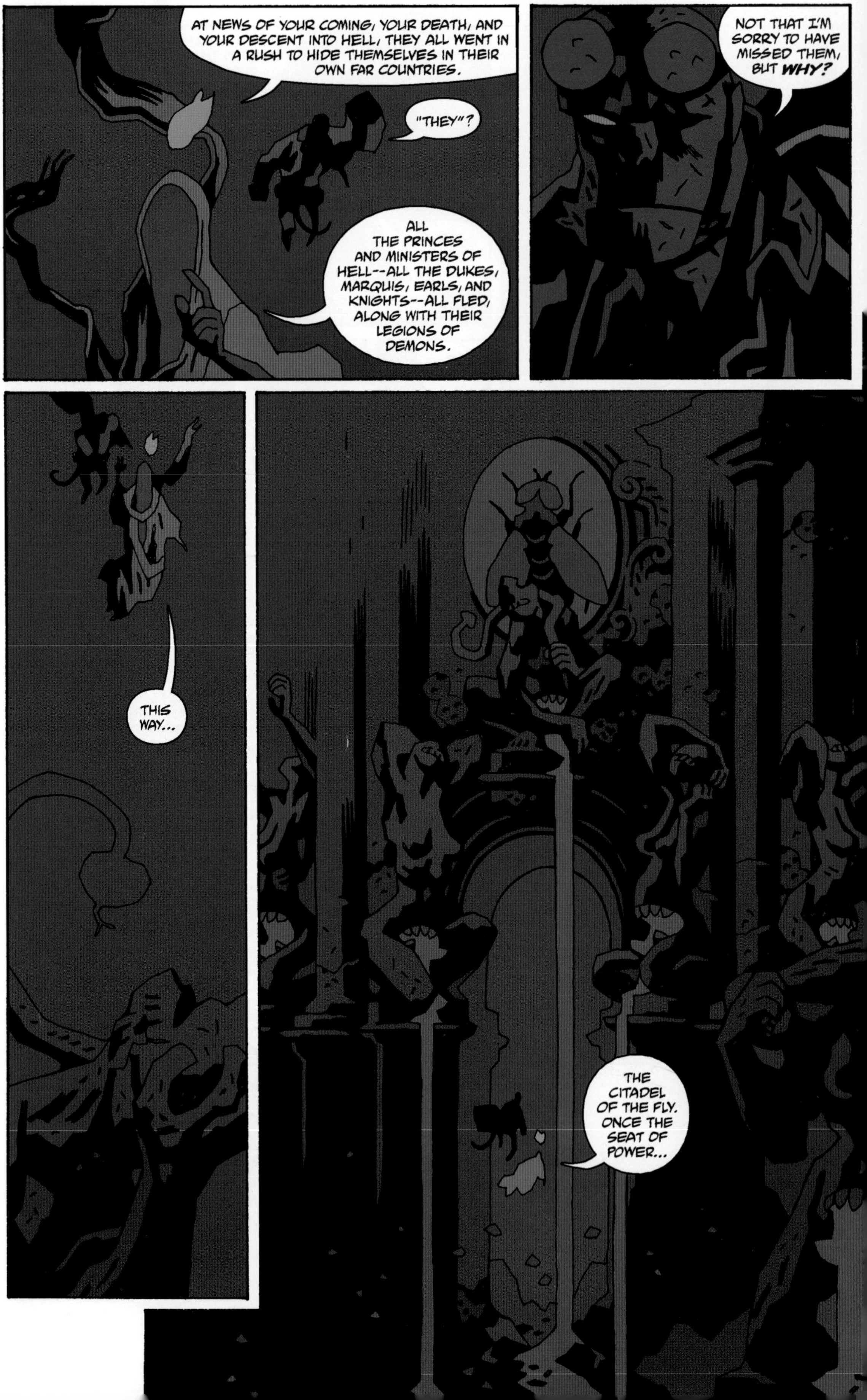
AT NEWS OF YOUR COMING, YOUR DEATH, AND YOUR DESCENT INTO HELL, THEY ALL WENT IN A RUSH TO HIDE THEMSELVES IN THEIR OWN FAR COUNTRIES.
"THEY"?
ALL THE PRINCES AND MINISTERS OF HELL--ALL THE DUKES, MARQUIS, EARLS, AND KNIGHTS--ALL FLED, ALONG WITH THEIR LEGIONS OF DEMONS.
NOT THAT I'M SORRY TO HAVE MISSED THEM, BUT ***WHY?***
THIS WAY...
THE CITADEL OF THE FLY. ONCE THE SEAT OF POWER...

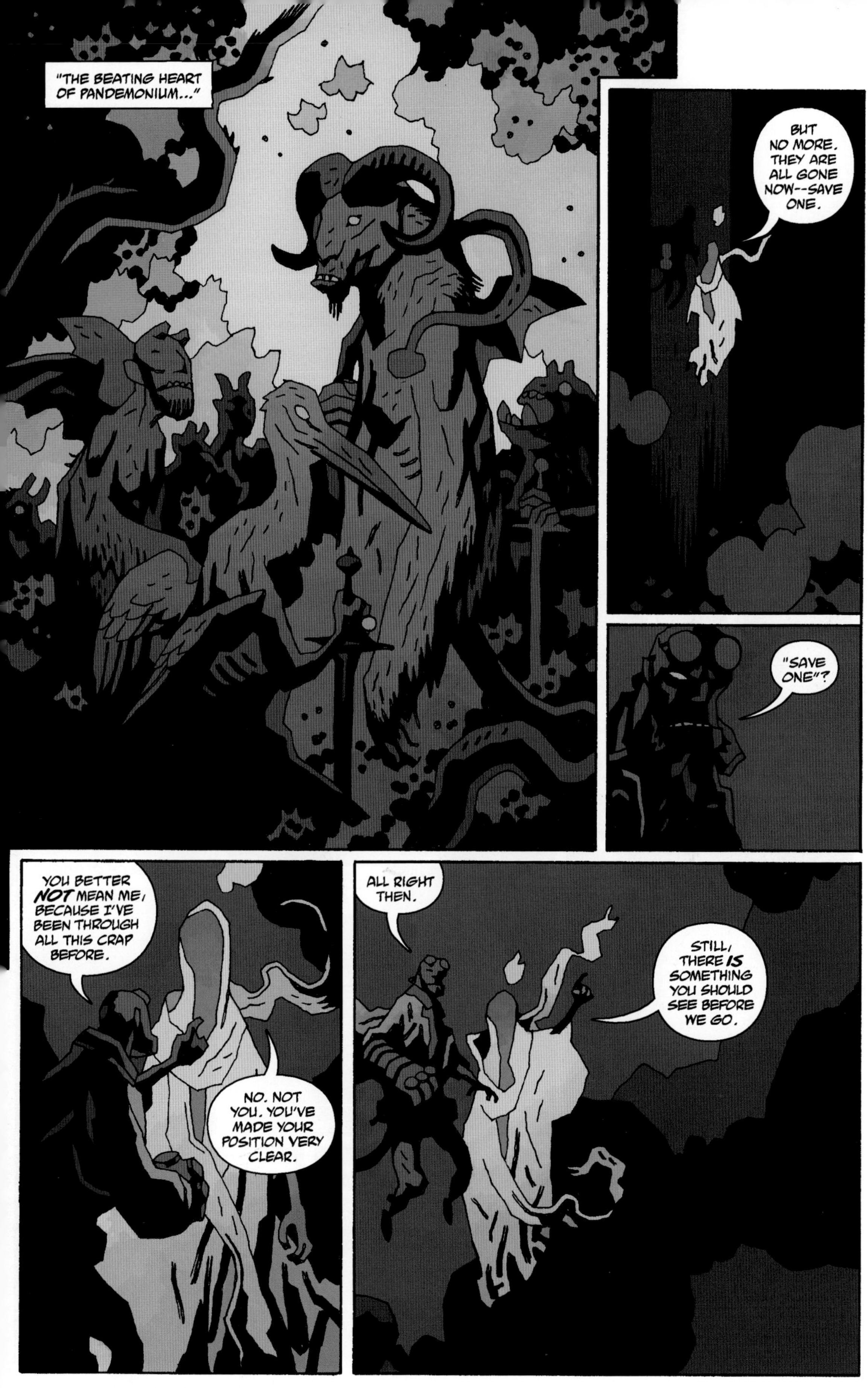
"THE BEATING HEART OF PANDEMONIUM..."
BUT NO MORE. THEY ARE ALL GONE NOW--SAVE ONE.
"SAVE ONE"?
YOU BETTER **NOT** MEAN ME, BECAUSE I'VE BEEN THROUGH ALL THIS CRAP BEFORE.
NO. NOT YOU. YOU'VE MADE YOUR POSITION VERY CLEAR.
ALL RIGHT THEN.
STILL, THERE **IS** SOMETHING YOU SHOULD SEE BEFORE WE GO.

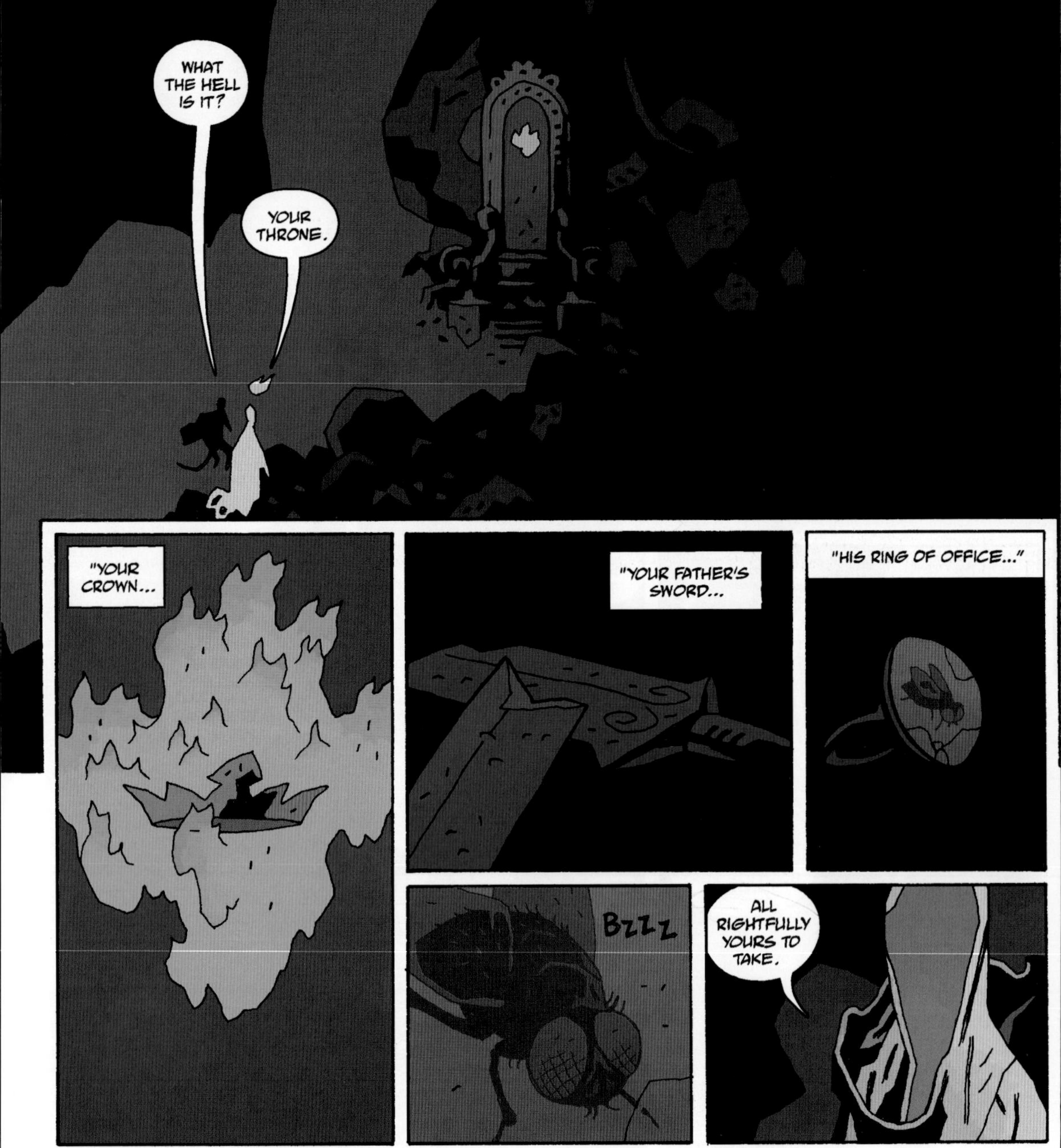
WHAT THE HELL IS IT?
YOUR THRONE.
"YOUR CROWN...
"YOUR FATHER'S SWORD...
"HIS RING OF OFFICE..."
BZZZ
ALL RIGHTFULLY YOURS TO TAKE.

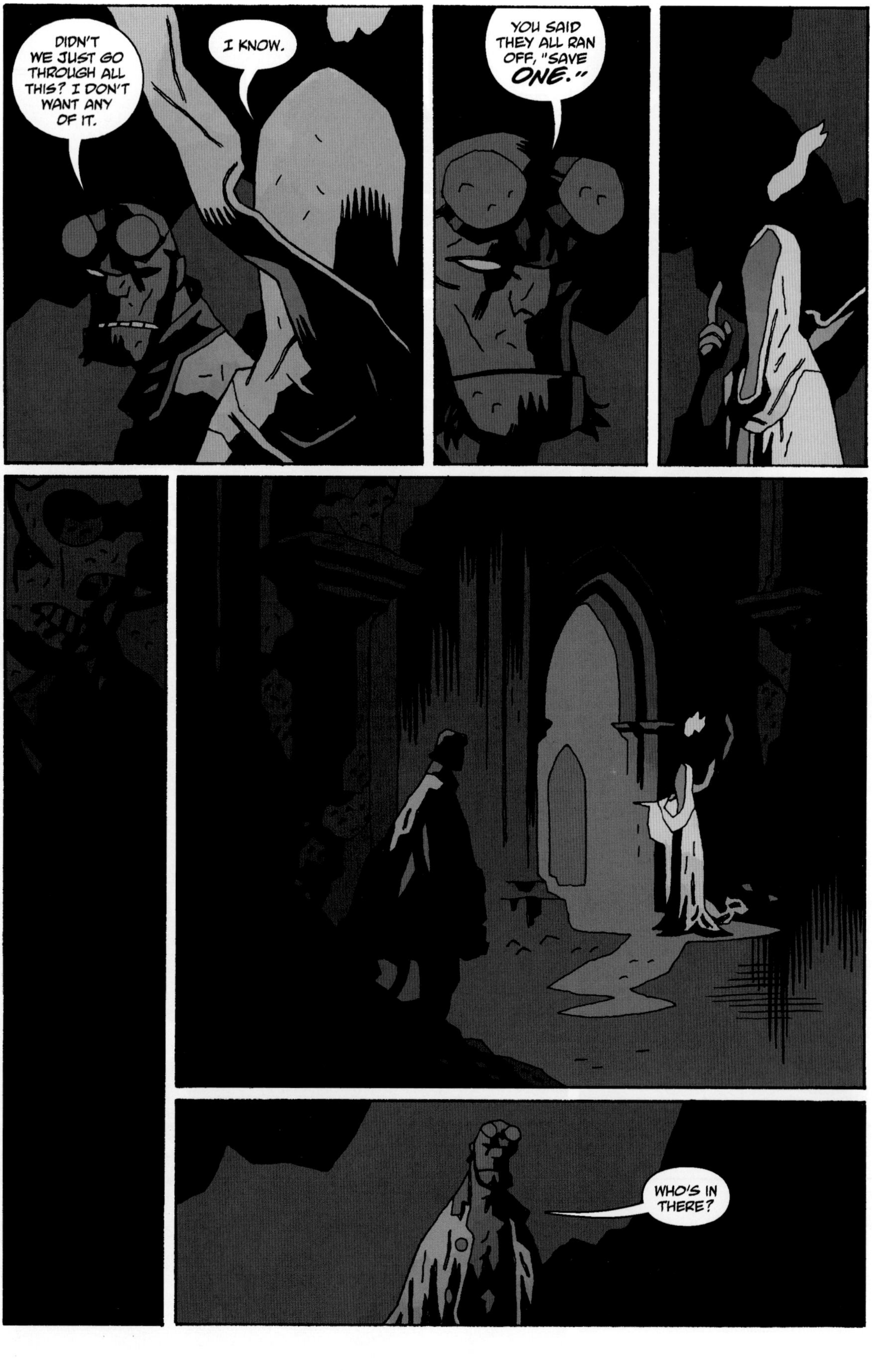
DIDN'T WE JUST GO THROUGH ALL THIS? I DON'T WANT ANY OF IT.
I KNOW.
YOU SAID THEY ALL RAN OFF, "SAVE ONE."
WHO'S IN THERE?

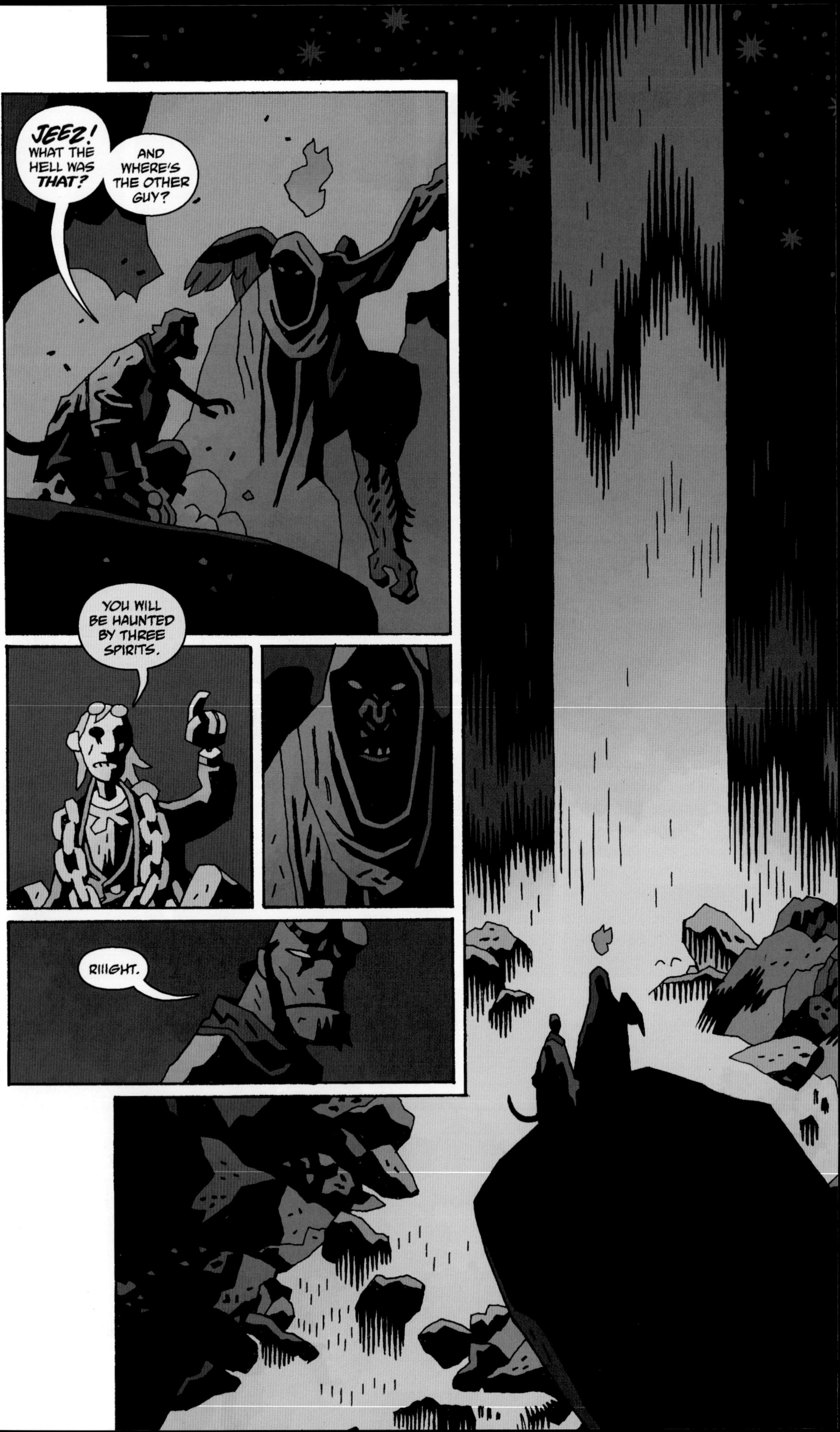
JEEZ! WHAT THE HELL WAS THAT?
AND WHERE'S THE OTHER GUY?
YOU WILL BE HAUNTED BY THREE SPIRITS.
RIIIGHT.

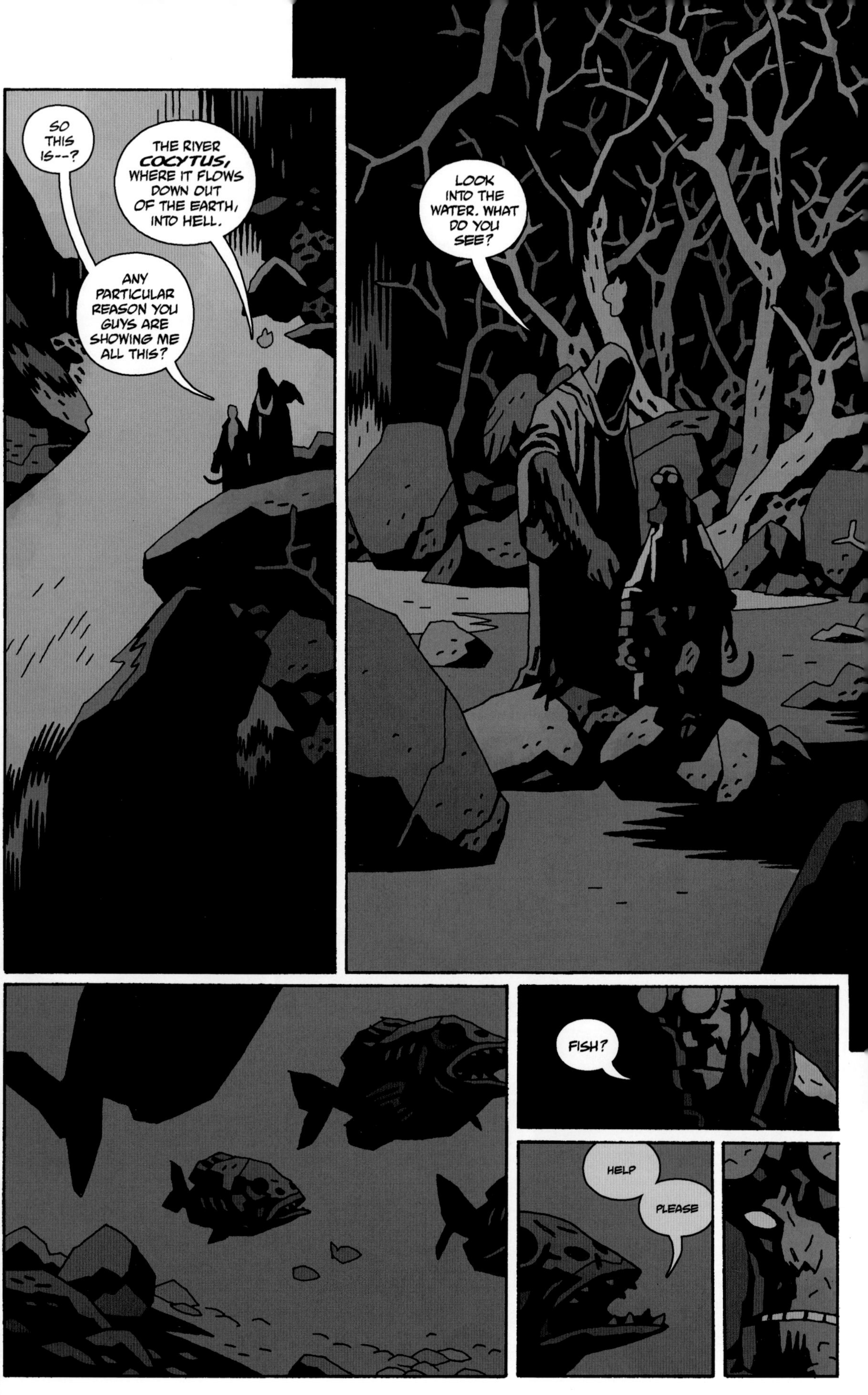
SO THIS IS--?
THE RIVER COCYTUS, WHERE IT FLOWS DOWN OUT OF THE EARTH, INTO HELL.
ANY PARTICULAR REASON YOU GUYS ARE SHOWING ME ALL THIS?
LOOK INTO THE WATER. WHAT DO YOU SEE?
FISH?
HELP
PLEASE

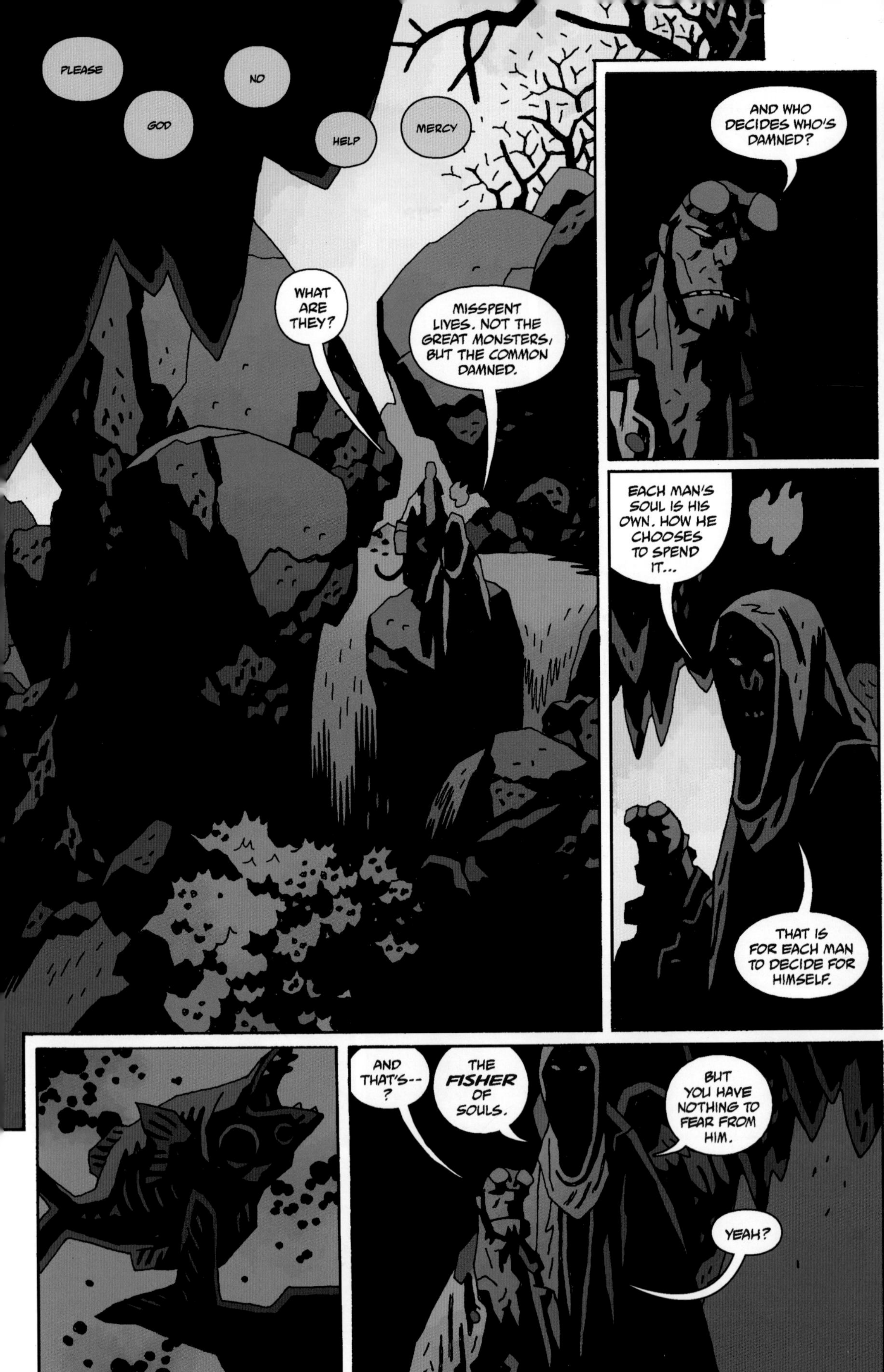
PLEASE
GOD
NO
HELP
MERCY
WHAT ARE THEY?
MISSPENT LIVES. NOT THE GREAT MONSTERS, BUT THE COMMON DAMNED.
AND WHO DECIDES WHO'S DAMNED?
EACH MAN'S SOUL IS HIS OWN. HOW HE CHOOSES TO SPEND IT...
THAT IS FOR EACH MAN TO DECIDE FOR HIMSELF.
AND THAT'S-- ?
THE **FISHER** OF SOULS.
BUT YOU HAVE NOTHING TO FEAR FROM HIM.
YEAH?

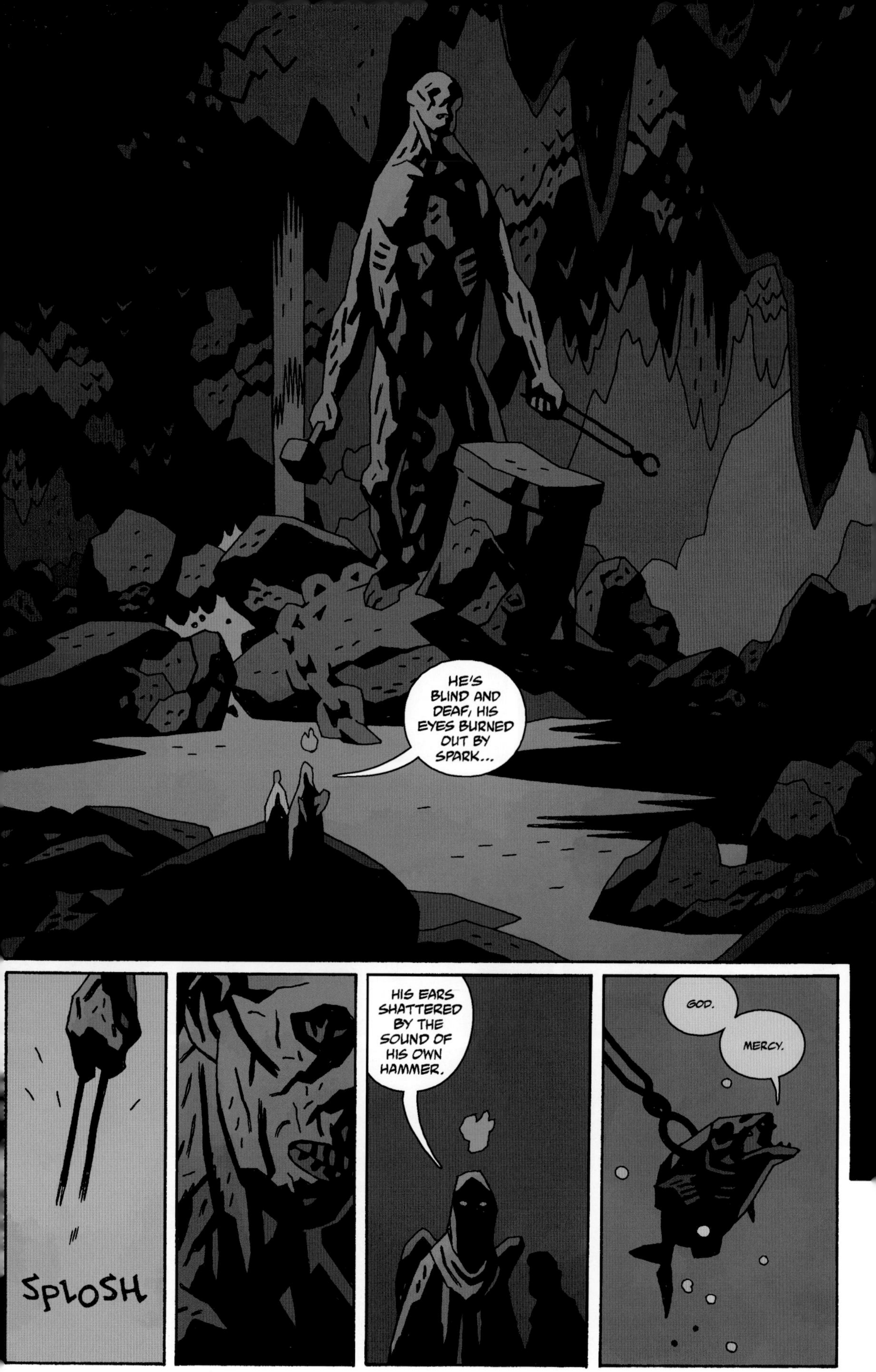
HE'S BLIND AND DEAF, HIS EYES BURNED OUT BY SPARK...
SPLOSH
HIS EARS SHATTERED BY THE SOUND OF HIS OWN HAMMER.
GOD.
MERCY.

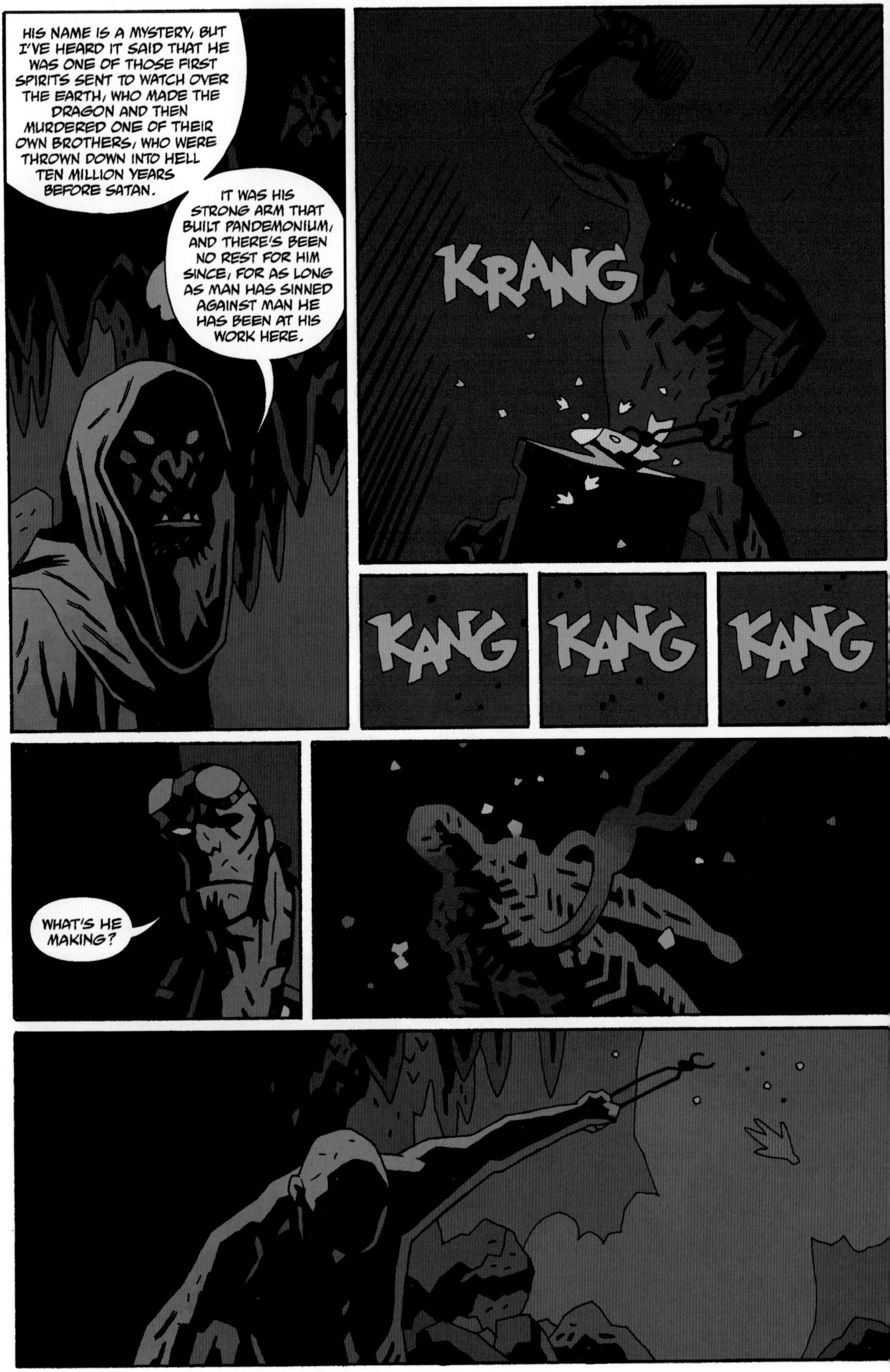

HIS NAME IS A MYSTERY, BUT I'VE HEARD IT SAID THAT HE WAS ONE OF THOSE FIRST SPIRITS SENT TO WATCH OVER THE EARTH, WHO MADE THE DRAGON AND THEN MURDERED ONE OF THEIR OWN BROTHERS, WHO WERE THROWN DOWN INTO HELL TEN MILLION YEARS BEFORE SATAN.
IT WAS HIS STRONG ARM THAT BUILT PANDEMONIUM, AND THERE'S BEEN NO REST FOR HIM SINCE, FOR AS LONG AS MAN HAS SINNED AGAINST MAN HE HAS BEEN AT HIS WORK HERE.
KRANG
KANG
KANG
KANG
WHAT'S HE MAKING?

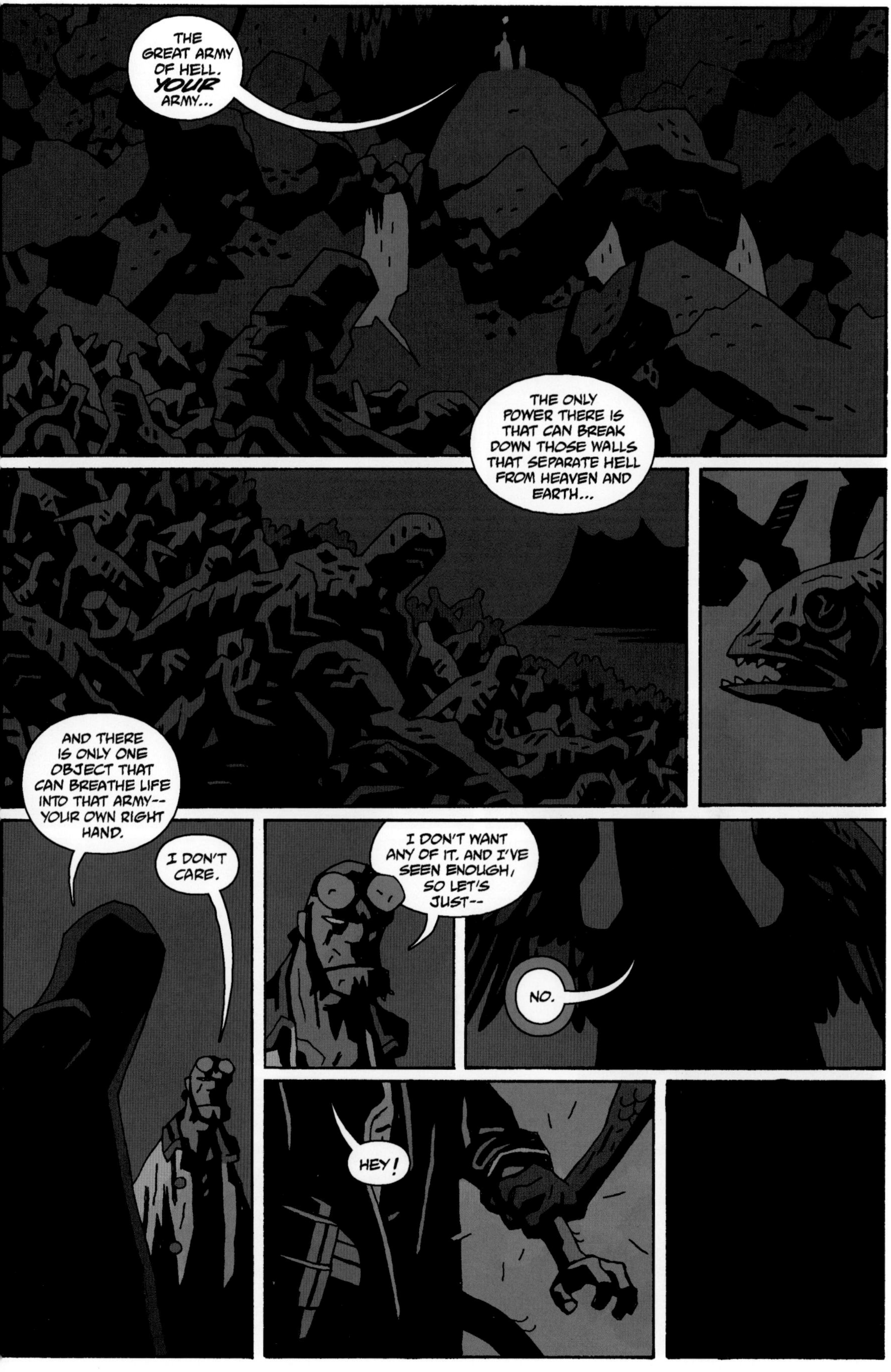
THE GREAT ARMY OF HELL. YOUR ARMY...
THE ONLY POWER THERE IS THAT CAN BREAK DOWN THOSE WALLS THAT SEPARATE HELL FROM HEAVEN AND EARTH...
AND THERE IS ONLY ONE OBJECT THAT CAN BREATHE LIFE INTO THAT ARMY-- YOUR OWN RIGHT HAND.
I DON'T CARE.
I DON'T WANT ANY OF IT. AND I'VE SEEN ENOUGH, SO LET'S JUST--
NO.
HEY!

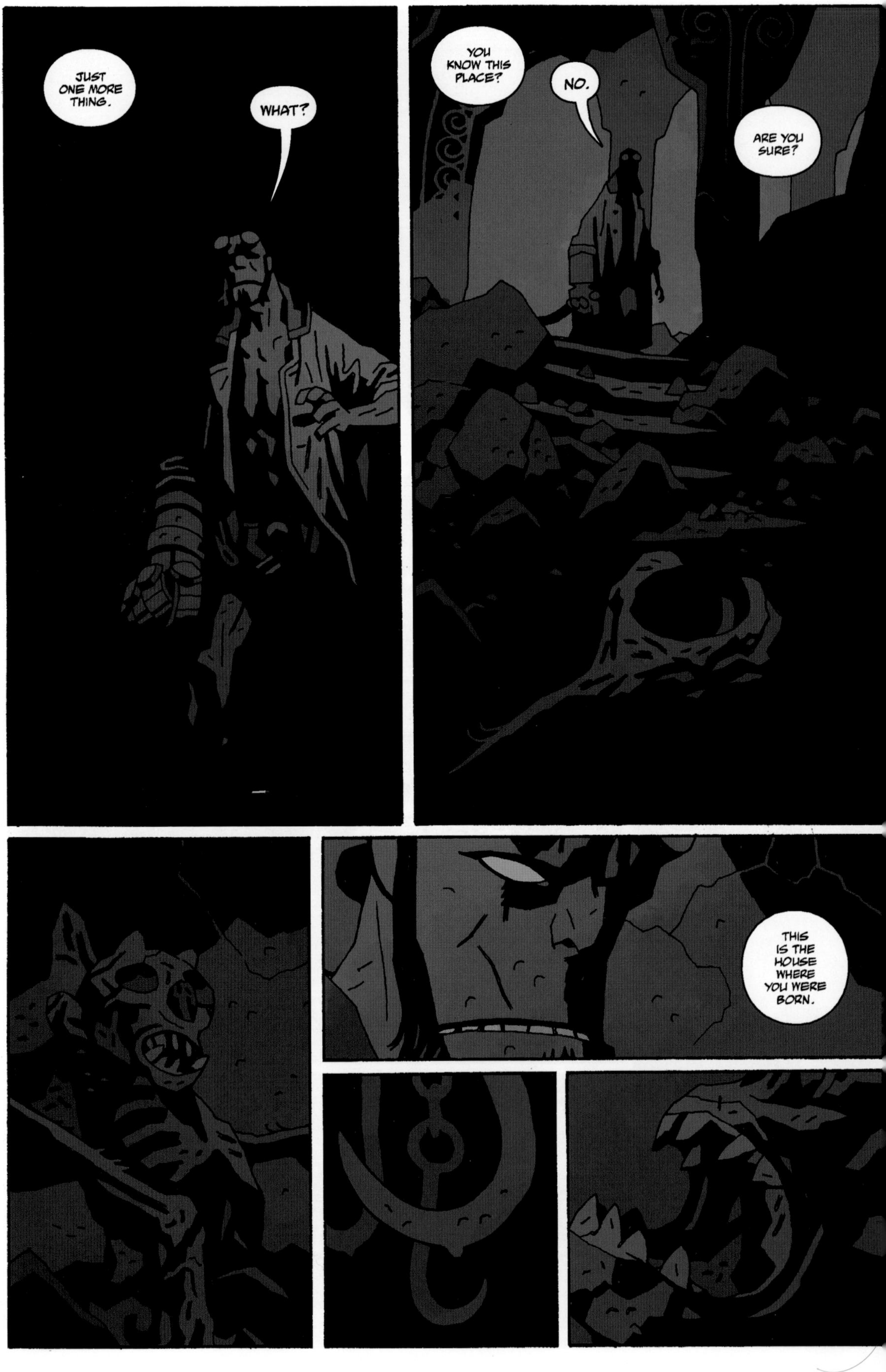
JUST ONE MORE THING.
WHAT?
YOU KNOW THIS PLACE?
NO.
ARE YOU SURE?
THIS IS THE HOUSE WHERE YOU WERE BORN.

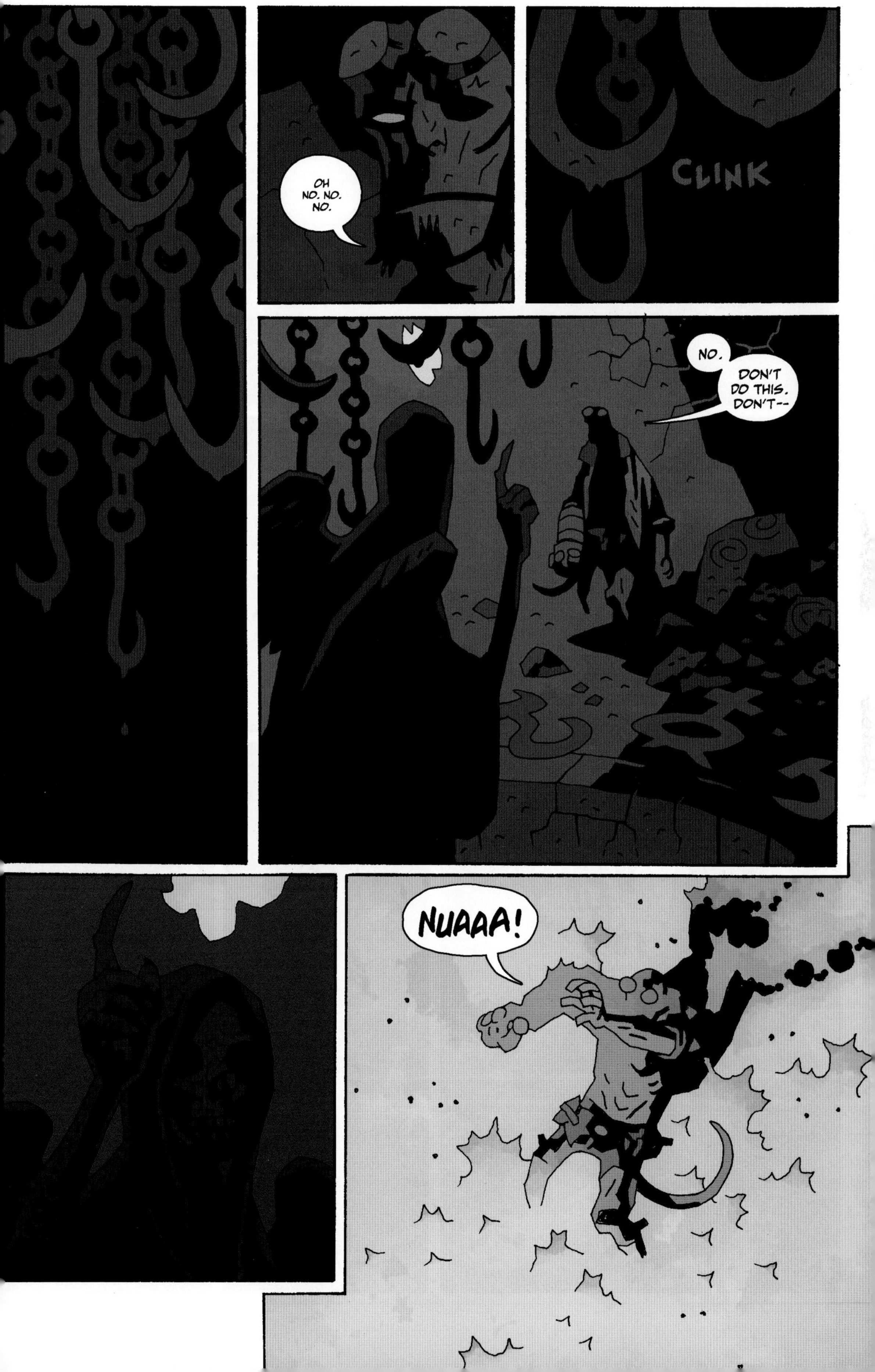
OH NO. NO. NO.
CLINK
NO.
DON'T DO THIS. DON'T--
NUAAA!

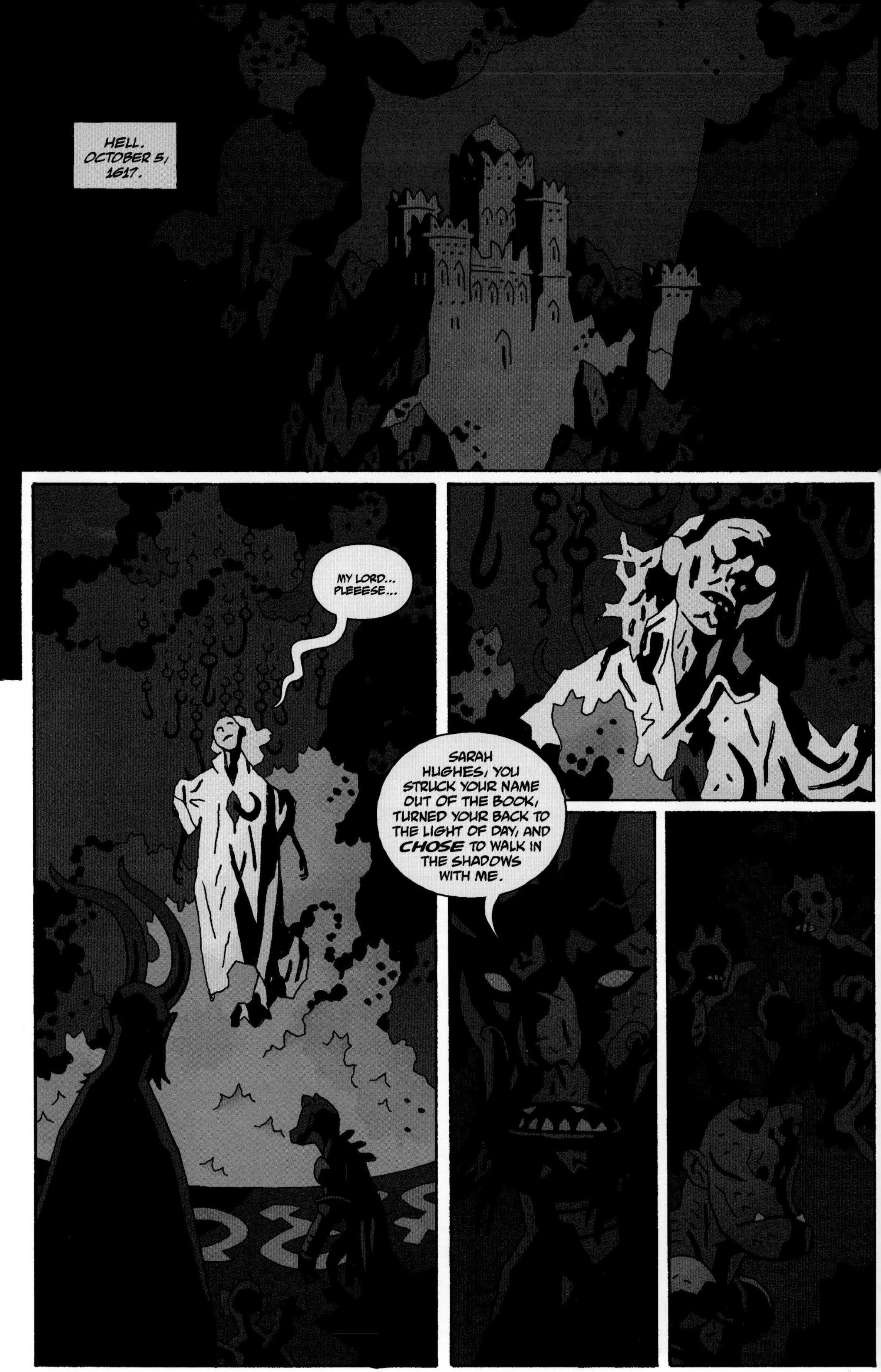
HELL. OCTOBER 5, 1617.
MY LORD... PLEEESE...
SARAH HUGHES, YOU STRUCK YOUR NAME OUT OF THE BOOK, TURNED YOUR BACK TO THE LIGHT OF DAY, AND CHOSE TO WALK IN THE SHADOWS WITH ME.

Chapter Three

FAMILY TIES

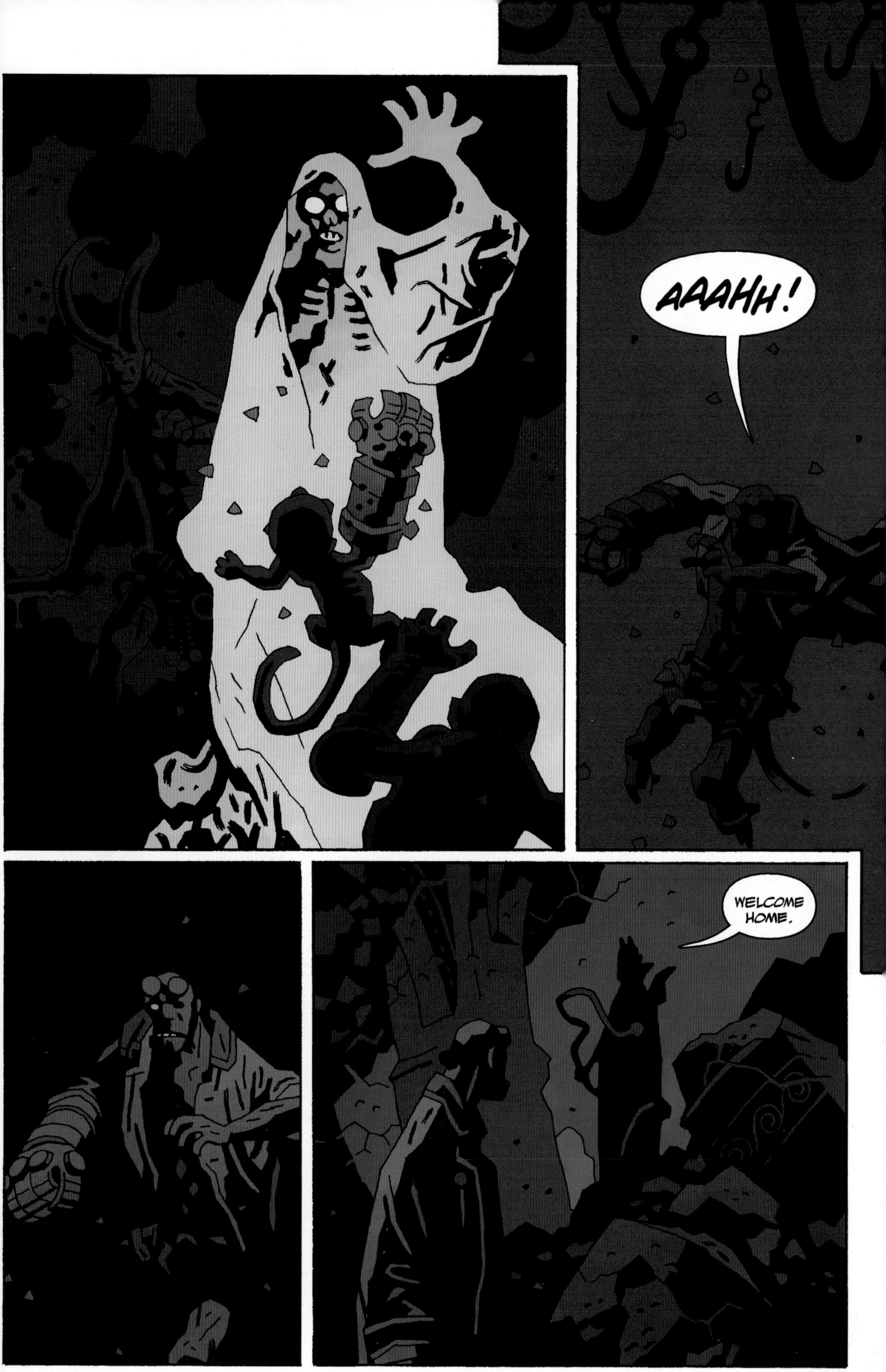
AAAHH!
WELCOME HOME.

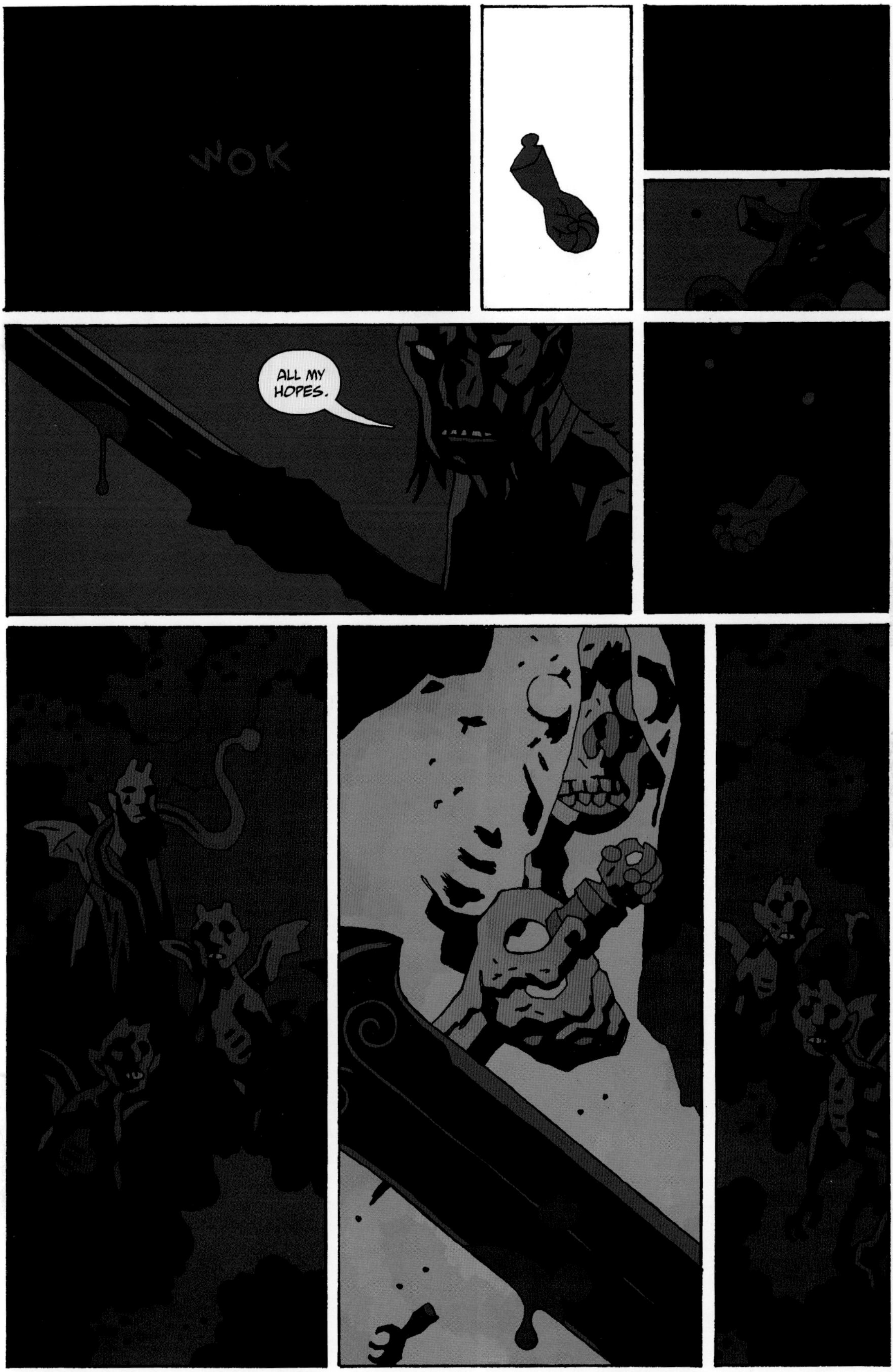

WOK
ALL MY HOPES.

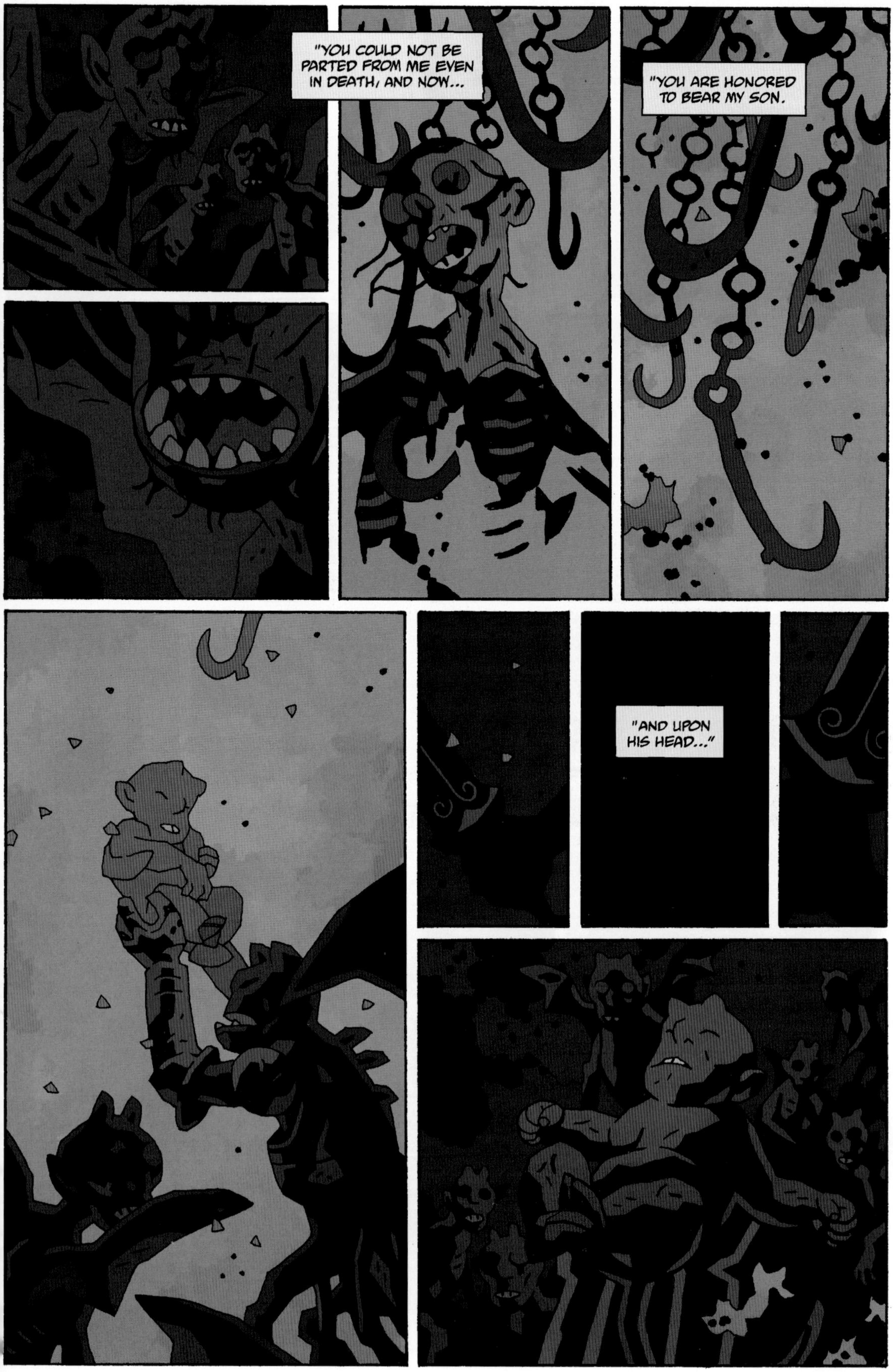
"YOU COULD NOT BE PARTED FROM ME EVEN IN DEATH, AND NOW...
"YOU ARE HONORED TO BEAR MY SON.
"AND UPON HIS HEAD..."

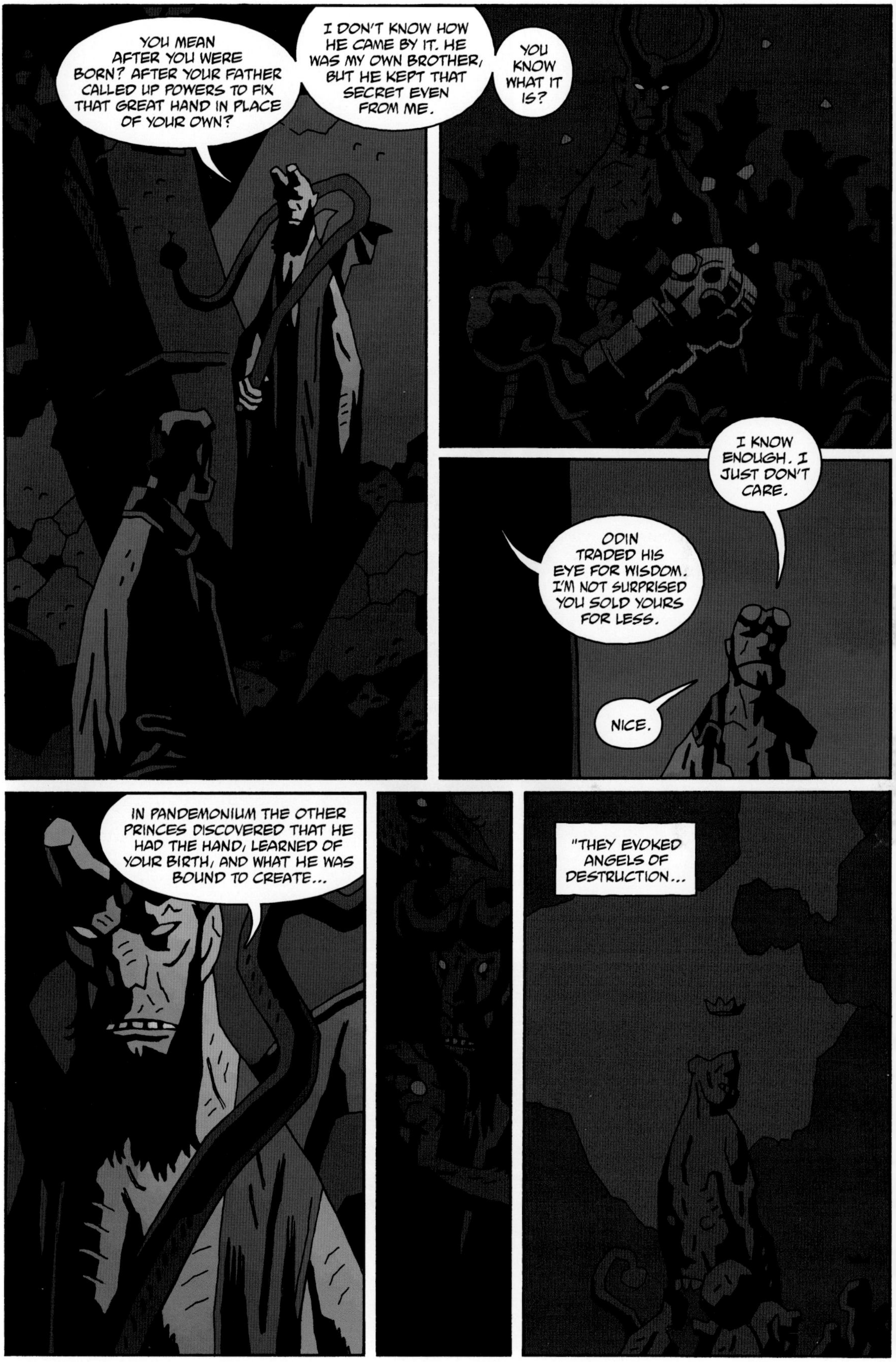
YOU MEAN AFTER YOU WERE BORN? AFTER YOUR FATHER CALLED UP POWERS TO FIX THAT GREAT HAND IN PLACE OF YOUR OWN?
I DON'T KNOW HOW HE CAME BY IT. HE WAS MY OWN BROTHER, BUT HE KEPT THAT SECRET EVEN FROM ME.
YOU KNOW WHAT IT IS?
I KNOW ENOUGH. I JUST DON'T CARE.
ODIN TRADED HIS EYE FOR WISDOM. I'M NOT SURPRISED YOU SOLD YOURS FOR LESS.
NICE.
IN PANDEMONIUM THE OTHER PRINCES DISCOVERED THAT HE HAD THE HAND, LEARNED OF YOUR BIRTH, AND WHAT HE WAS BOUND TO CREATE...
"THEY EVOKED ANGELS OF DESTRUCTION...

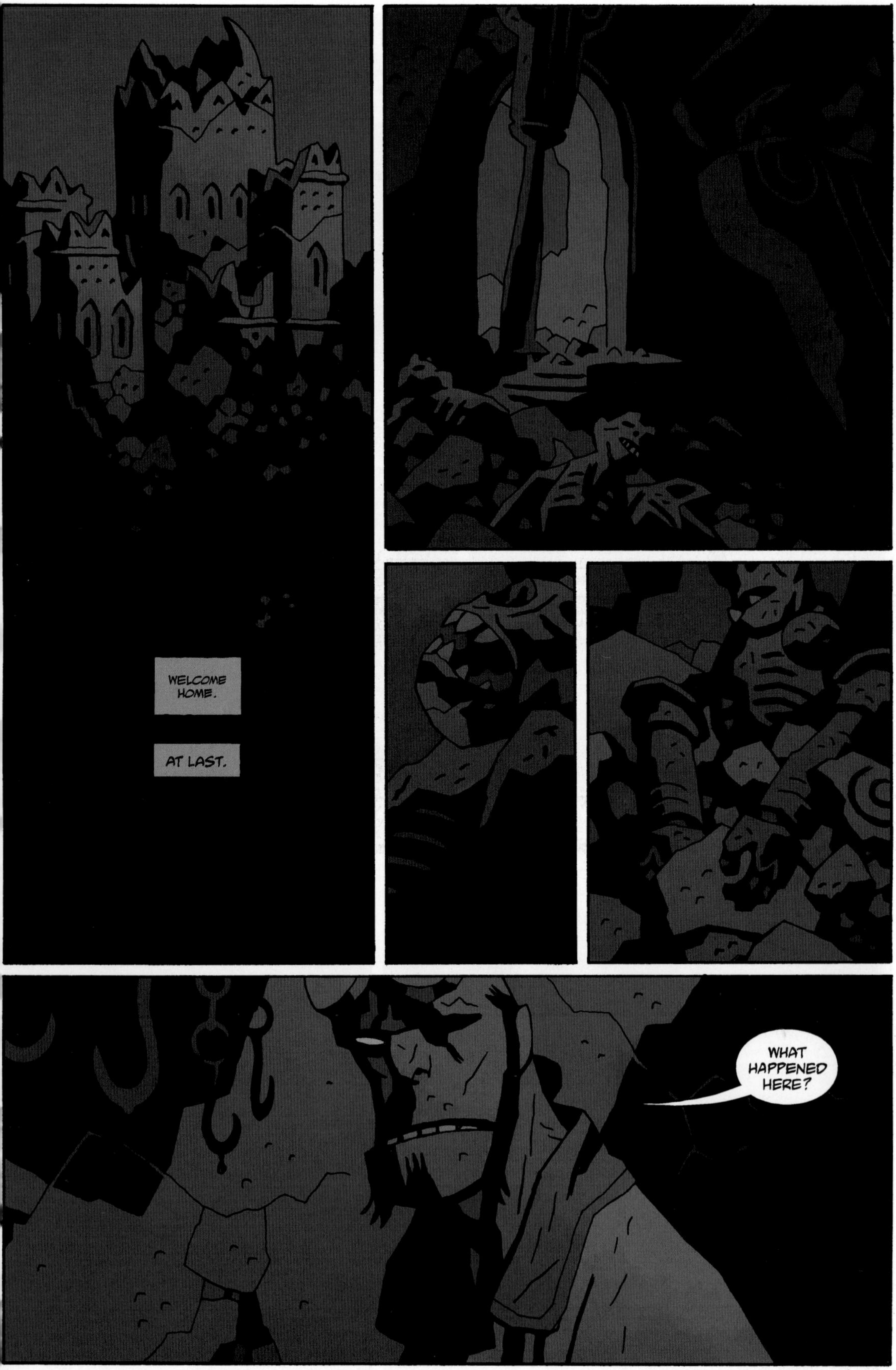
WELCOME HOME.
AT LAST.
WHAT HAPPENED HERE?

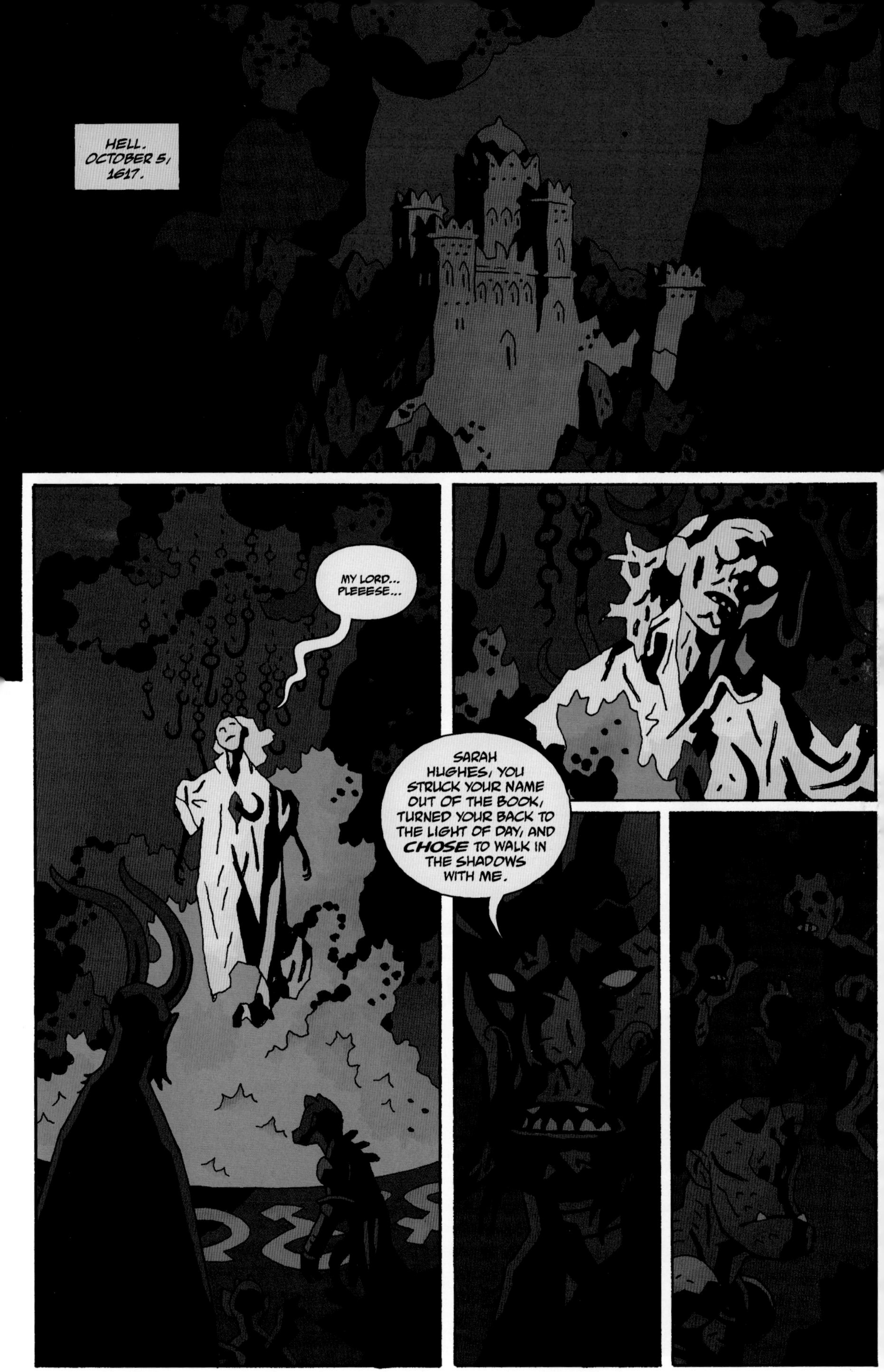
HELL.
OCTOBER 5, 1617.
MY LORD... PLEEESE...
SARAH HUGHES, YOU STRUCK YOUR NAME OUT OF THE BOOK, TURNED YOUR BACK TO THE LIGHT OF DAY, AND CHOSE TO WALK IN THE SHADOWS WITH ME.

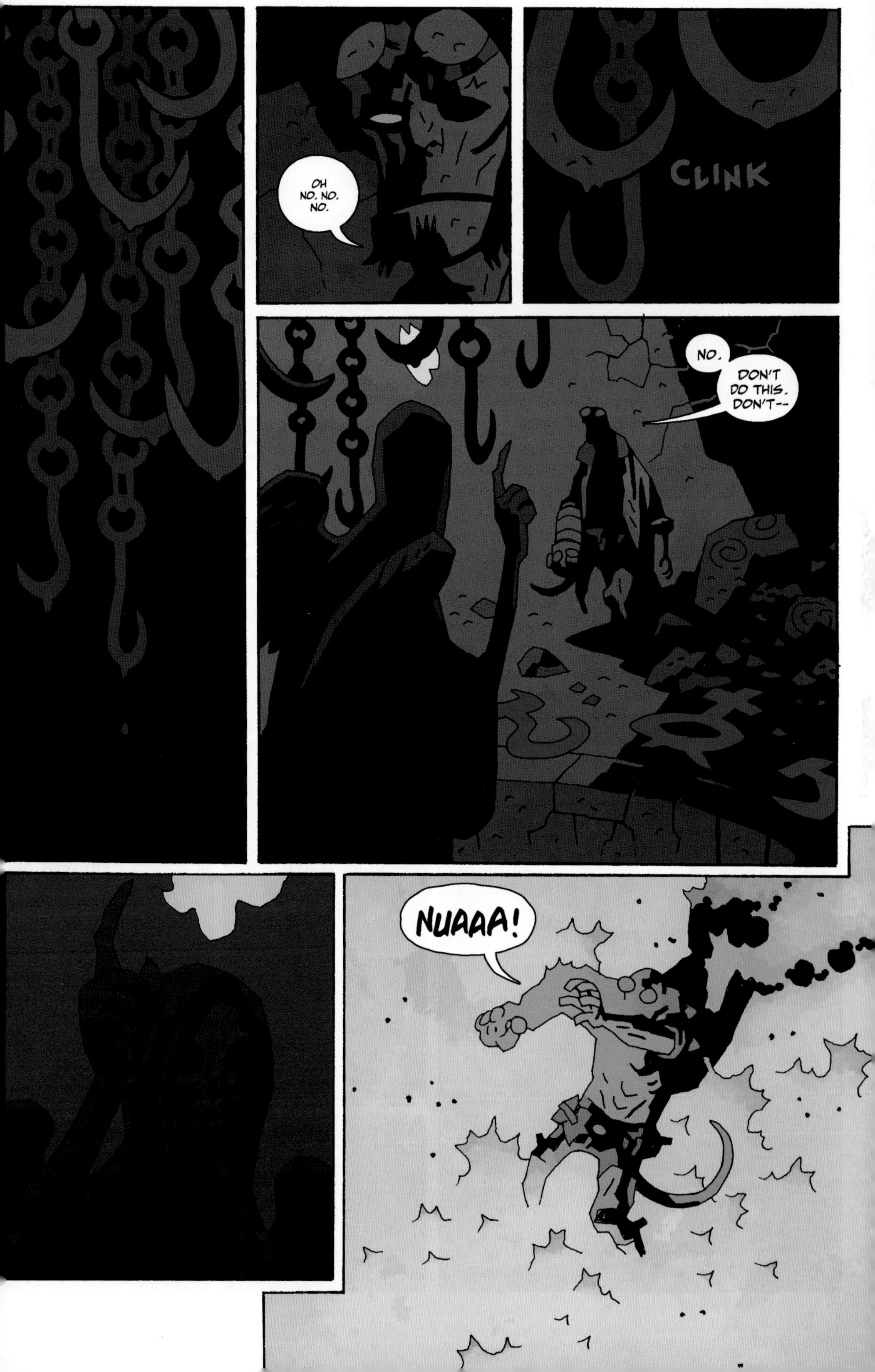
OH NO. NO. NO.
CLINK
NO.
DON'T DO THIS. DON'T--
NUAAA!

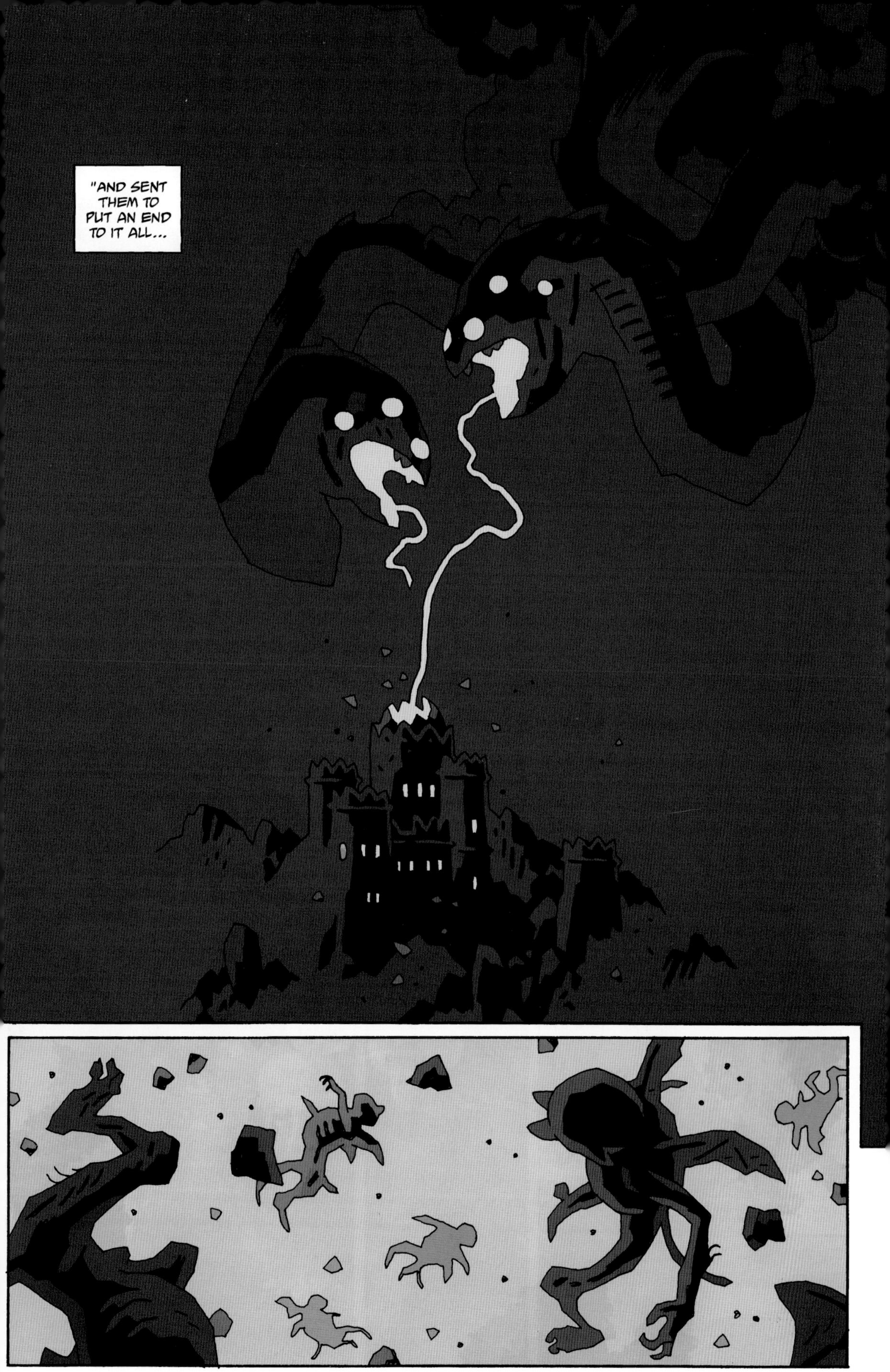
"AND SENT THEM TO PUT AN END TO IT ALL...

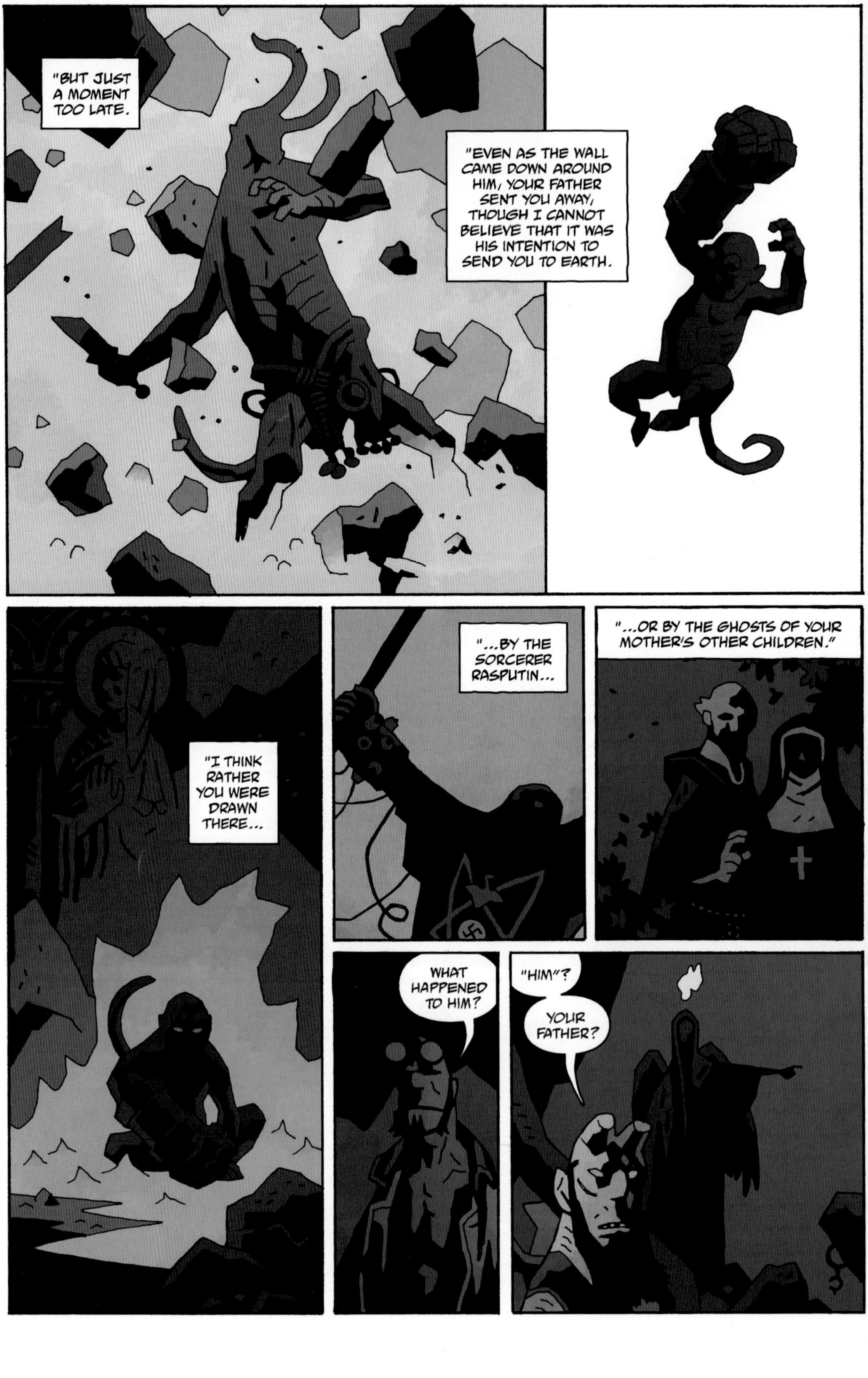
"BUT JUST A MOMENT TOO LATE.
"EVEN AS THE WALL CAME DOWN AROUND HIM, YOUR FATHER SENT YOU AWAY, THOUGH I CANNOT BELIEVE THAT IT WAS HIS INTENTION TO SEND YOU TO EARTH.
"I THINK RATHER YOU WERE DRAWN THERE...
"...BY THE SORCERER RASPUTIN...
"...OR BY THE GHOSTS OF YOUR MOTHER'S OTHER CHILDREN."
WHAT HAPPENED TO HIM?
"HIM"?
YOUR FATHER?

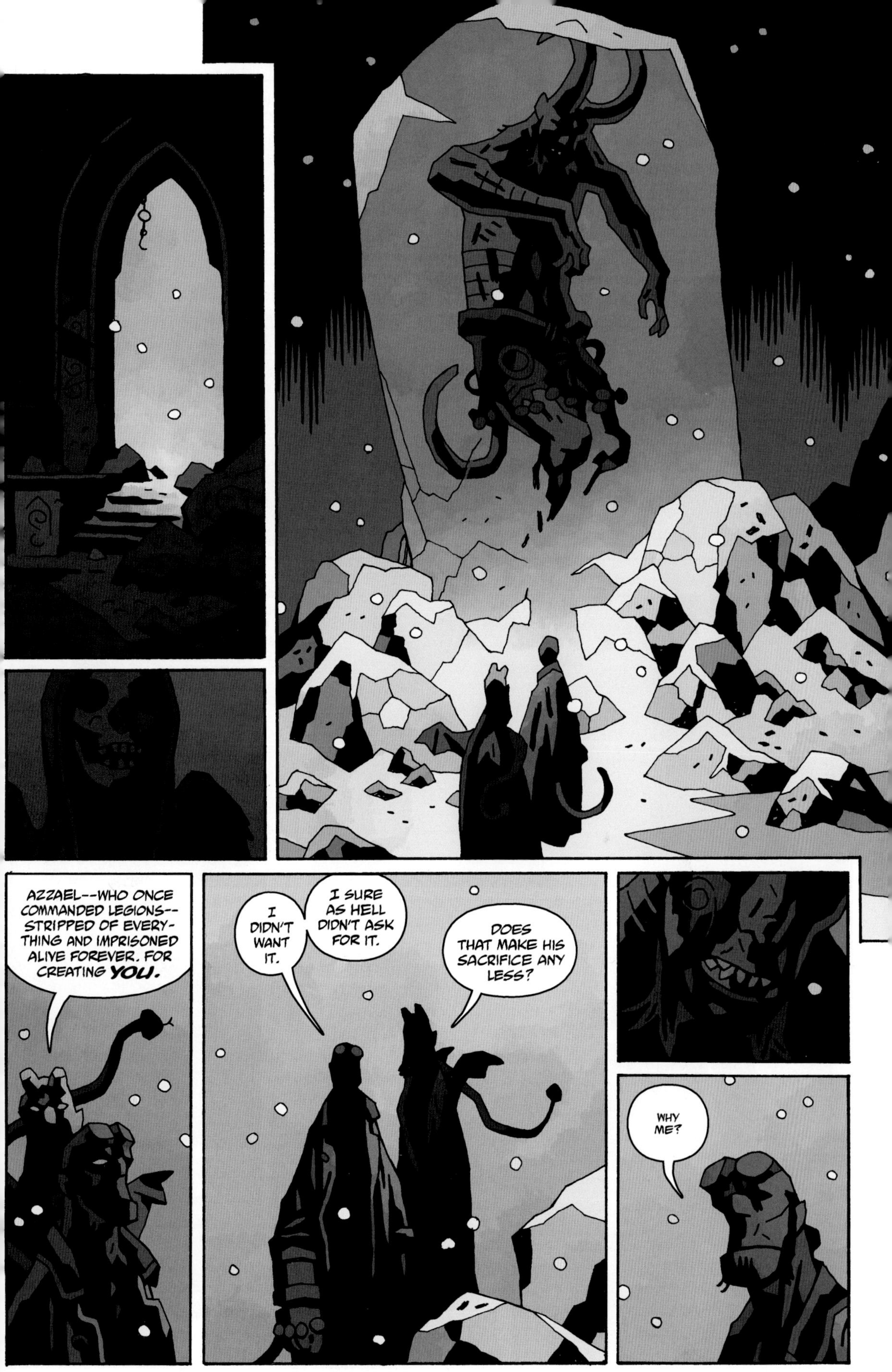
AZZAEL--WHO ONCE COMMANDED LEGIONS--STRIPPED OF EVERYTHING AND IMPRISONED ALIVE FOREVER. FOR CREATING **YOU.**
I DIDN'T WANT IT.
I SURE AS HELL DIDN'T ASK FOR IT.
DOES THAT MAKE HIS SACRIFICE ANY LESS?
WHY ME?

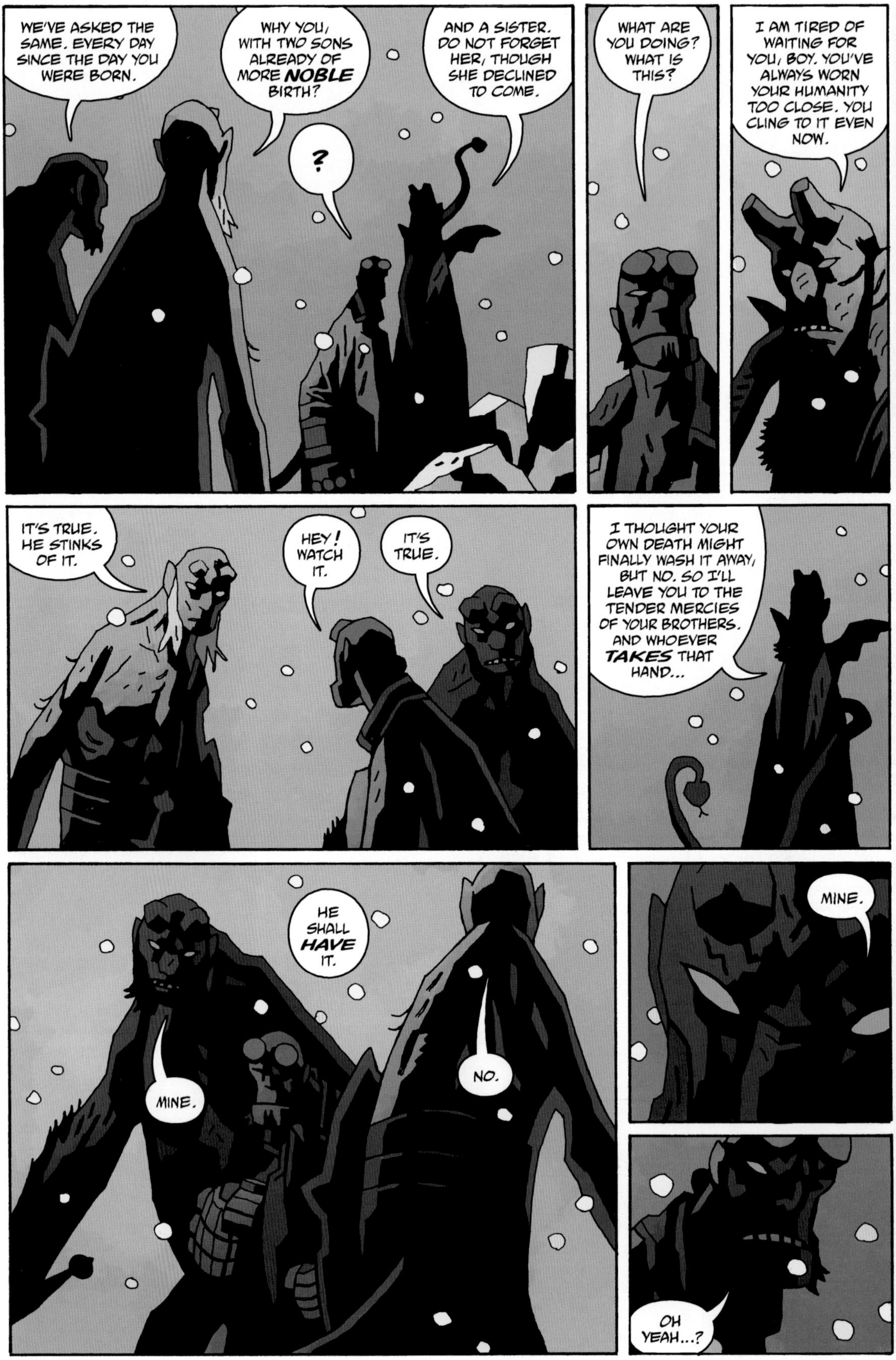

WE'VE ASKED THE SAME. EVERY DAY SINCE THE DAY YOU WERE BORN.
WHY YOU, WITH TWO SONS ALREADY OF MORE NOBLE BIRTH?
?
AND A SISTER. DO NOT FORGET HER, THOUGH SHE DECLINED TO COME.
WHAT ARE YOU DOING? WHAT IS THIS?
I AM TIRED OF WAITING FOR YOU, BOY. YOU'VE ALWAYS WORN YOUR HUMANITY TOO CLOSE. YOU CLING TO IT EVEN NOW.
IT'S TRUE. HE STINKS OF IT.
HEY! WATCH IT.
IT'S TRUE.
I THOUGHT YOUR OWN DEATH MIGHT FINALLY WASH IT AWAY, BUT NO. SO I'LL LEAVE YOU TO THE TENDER MERCIES OF YOUR BROTHERS, AND WHOEVER TAKES THAT HAND...
HE SHALL HAVE IT.
MINE.
NO.
MINE.
OH YEAH...?

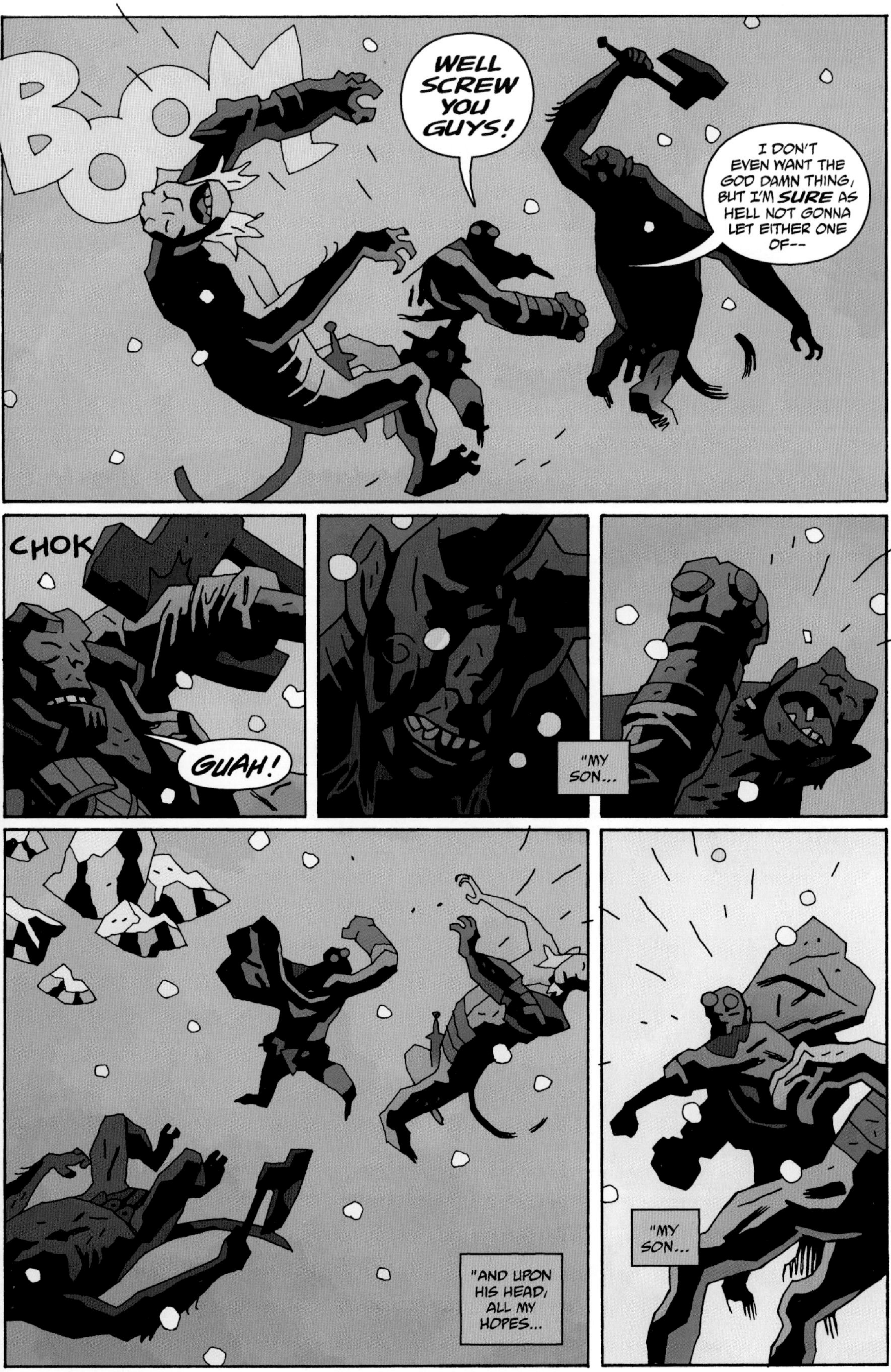
BOOM
WELL SCREW YOU GUYS!
I DON'T EVEN WANT THE GOD DAMN THING, BUT I'M SURE AS HELL NOT GONNA LET EITHER ONE OF--
CHOK
GUAH!
"MY SON...
"AND UPON HIS HEAD, ALL MY HOPES...
"MY SON...

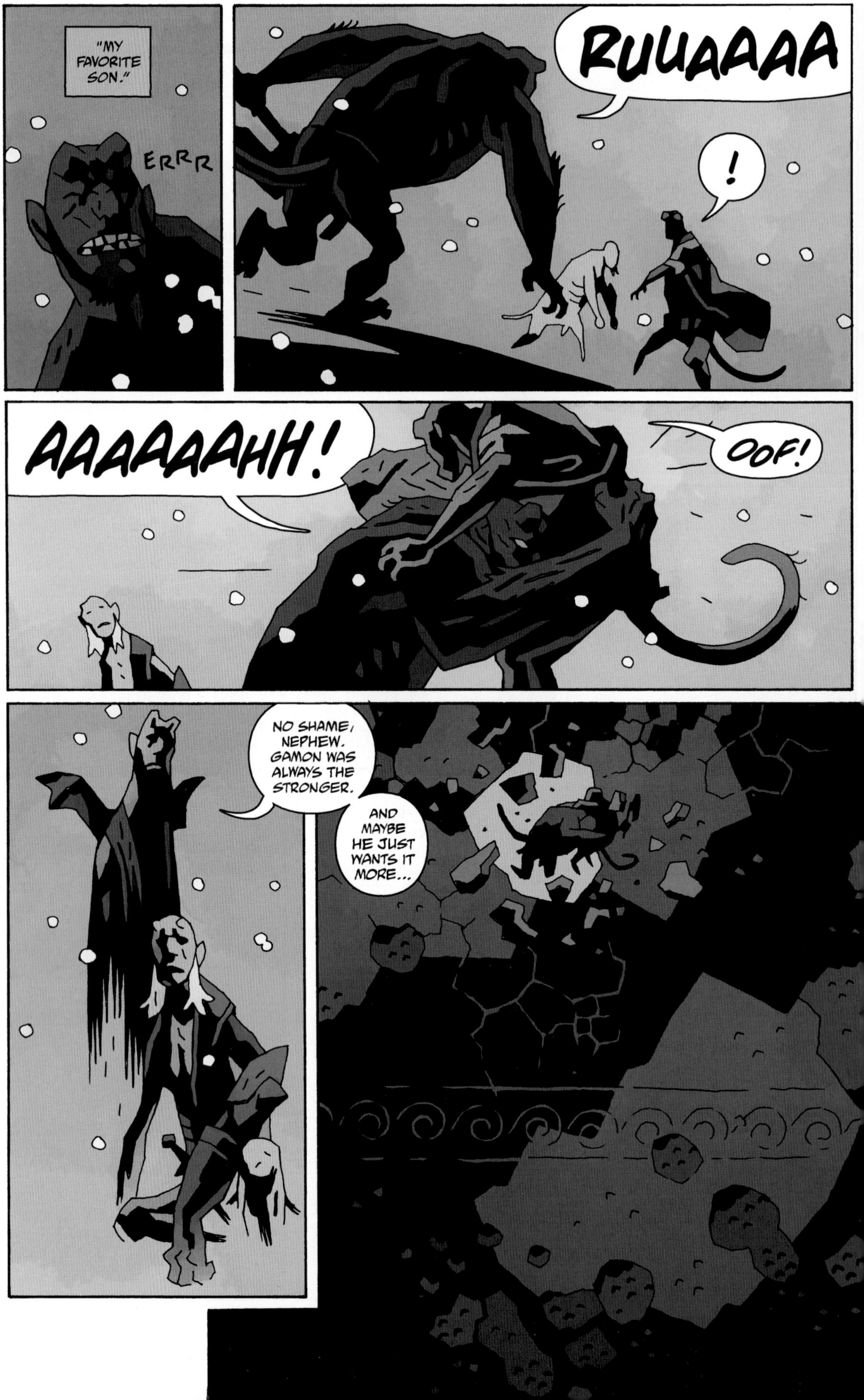
"MY FAVORITE SON."
ERRR
RUUAAAA
!
AAAAAAHH!
OOF!
NO SHAME, NEPHEW. GAMON WAS ALWAYS THE STRONGER.
AND MAYBE HE JUST WANTS IT MORE...

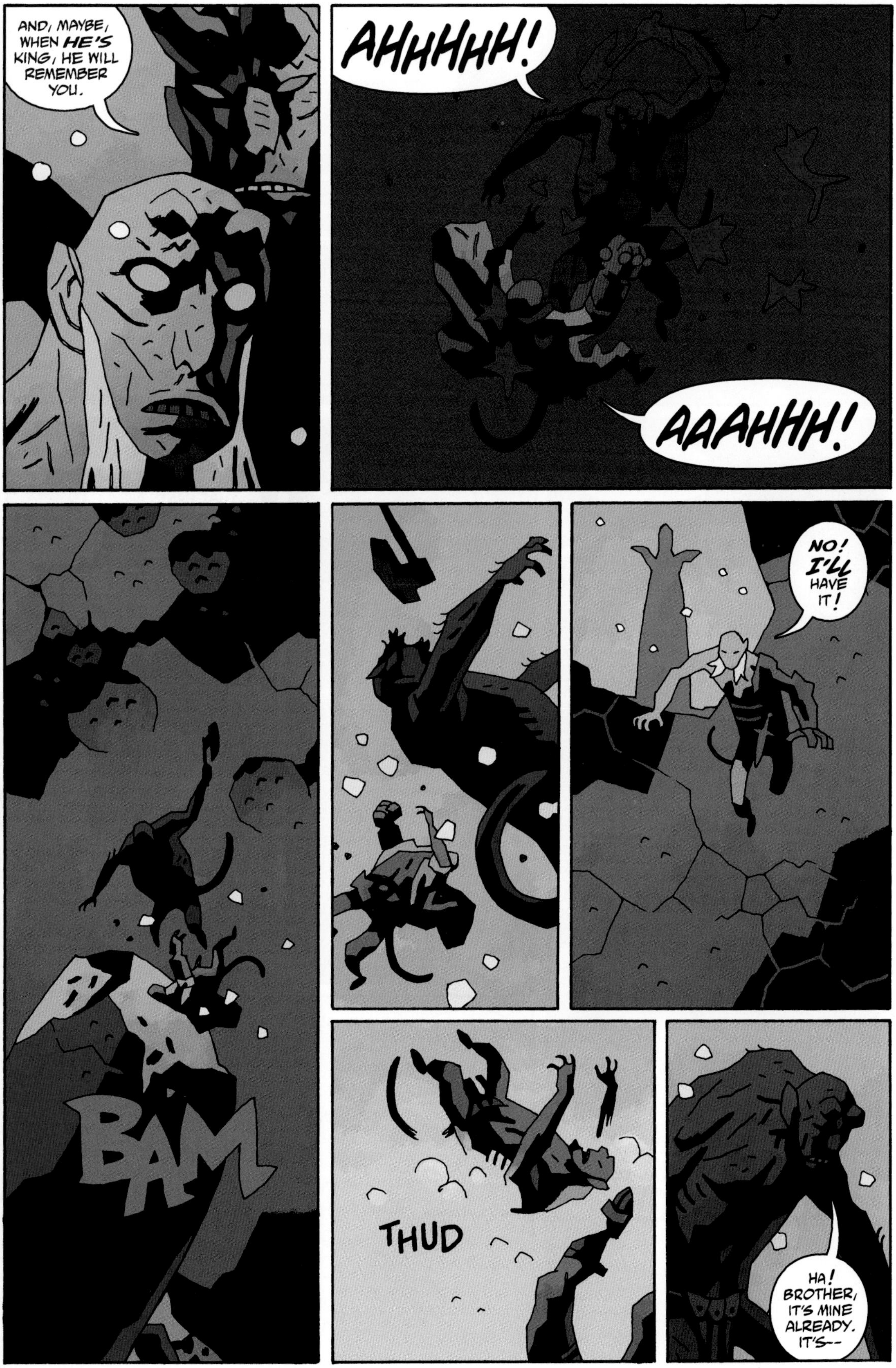
AND, MAYBE, WHEN HE'S KING, HE WILL REMEMBER YOU.
AHHHHH!
AAAHHH!
BAM
NO! I'LL HAVE IT!
THUD
HA! BROTHER, IT'S MINE ALREADY. IT'S--

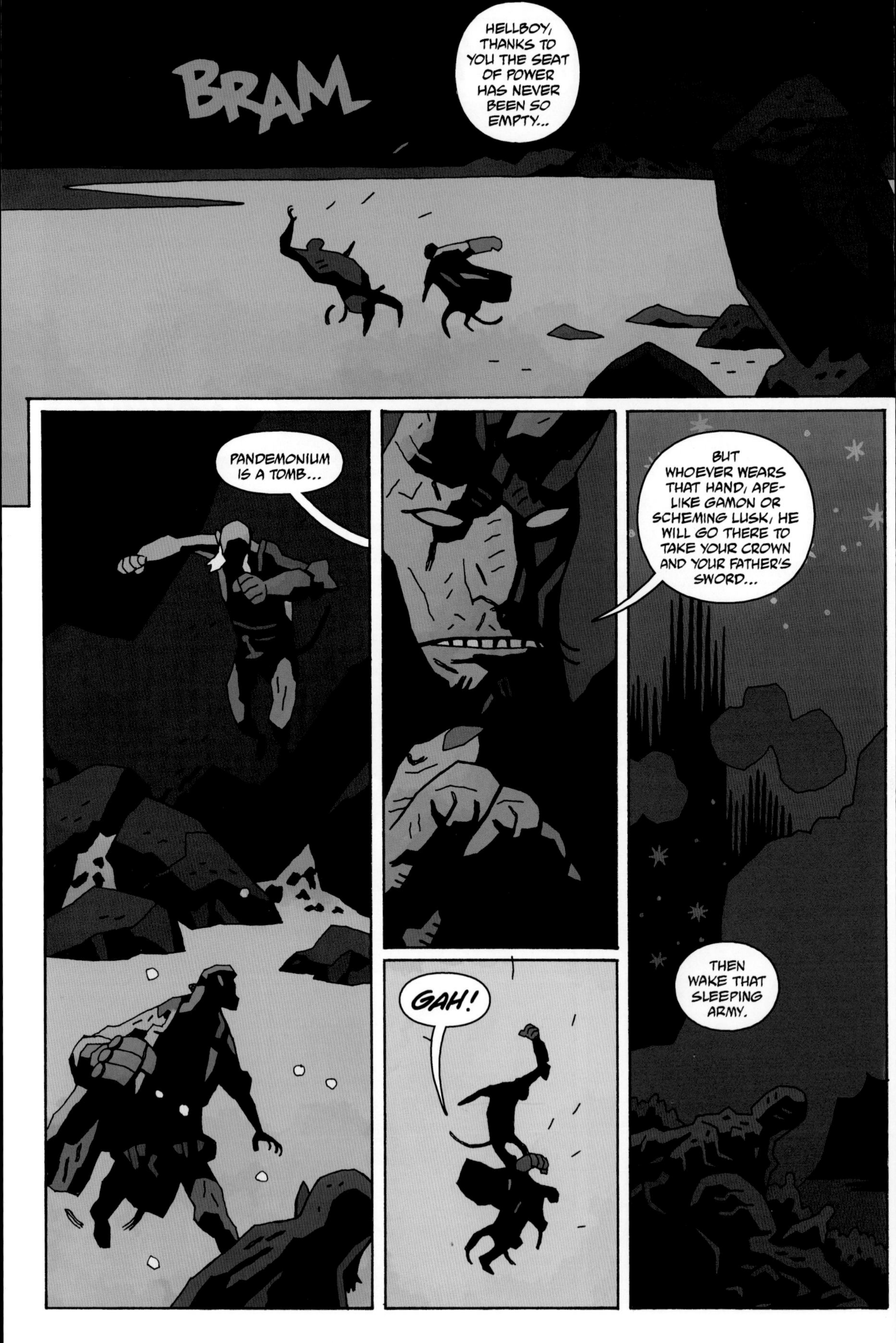
BRAM
HELLBOY, THANKS TO YOU THE SEAT OF POWER HAS NEVER BEEN SO EMPTY...
PANDEMONIUM IS A TOMB...
BUT WHOEVER WEARS THAT HAND, APE-LIKE GAMON OR SCHEMING LUSK, HE WILL GO THERE TO TAKE YOUR CROWN AND YOUR FATHER'S SWORD...
GAH!
THEN WAKE THAT SLEEPING ARMY.

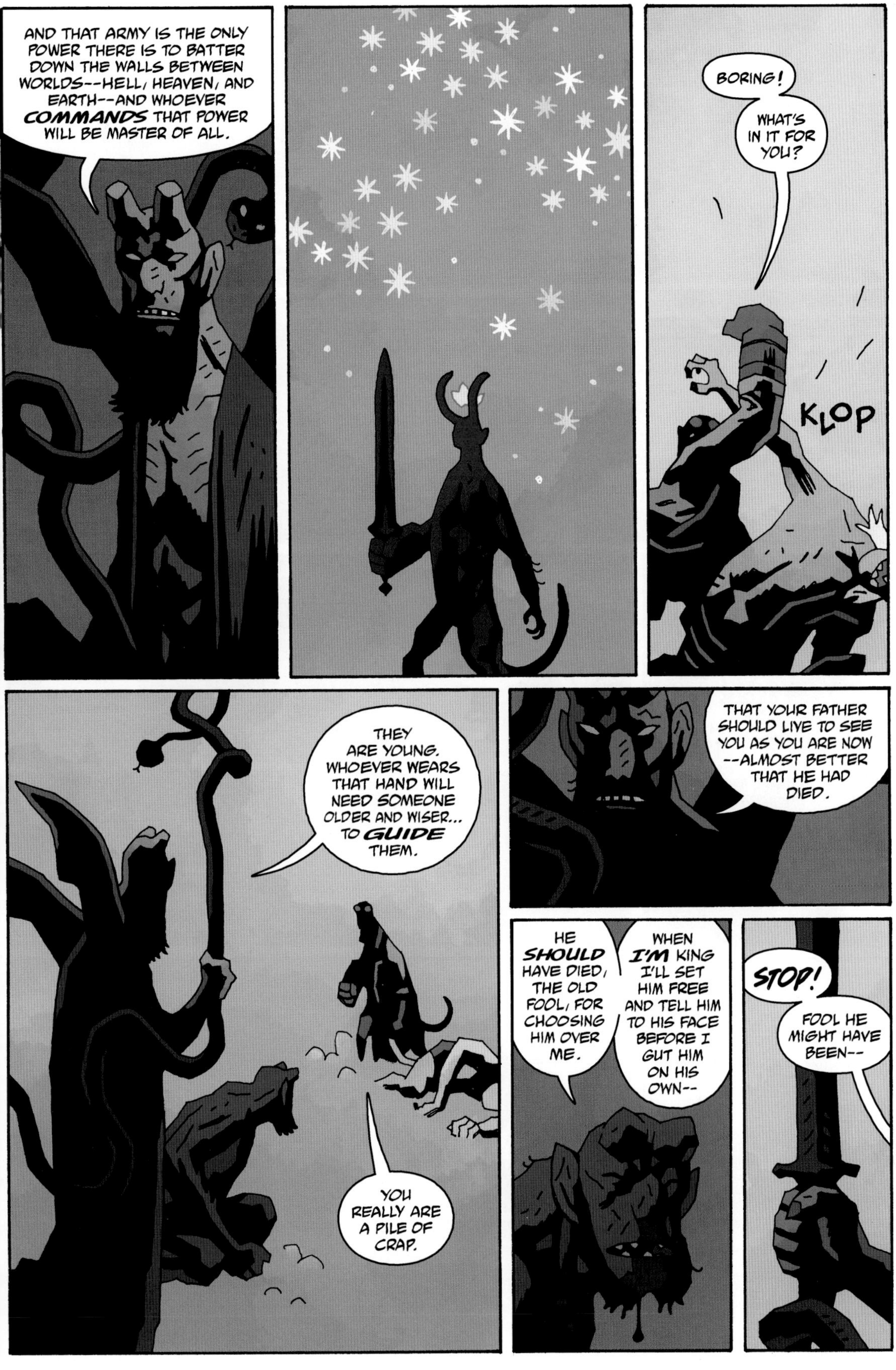
AND THAT ARMY IS THE ONLY POWER THERE IS TO BATTER DOWN THE WALLS BETWEEN WORLDS--HELL, HEAVEN, AND EARTH--AND WHOEVER COMMANDS THAT POWER WILL BE MASTER OF ALL.
BORING!
WHAT'S IN IT FOR YOU?
KLOP
THEY ARE YOUNG. WHOEVER WEARS THAT HAND WILL NEED SOMEONE OLDER AND WISER... TO GUIDE THEM.
YOU REALLY ARE A PILE OF CRAP.
THAT YOUR FATHER SHOULD LIVE TO SEE YOU AS YOU ARE NOW --ALMOST BETTER THAT HE HAD DIED.
HE SHOULD HAVE DIED, THE OLD FOOL, FOR CHOOSING HIM OVER ME.
WHEN I'M KING I'LL SET HIM FREE AND TELL HIM TO HIS FACE BEFORE I GUT HIM ON HIS OWN--
STOP!
FOOL HE MIGHT HAVE BEEN--

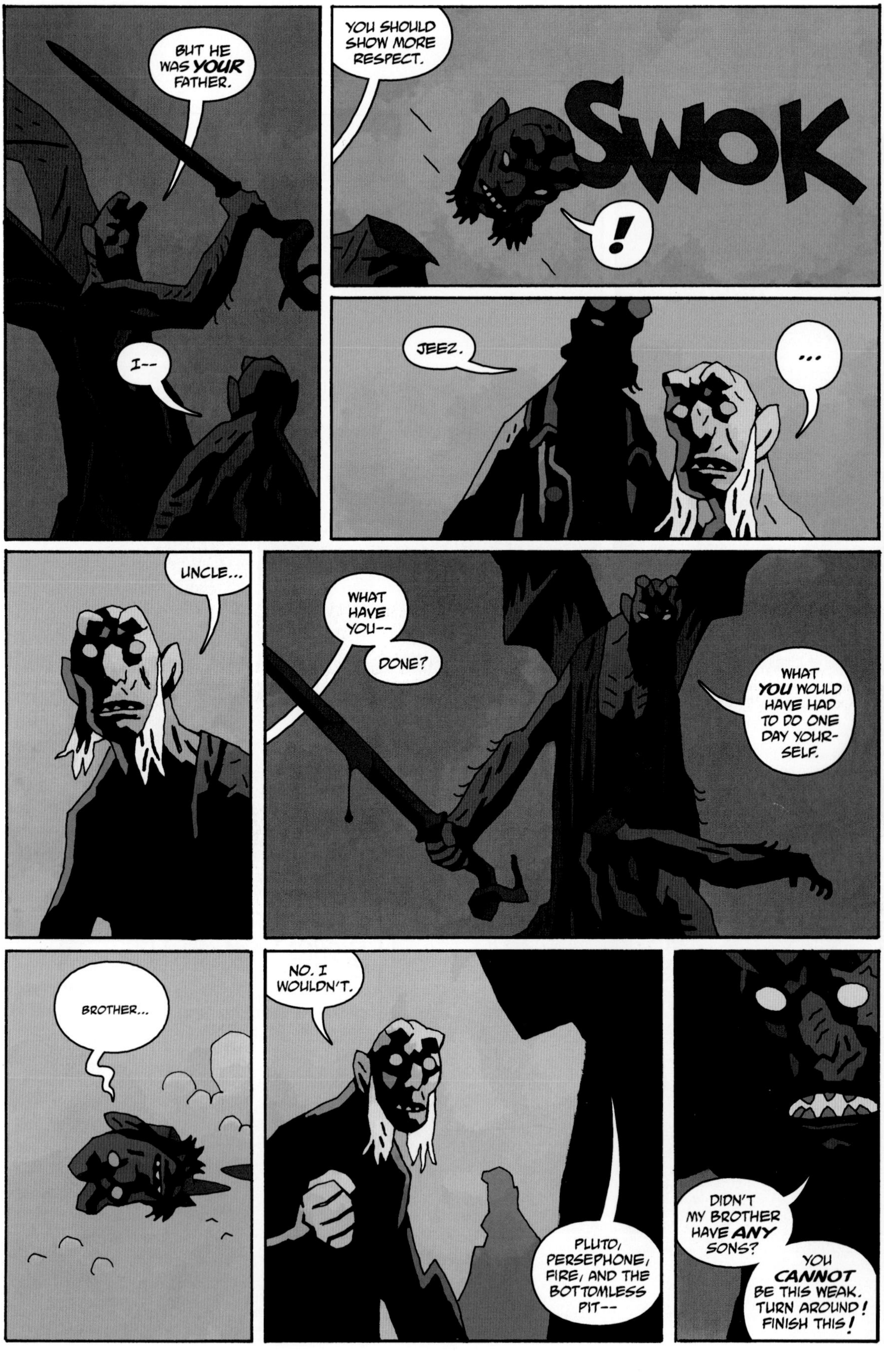
BUT HE WAS YOUR FATHER.
I--
YOU SHOULD SHOW MORE RESPECT.
SWOK
!
JEEZ.
...
UNCLE...
WHAT HAVE YOU--
DONE?
WHAT YOU WOULD HAVE HAD TO DO ONE DAY YOUR-SELF.
BROTHER...
NO. I WOULDN'T.
PLUTO, PERSEPHONE, FIRE, AND THE BOTTOMLESS PIT--
DIDN'T MY BROTHER HAVE ANY SONS?
YOU CANNOT BE THIS WEAK. TURN AROUND! FINISH THIS!

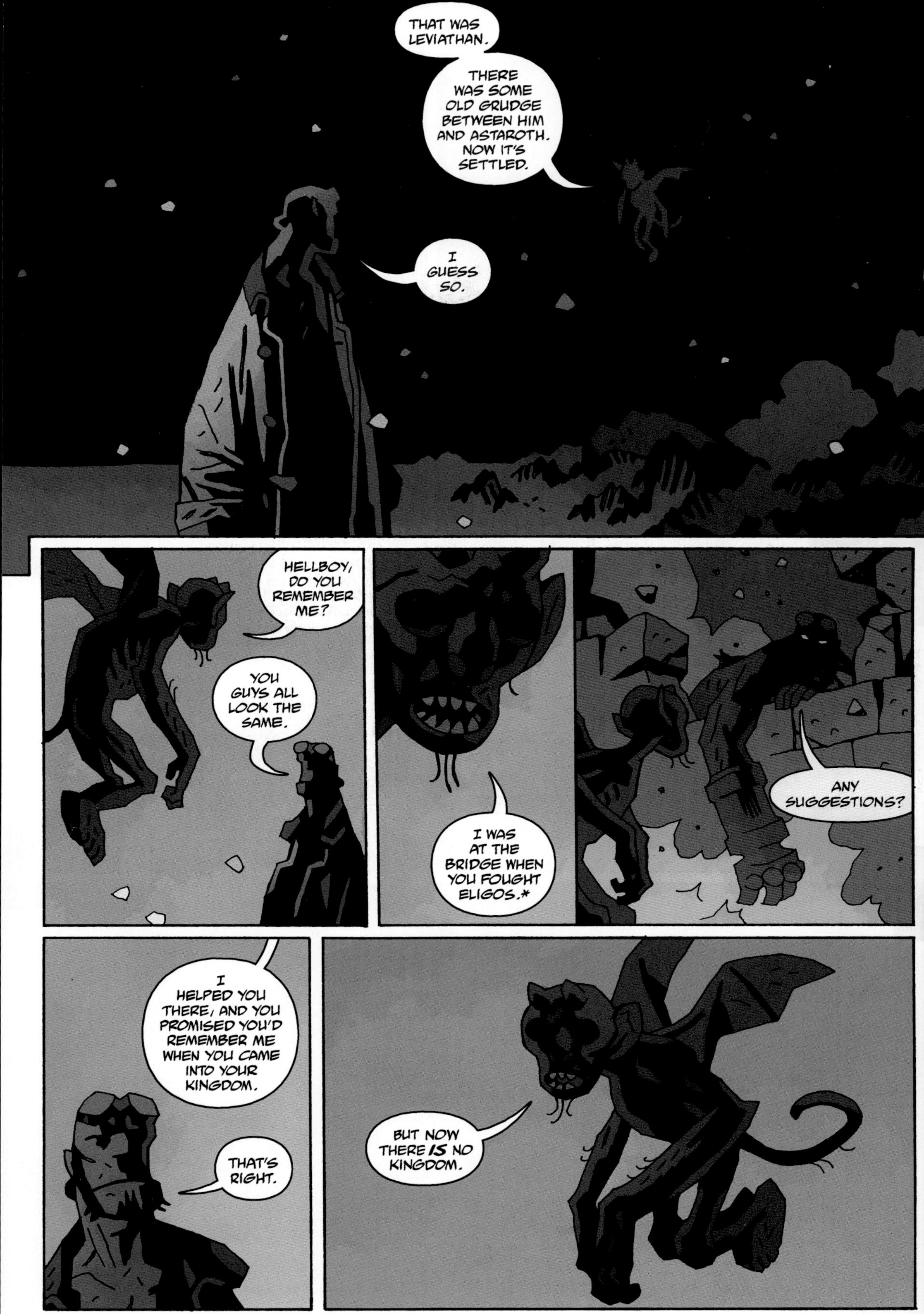
THAT WAS LEVIATHAN.
THERE WAS SOME OLD GRUDGE BETWEEN HIM AND ASTAROTH. NOW IT'S SETTLED.
I GUESS SO.
HELLBOY, DO YOU REMEMBER ME?
YOU GUYS ALL LOOK THE SAME.
I WAS AT THE BRIDGE WHEN YOU FOUGHT ELIGOS.*
ANY SUGGESTIONS?
I HELPED YOU THERE, AND YOU PROMISED YOU'D REMEMBER ME WHEN YOU CAME INTO YOUR KINGDOM.
THAT'S RIGHT.
BUT NOW THERE *IS* NO KINGDOM.

*HELLBOY: THE WILD HUNT

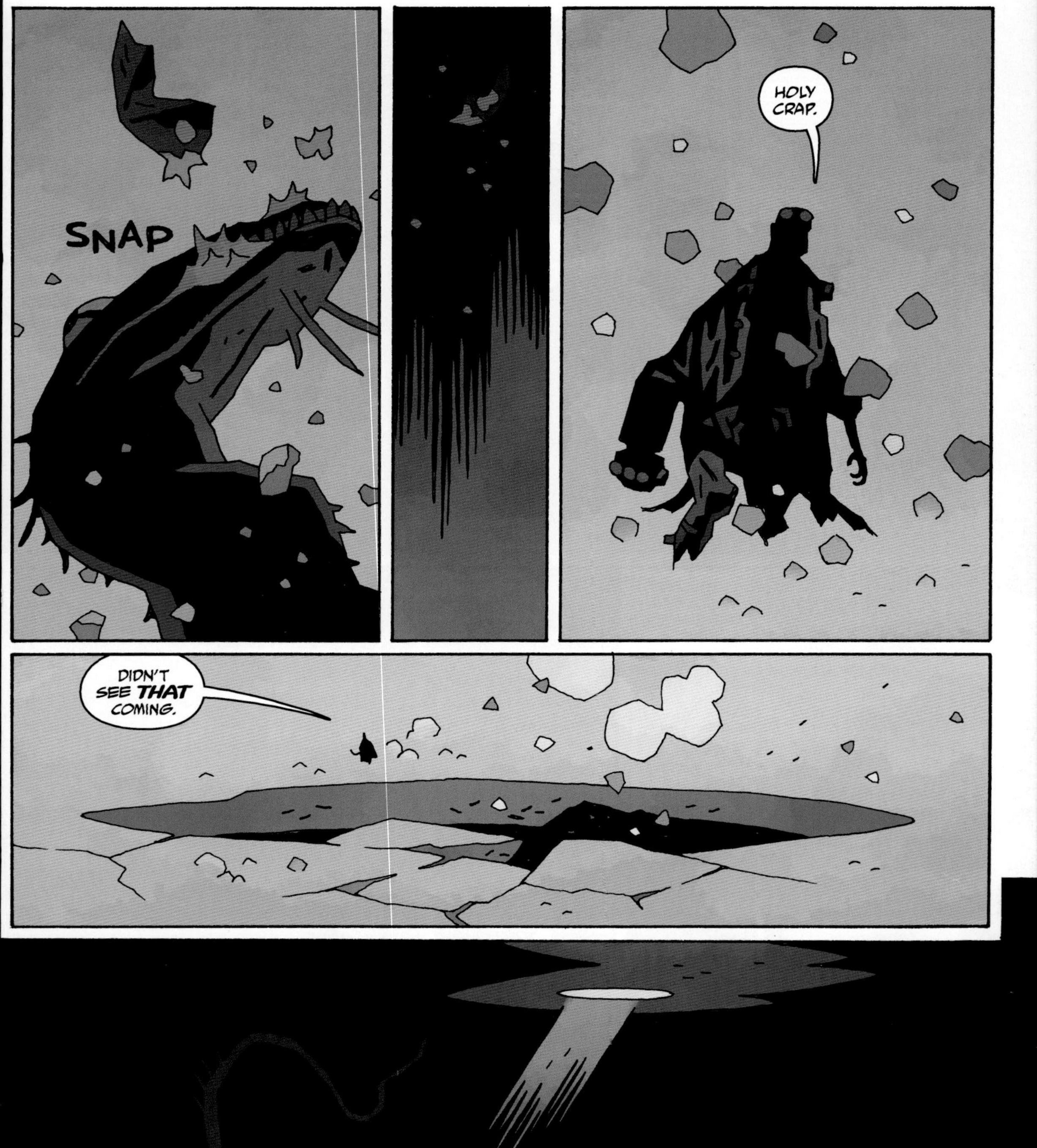
SNAP
HOLY CRAP.
DIDN'T SEE THAT COMING.

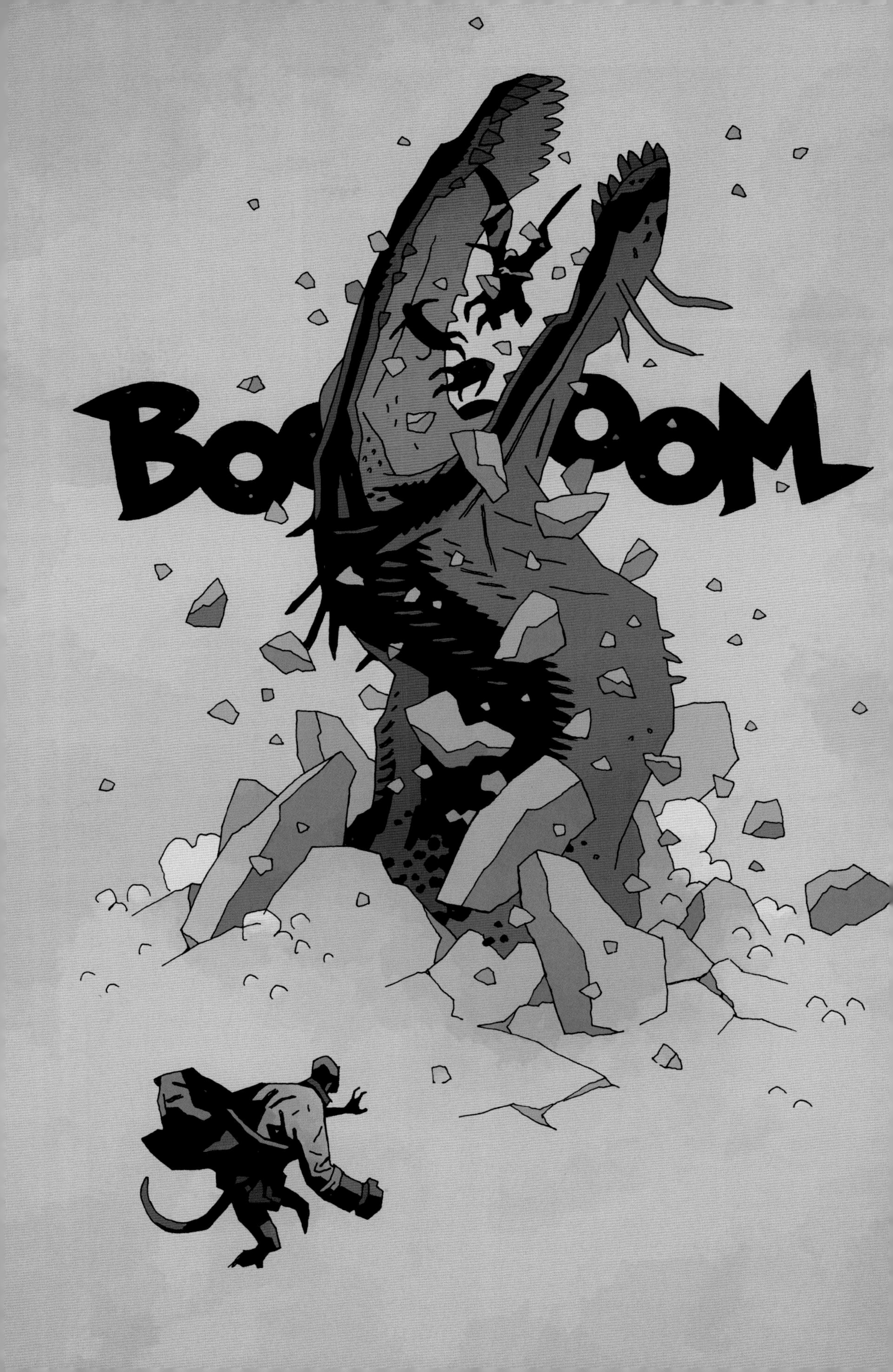
BO OOM

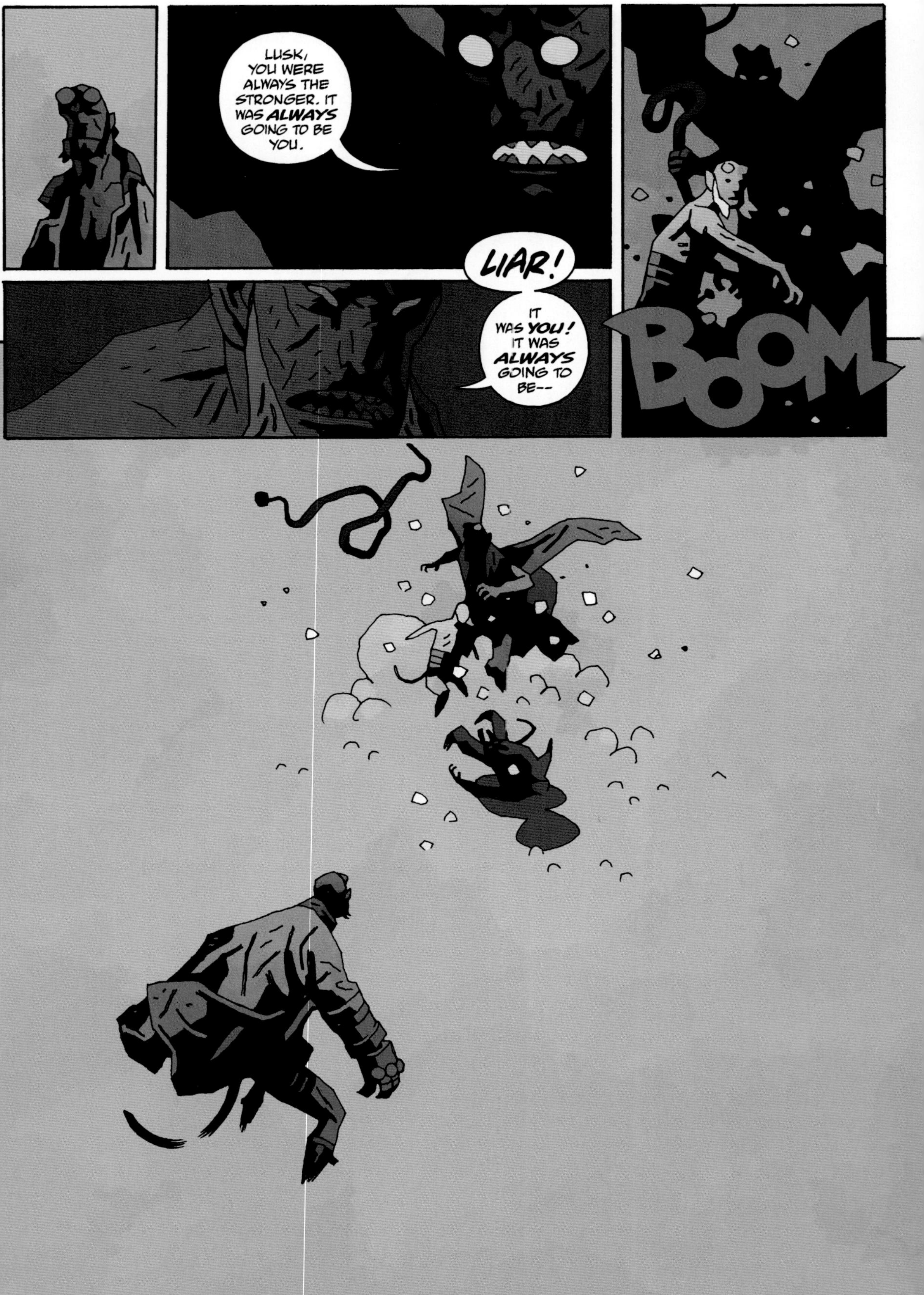
LUSK, YOU WERE ALWAYS THE STRONGER. IT WAS ALWAYS GOING TO BE YOU.
LIAR!
IT WAS YOU! IT WAS ALWAYS GOING TO BE--
BOOM

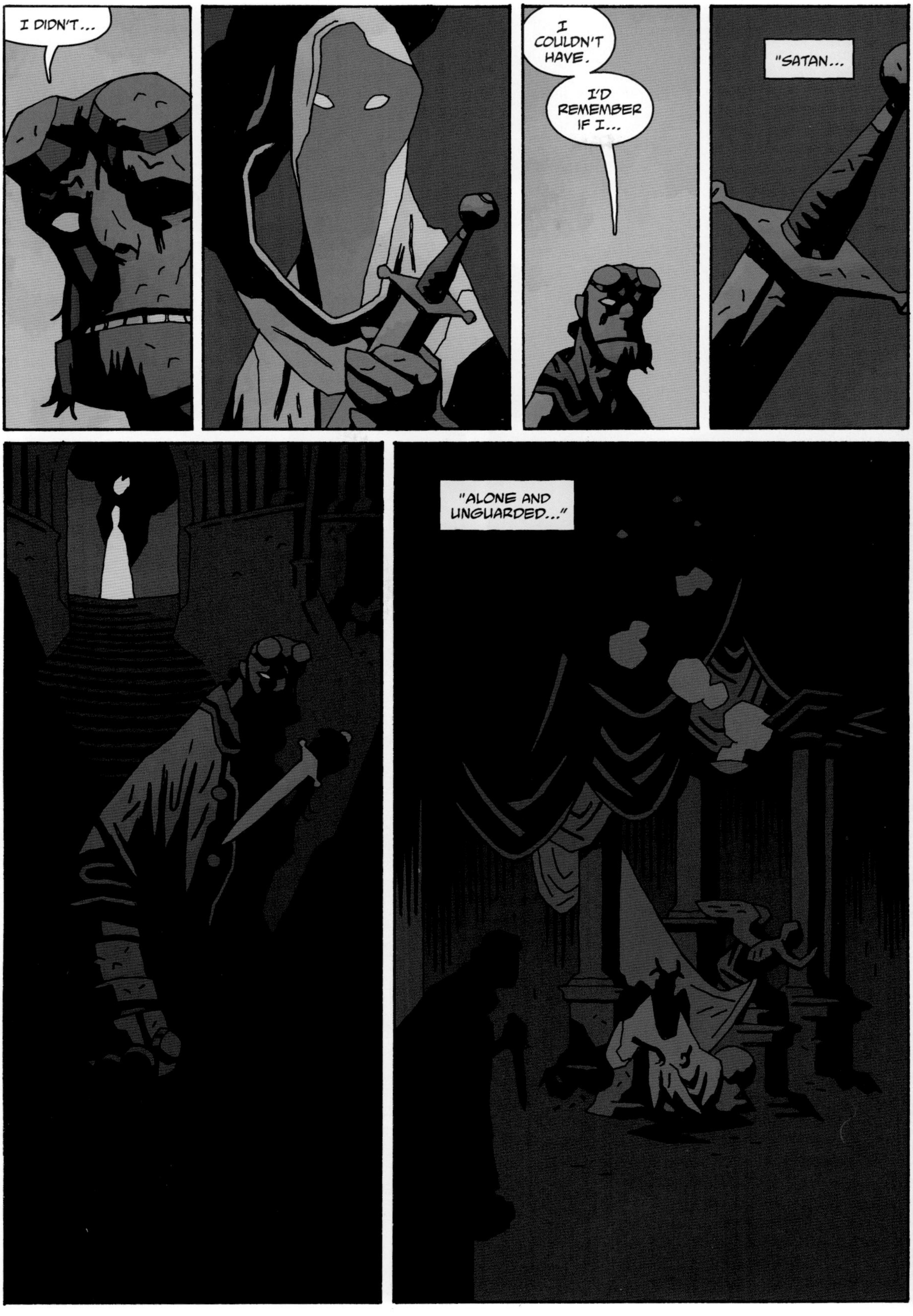
I DIDN'T...
I COULDN'T HAVE.
I'D REMEMBER IF I...
"SATAN...
"ALONE AND UNGUARDED..."

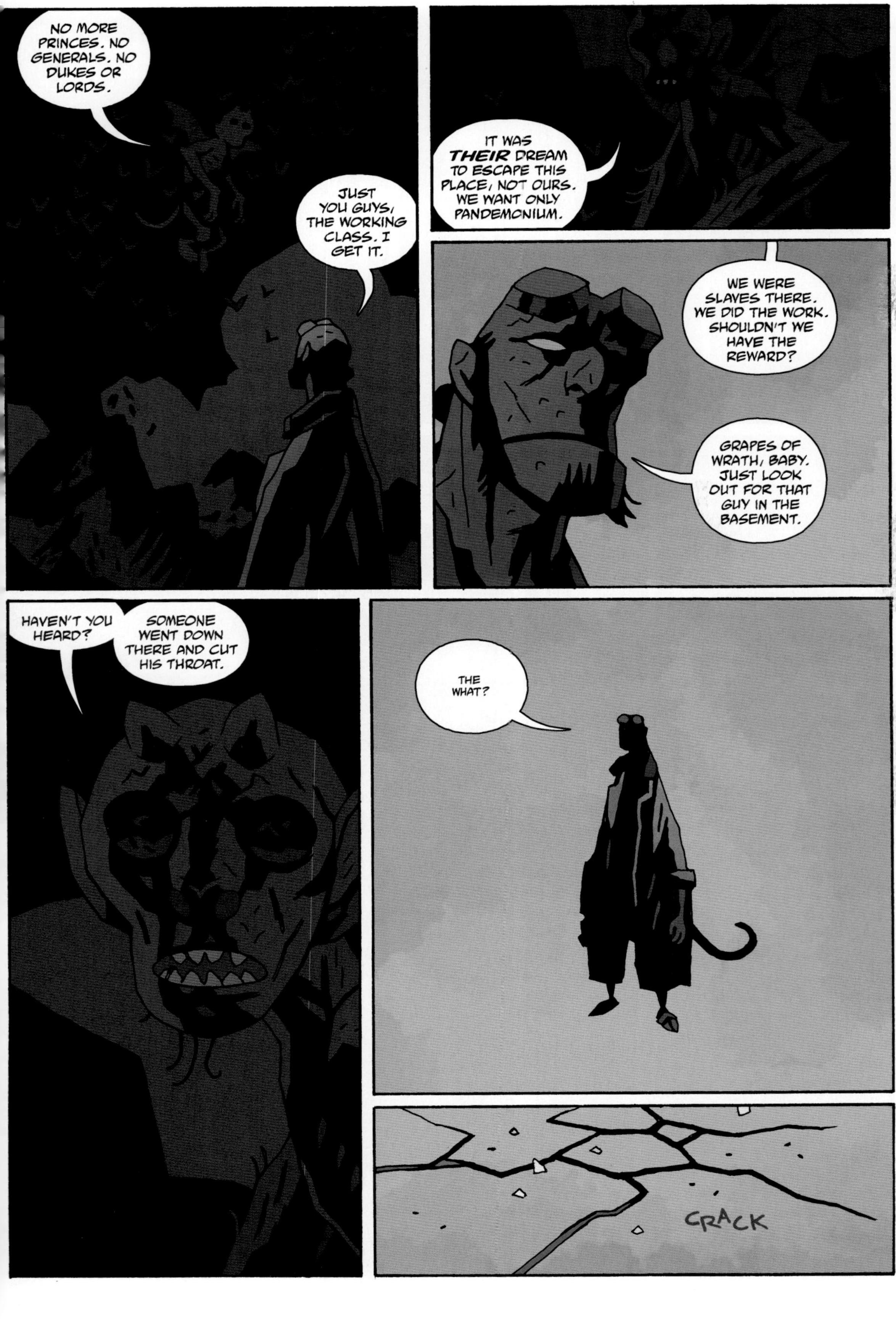
NO MORE PRINCES. NO GENERALS. NO DUKES OR LORDS.
JUST YOU GUYS, THE WORKING CLASS. I GET IT.
IT WAS **THEIR** DREAM TO ESCAPE THIS PLACE, NOT OURS. WE WANT ONLY PANDEMONIUM.
WE WERE SLAVES THERE. WE DID THE WORK. SHOULDN'T WE HAVE THE REWARD?
GRAPES OF WRATH, BABY. JUST LOOK OUT FOR THAT GUY IN THE BASEMENT.
HAVEN'T YOU HEARD?
SOMEONE WENT DOWN THERE AND CUT HIS THROAT.
THE WHAT?
CRACK

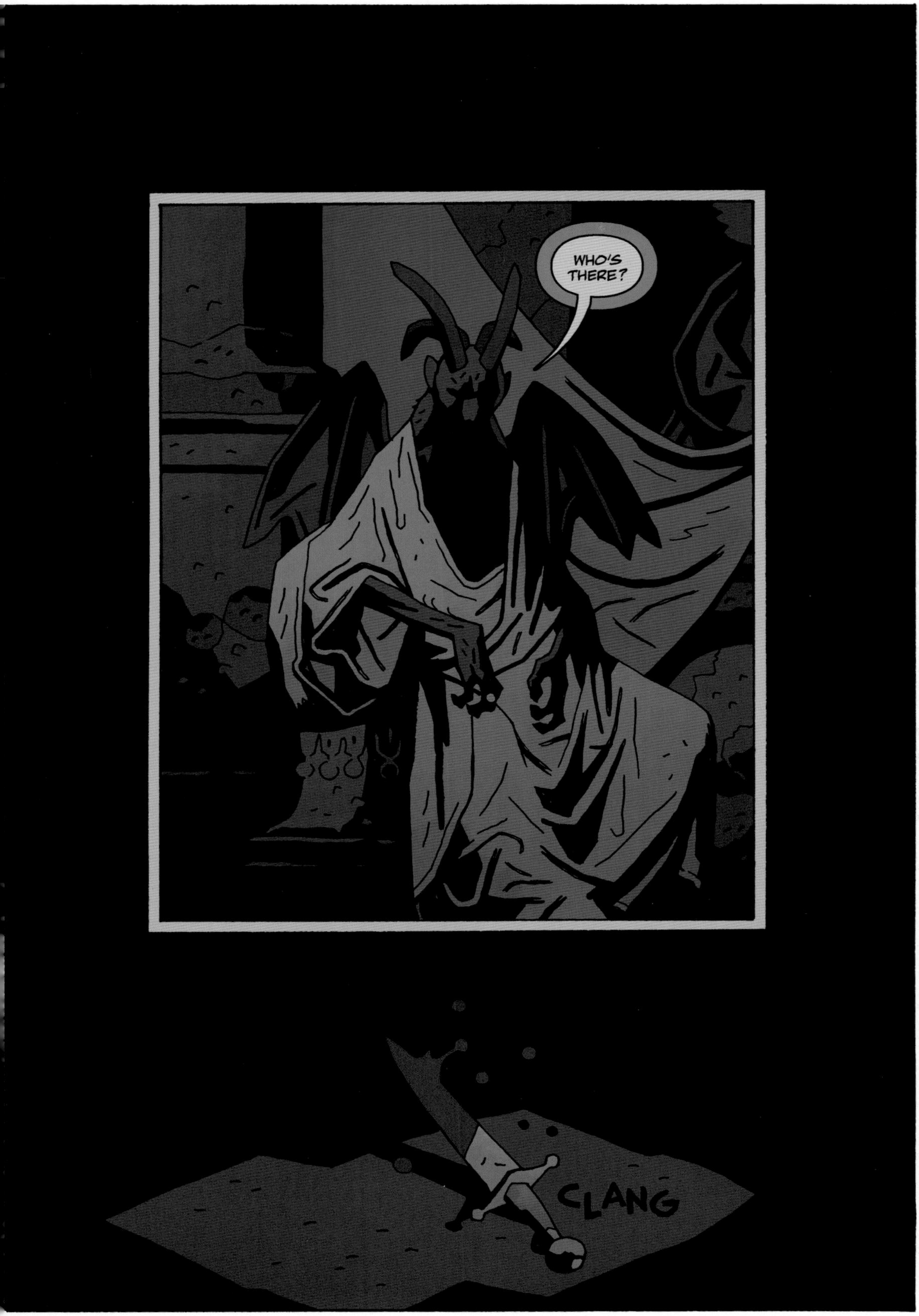
WHO'S THERE?
CLANG

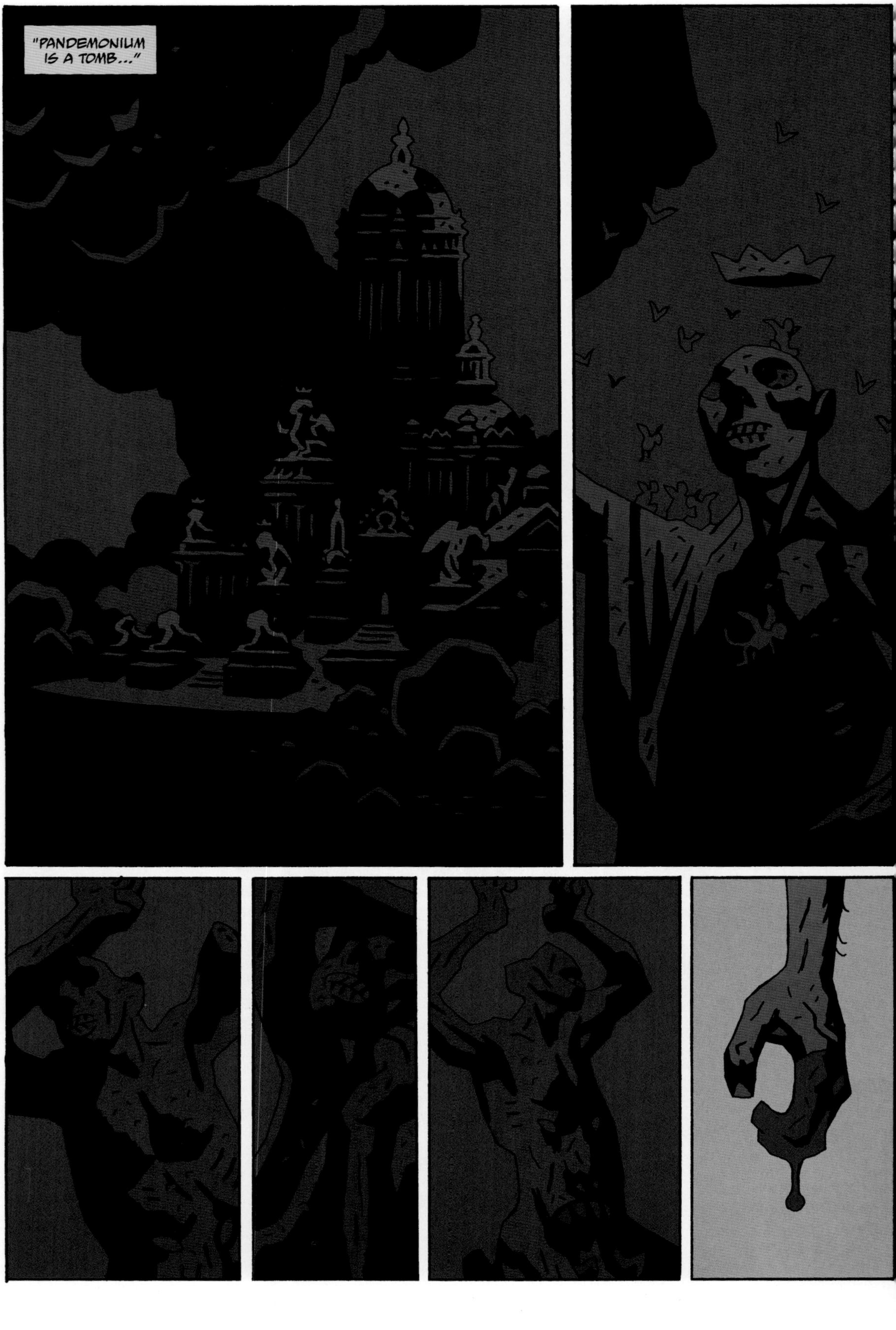
"PANDEMONIUM IS A TOMB..."

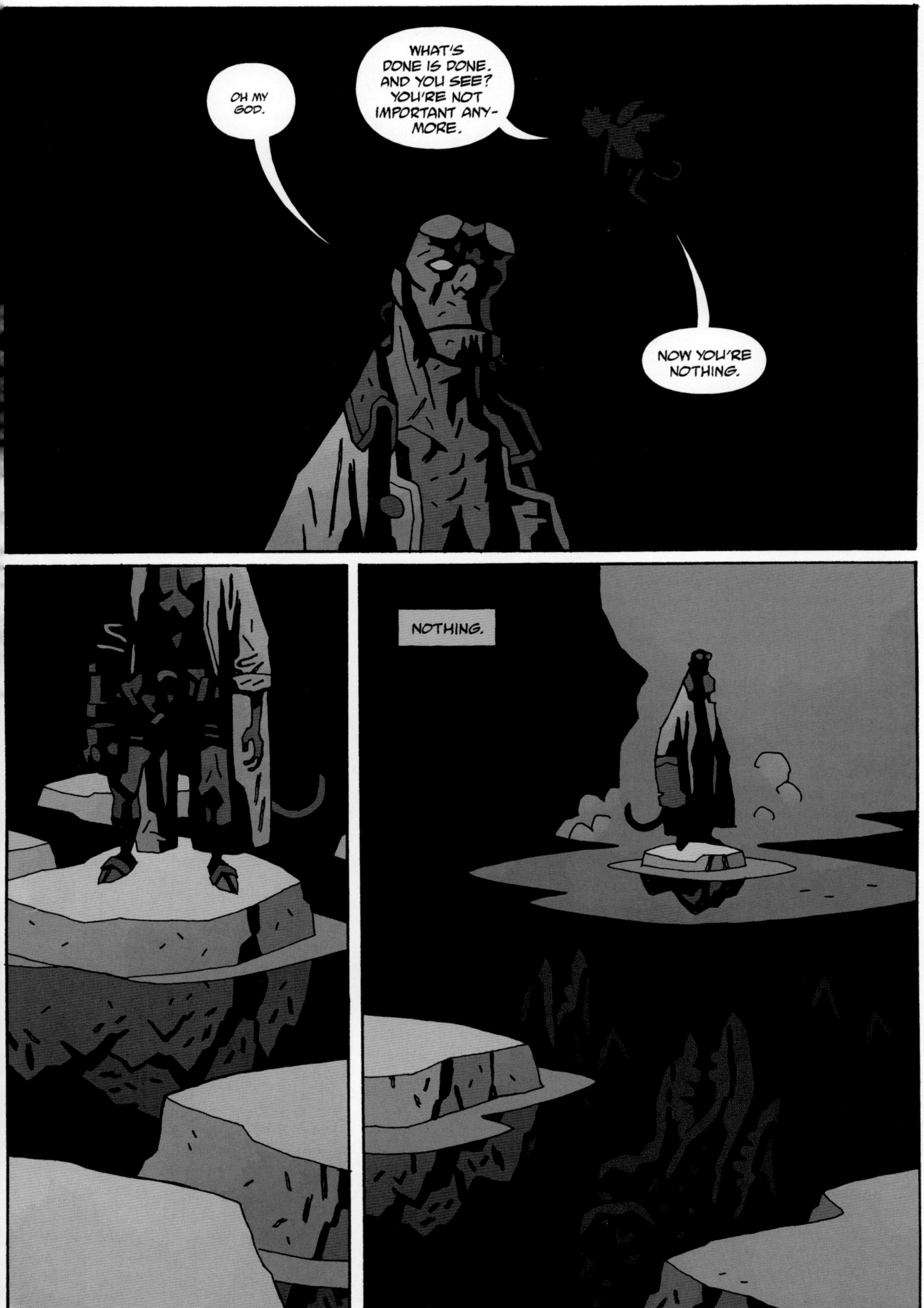
OH MY GOD.
WHAT'S DONE IS DONE. AND YOU SEE? YOU'RE NOT IMPORTANT ANY-MORE.
NOW YOU'RE NOTHING.
NOTHING.

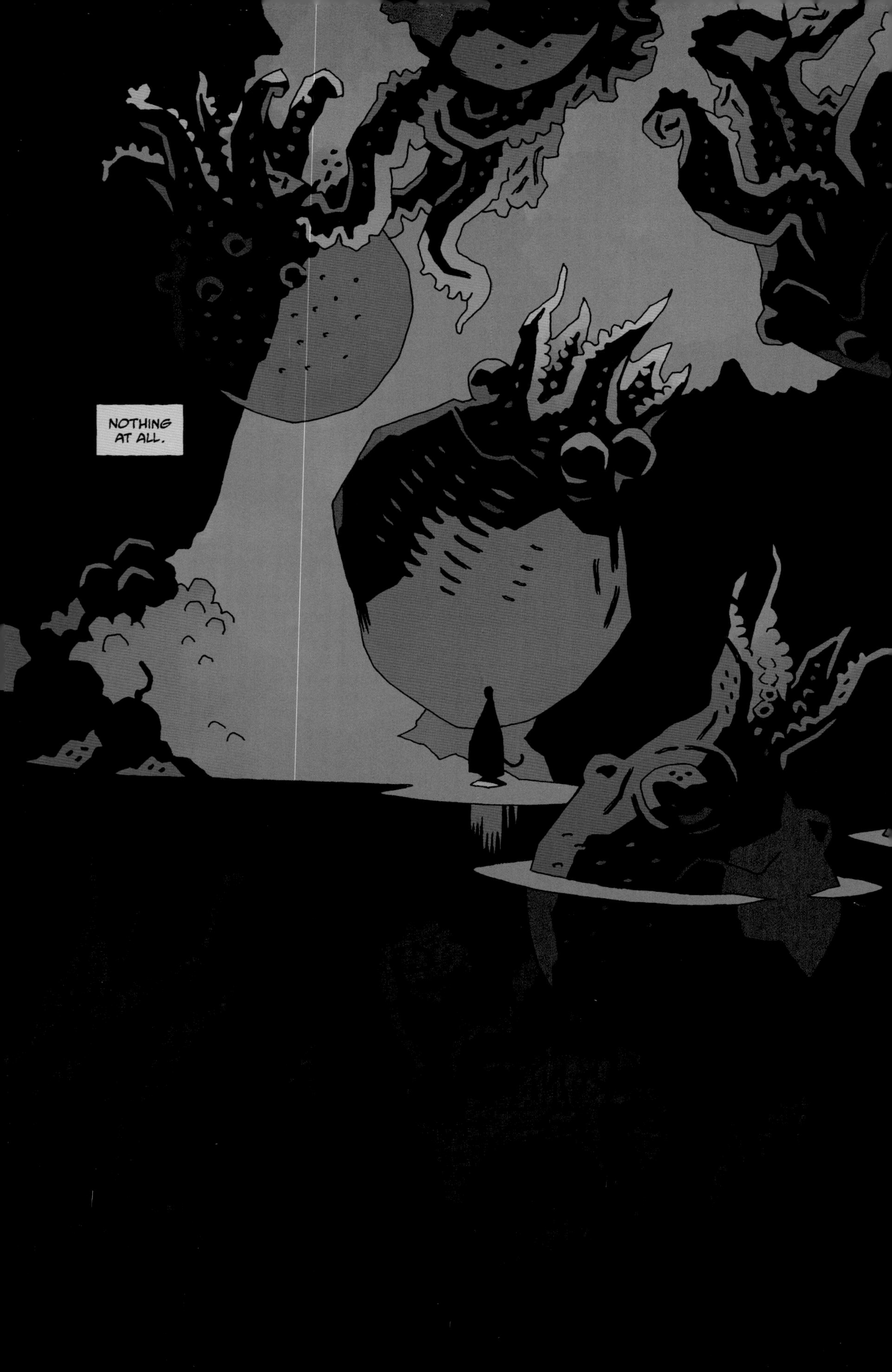
NOTHING AT ALL.

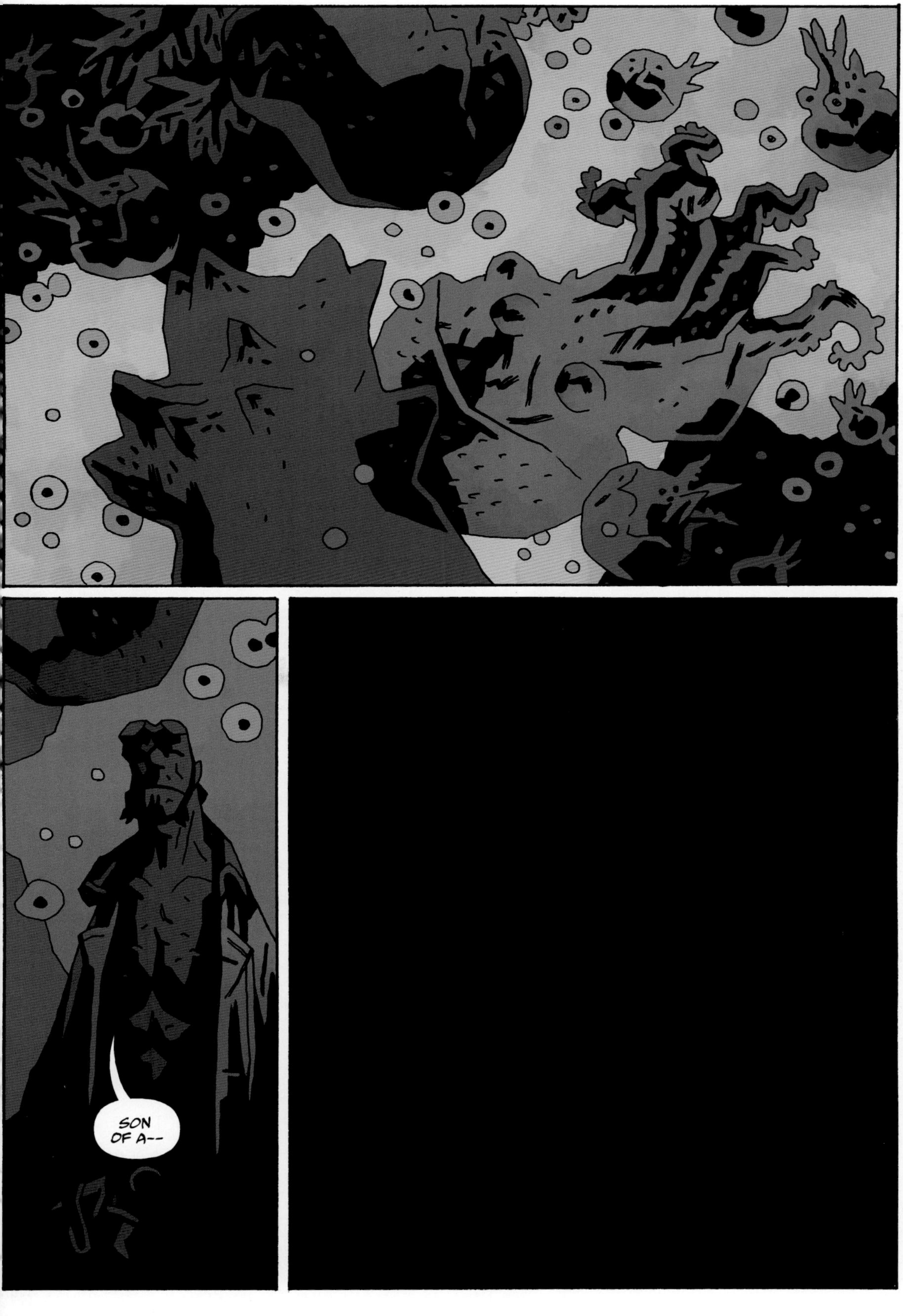
SON OF A--

CHAPTER FOUR

DEATH RIDING
AN ELEPHANT

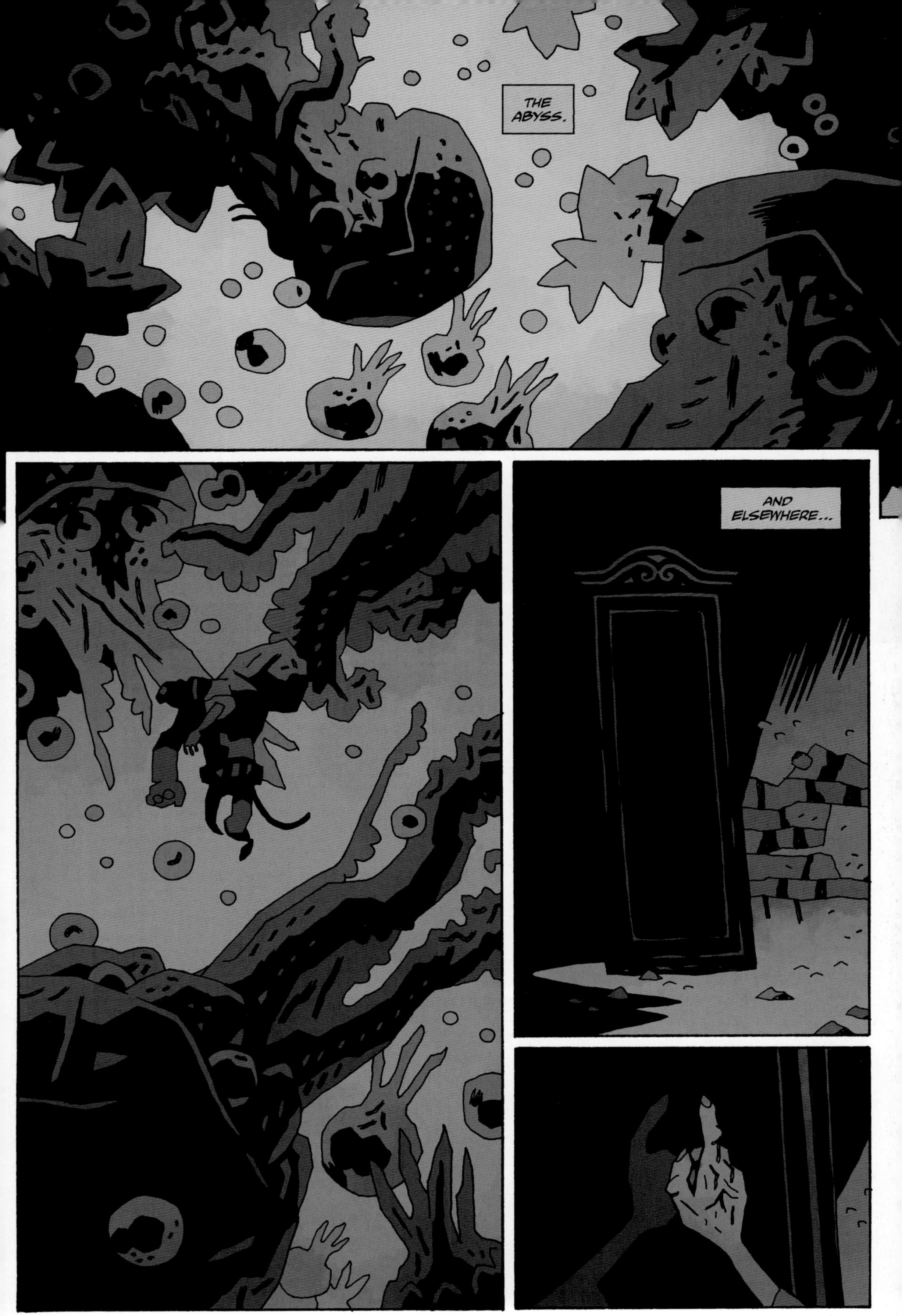
THE ABYSS.
AND ELSEWHERE...

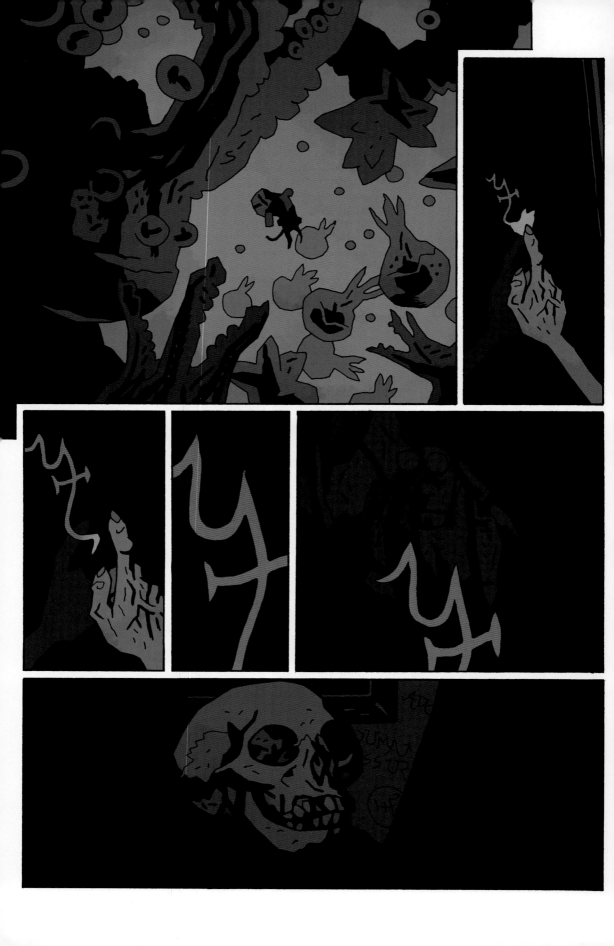

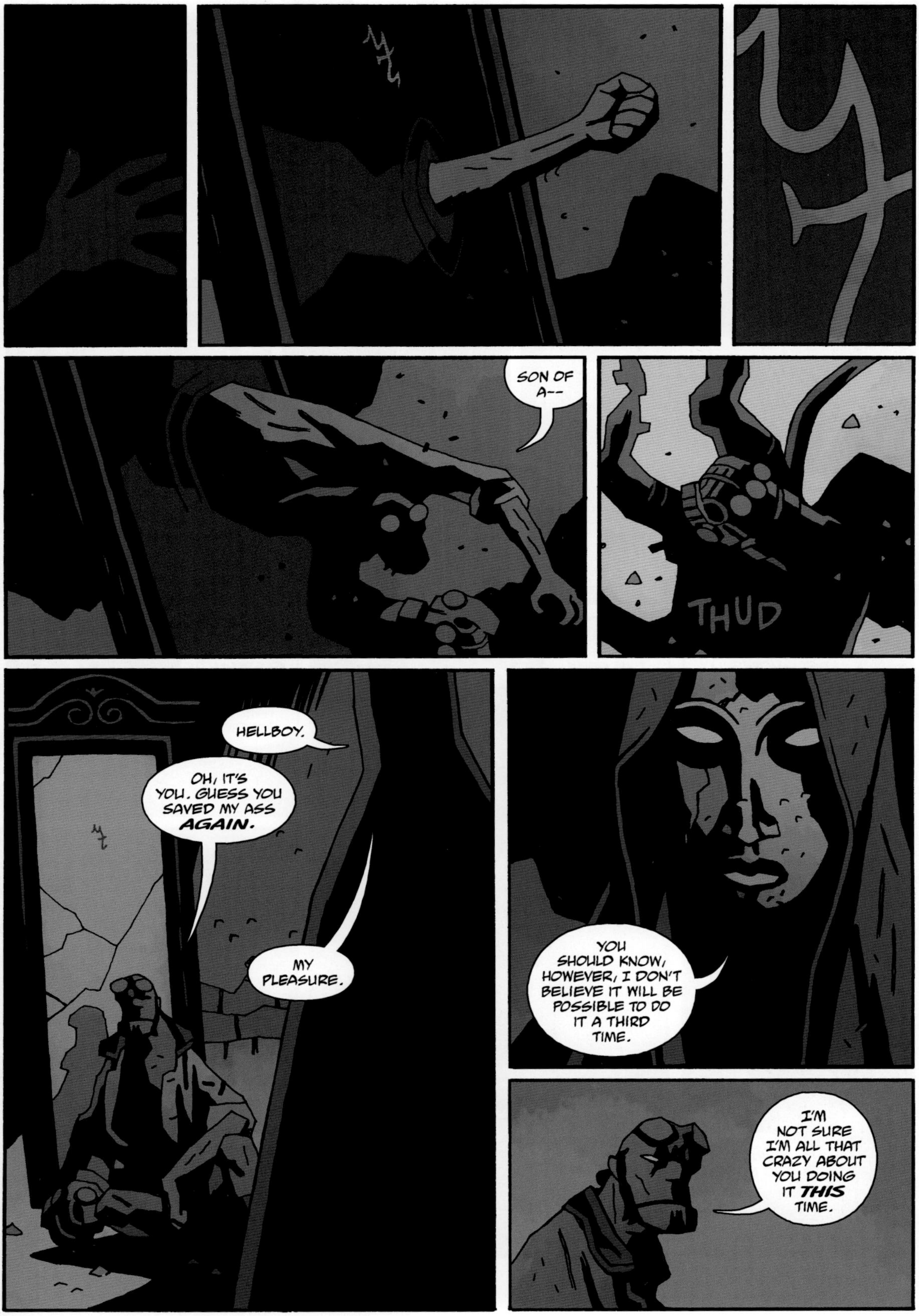
SON OF A--
THUD
HELLBOY.
OH, IT'S YOU. GUESS YOU SAVED MY ASS AGAIN.
MY PLEASURE.
YOU SHOULD KNOW, HOWEVER, I DON'T BELIEVE IT WILL BE POSSIBLE TO DO IT A THIRD TIME.
I'M NOT SURE I'M ALL THAT CRAZY ABOUT YOU DOING IT THIS TIME.

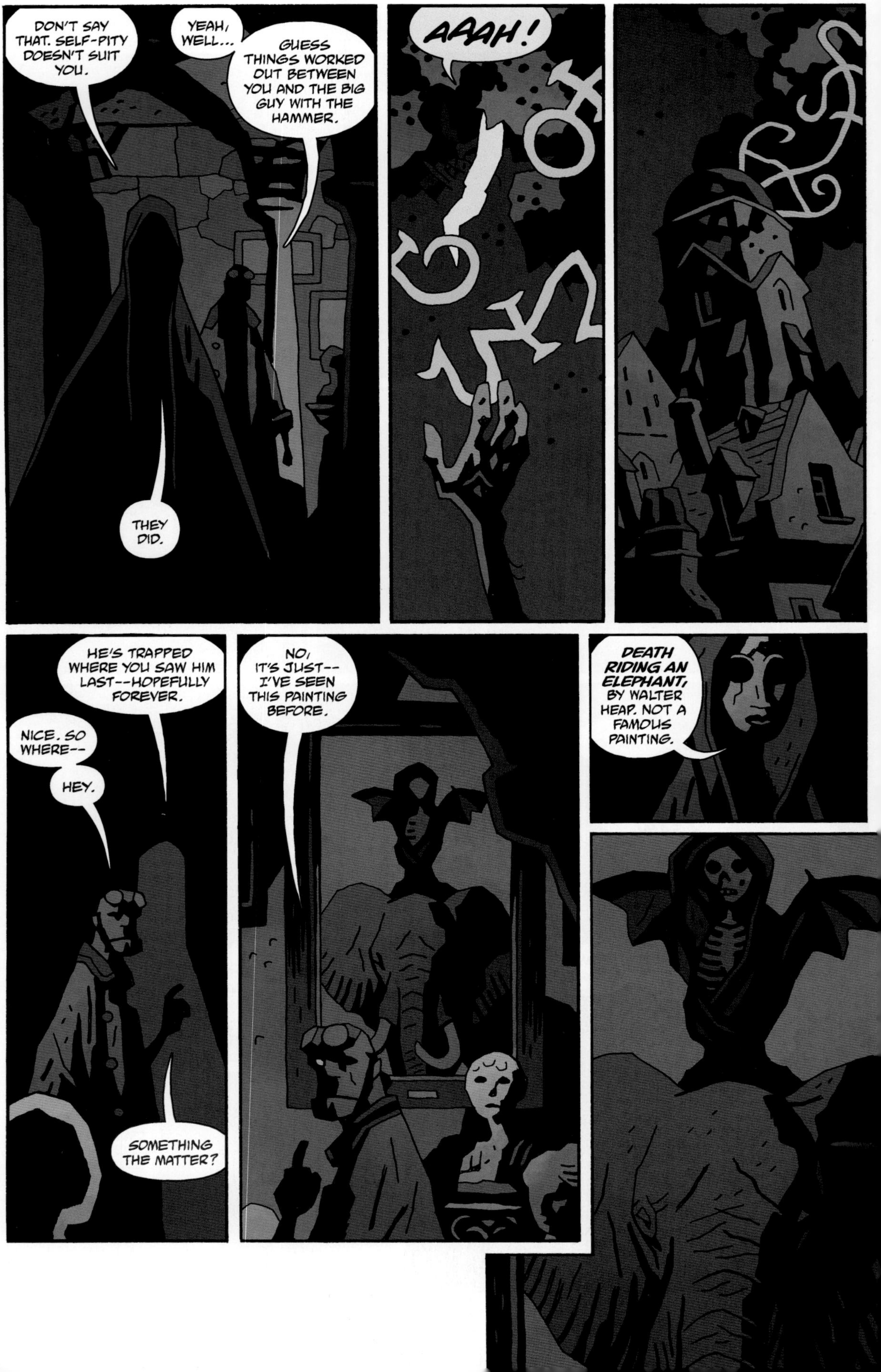

DON'T SAY THAT. SELF-PITY DOESN'T SUIT YOU.
YEAH, WELL...
GUESS THINGS WORKED OUT BETWEEN YOU AND THE BIG GUY WITH THE HAMMER.
THEY DID.
AAAH!
HE'S TRAPPED WHERE YOU SAW HIM LAST--HOPEFULLY FOREVER.
NICE. SO WHERE--
HEY.
SOMETHING THE MATTER?
NO, IT'S JUST-- I'VE SEEN THIS PAINTING BEFORE.
DEATH RIDING AN ELEPHANT, BY WALTER HEAP. NOT A FAMOUS PAINTING.

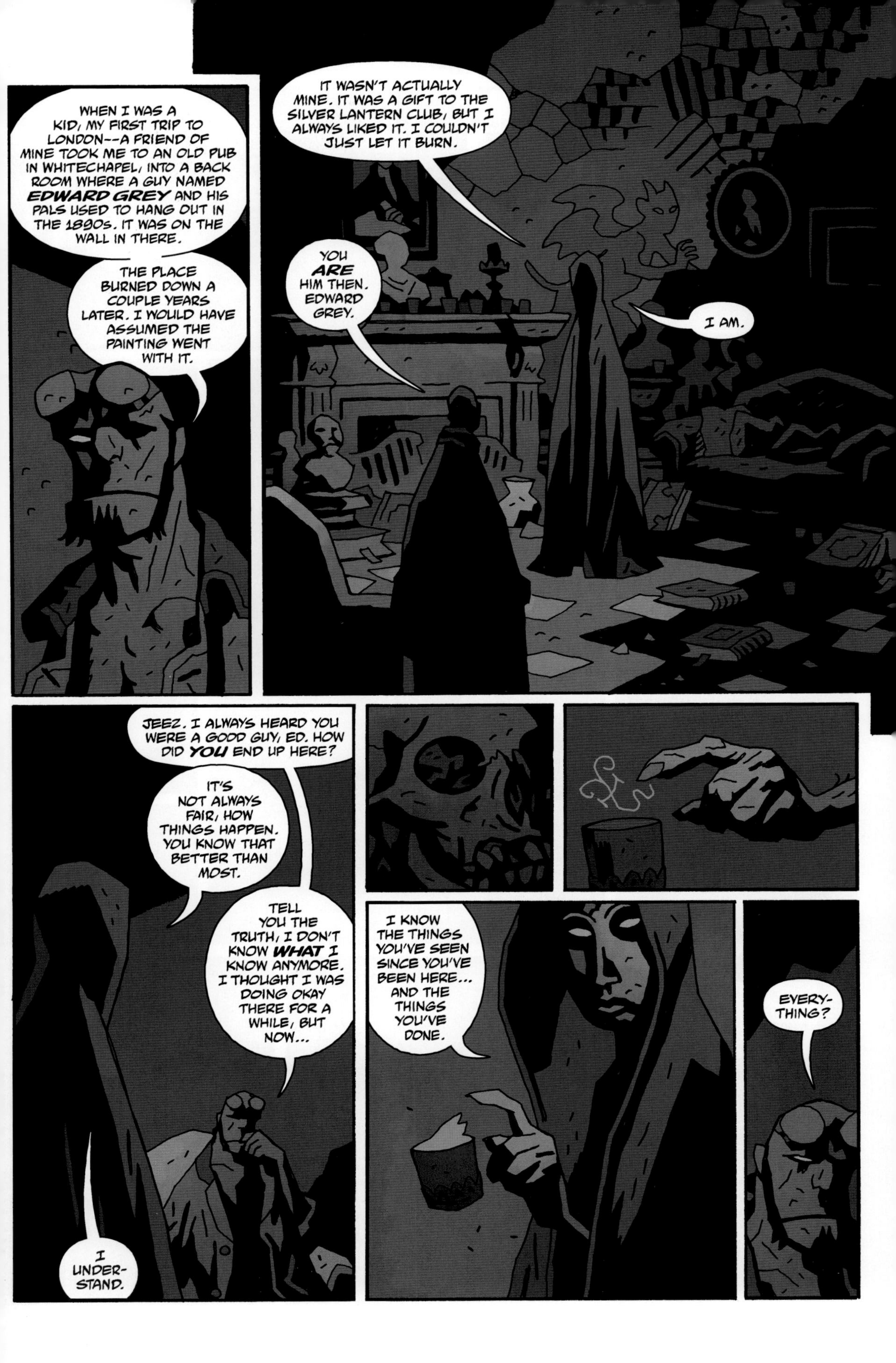
WHEN I WAS A KID, MY FIRST TRIP TO LONDON--A FRIEND OF MINE TOOK ME TO AN OLD PUB IN WHITECHAPEL, INTO A BACK ROOM WHERE A GUY NAMED EDWARD GREY AND HIS PALS USED TO HANG OUT IN THE 1890s. IT WAS ON THE WALL IN THERE.
THE PLACE BURNED DOWN A COUPLE YEARS LATER. I WOULD HAVE ASSUMED THE PAINTING WENT WITH IT.
IT WASN'T ACTUALLY MINE. IT WAS A GIFT TO THE SILVER LANTERN CLUB, BUT I ALWAYS LIKED IT. I COULDN'T JUST LET IT BURN.
YOU ARE HIM THEN. EDWARD GREY.
I AM.
JEEZ. I ALWAYS HEARD YOU WERE A GOOD GUY, ED. HOW DID YOU END UP HERE?
IT'S NOT ALWAYS FAIR, HOW THINGS HAPPEN. YOU KNOW THAT BETTER THAN MOST.
TELL YOU THE TRUTH, I DON'T KNOW WHAT I KNOW ANYMORE. I THOUGHT I WAS DOING OKAY THERE FOR A WHILE, BUT NOW...
I UNDER-STAND.
I KNOW THE THINGS YOU'VE SEEN SINCE YOU'VE BEEN HERE... AND THE THINGS YOU'VE DONE.
EVERY-THING?

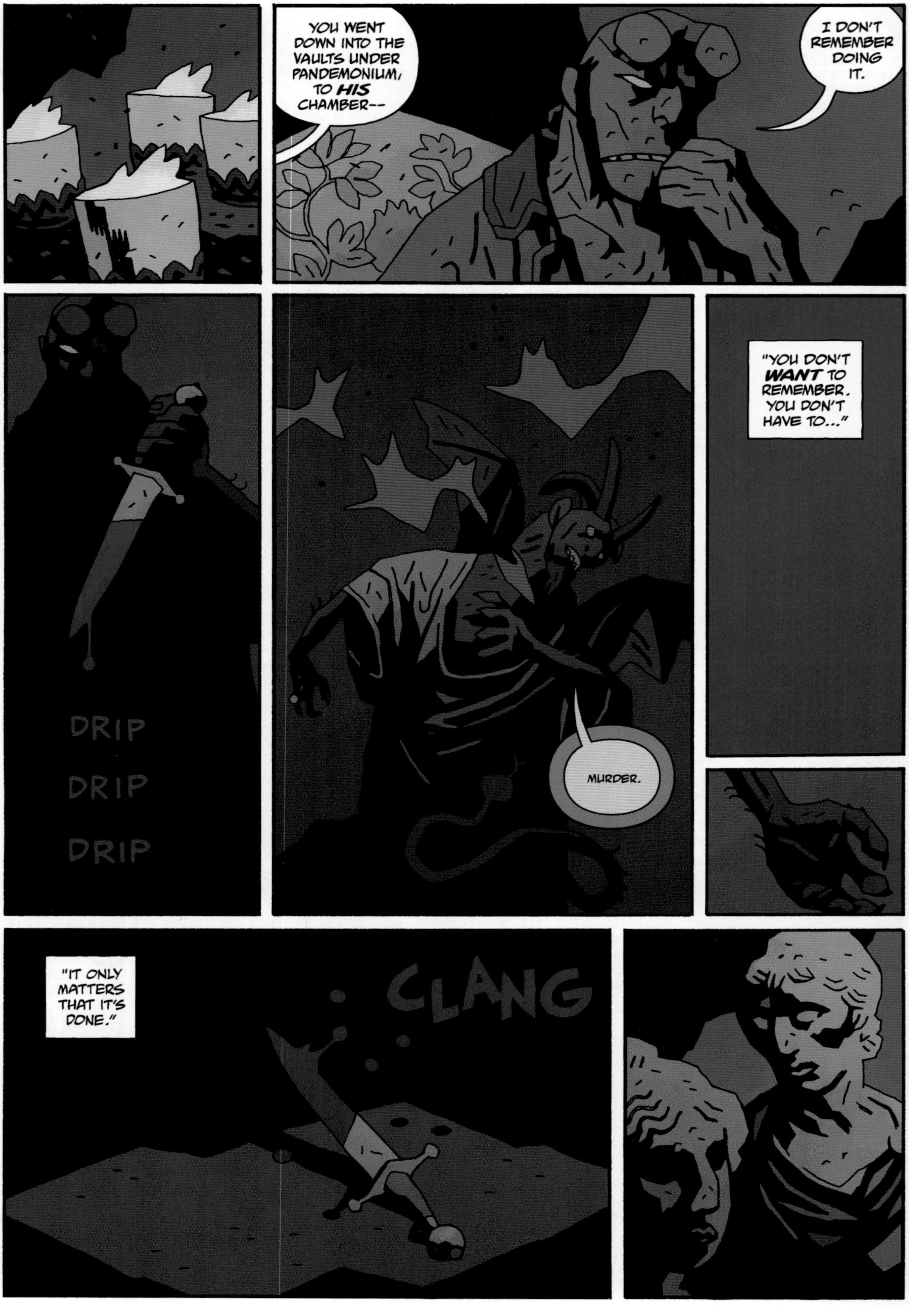
YOU WENT DOWN INTO THE VAULTS UNDER PANDEMONIUM, TO **HIS** CHAMBER--
I DON'T REMEMBER DOING IT.
DRIP
DRIP
DRIP
MURDER.
"YOU DON'T **WANT** TO REMEMBER. YOU DON'T HAVE TO..."
"IT ONLY MATTERS THAT IT'S DONE."
CLANG

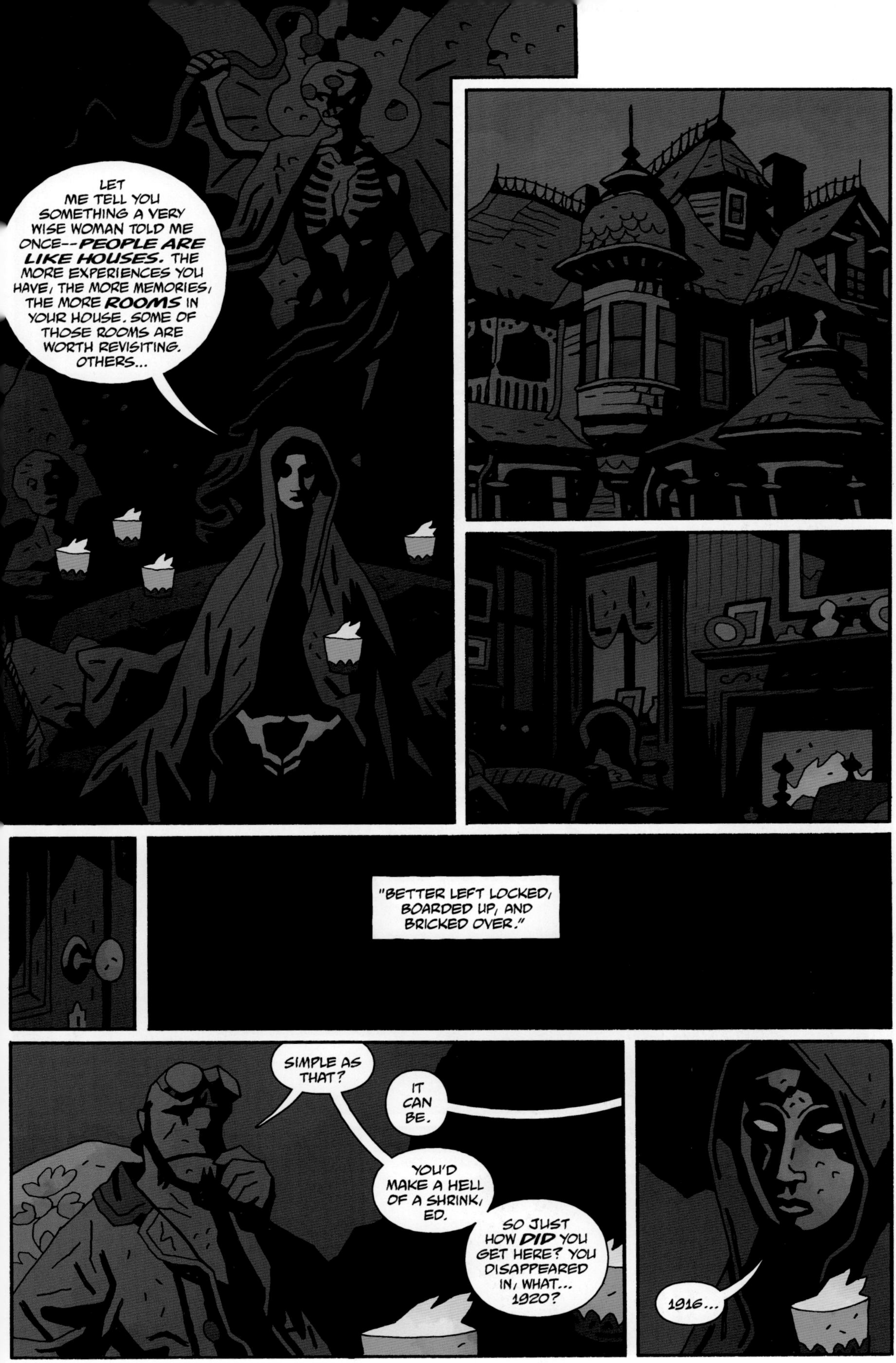
LET ME TELL YOU SOMETHING A VERY WISE WOMAN TOLD ME ONCE--PEOPLE ARE LIKE HOUSES. THE MORE EXPERIENCES YOU HAVE, THE MORE MEMORIES, THE MORE ROOMS IN YOUR HOUSE. SOME OF THOSE ROOMS ARE WORTH REVISITING. OTHERS...
"BETTER LEFT LOCKED, BOARDED UP, AND BRICKED OVER."
SIMPLE AS THAT?
IT CAN BE.
YOU'D MAKE A HELL OF A SHRINK, ED.
SO JUST HOW DID YOU GET HERE? YOU DISAPPEARED IN, WHAT... 1920?
1916...

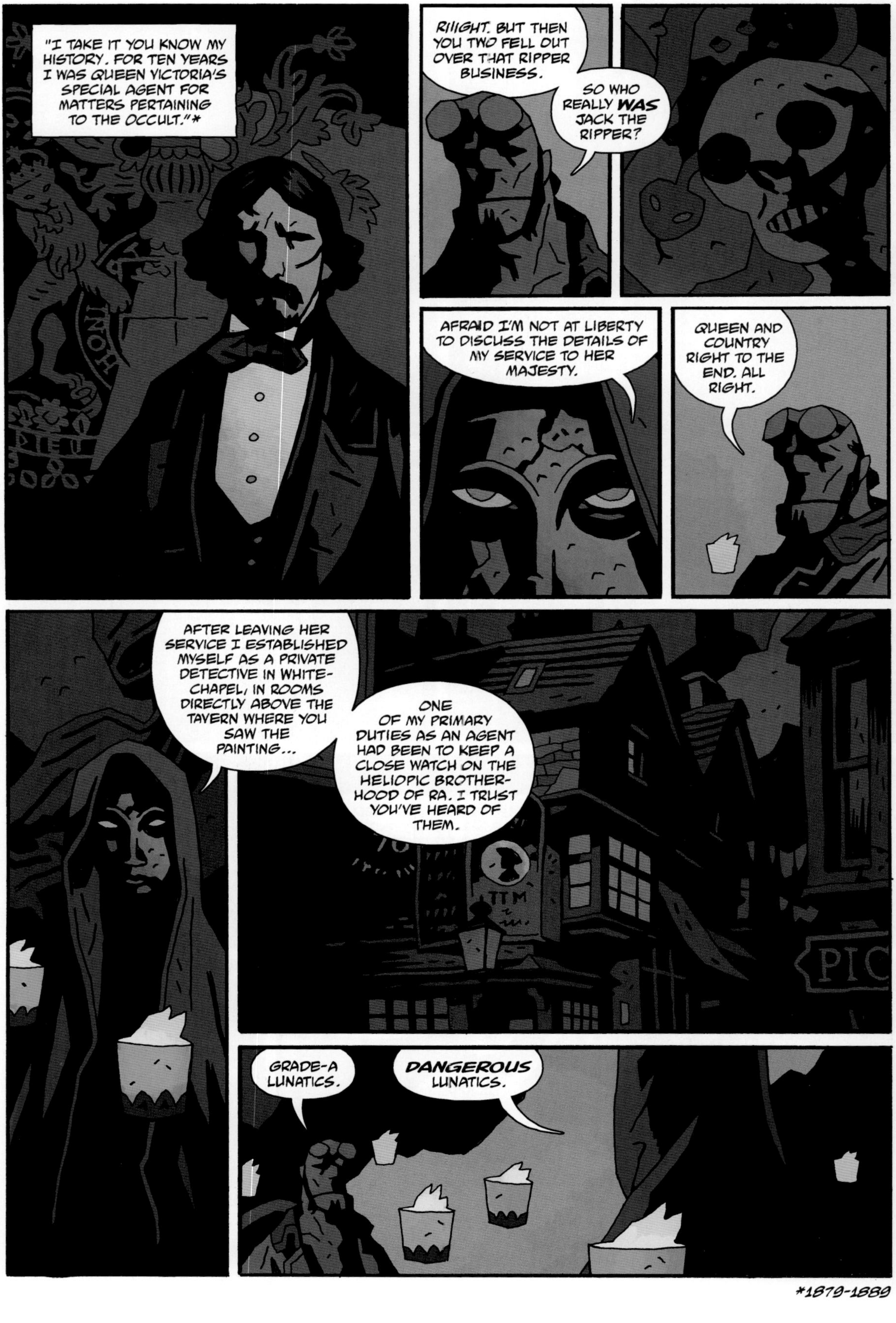
"I TAKE IT YOU KNOW MY HISTORY. FOR TEN YEARS I WAS QUEEN VICTORIA'S SPECIAL AGENT FOR MATTERS PERTAINING TO THE OCCULT."*
RIIIGHT. BUT THEN YOU TWO FELL OUT OVER THAT RIPPER BUSINESS.
SO WHO REALLY WAS JACK THE RIPPER?
AFRAID I'M NOT AT LIBERTY TO DISCUSS THE DETAILS OF MY SERVICE TO HER MAJESTY.
QUEEN AND COUNTRY RIGHT TO THE END. ALL RIGHT.
AFTER LEAVING HER SERVICE I ESTABLISHED MYSELF AS A PRIVATE DETECTIVE IN WHITE-CHAPEL, IN ROOMS DIRECTLY ABOVE THE TAVERN WHERE YOU SAW THE PAINTING...
ONE OF MY PRIMARY DUTIES AS AN AGENT HAD BEEN TO KEEP A CLOSE WATCH ON THE HELIOPIC BROTHER-HOOD OF RA. I TRUST YOU'VE HEARD OF THEM.
PIC
GRADE-A LUNATICS.
DANGEROUS LUNATICS.

*1879-1889

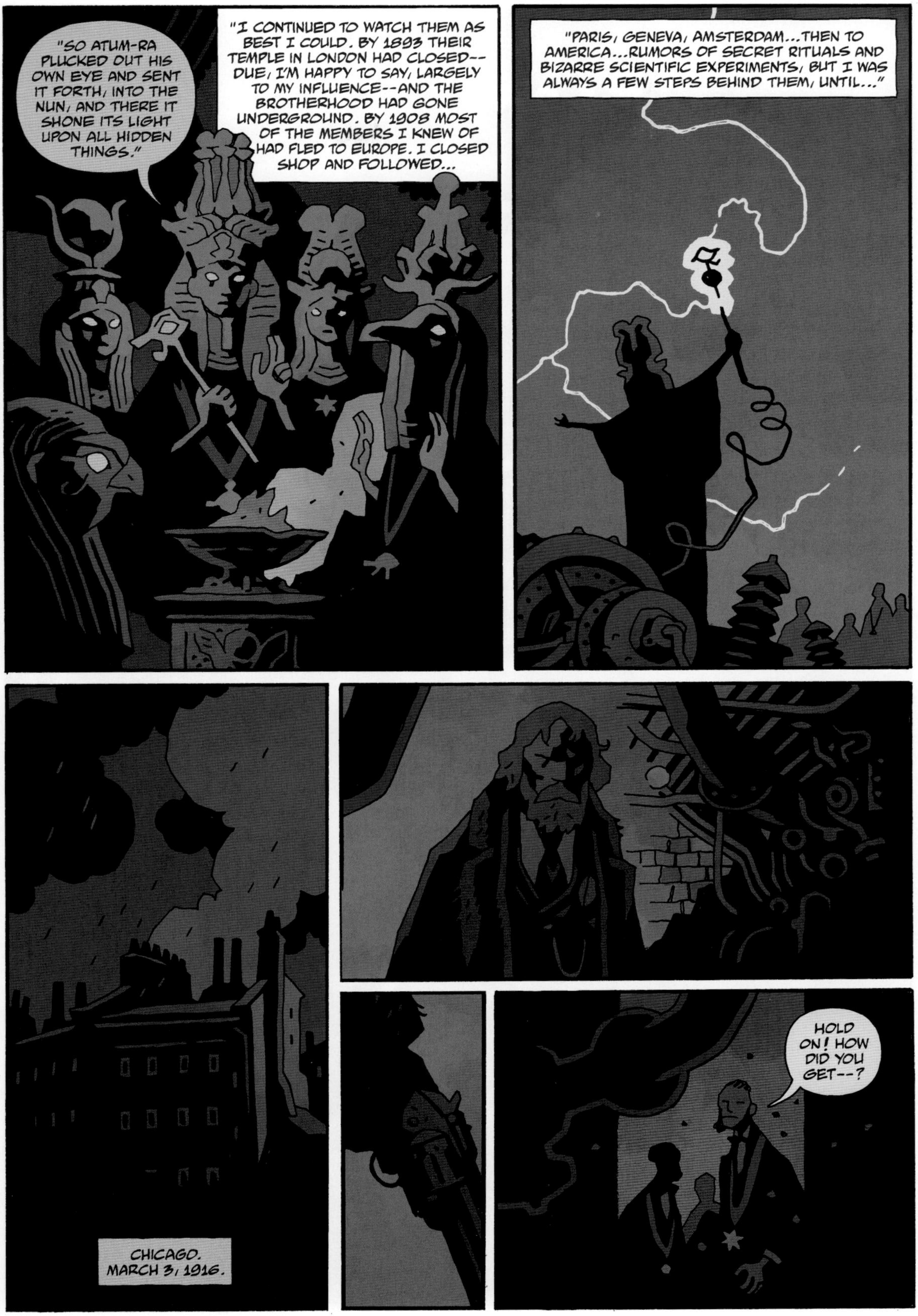
"SO ATUM-RA PLUCKED OUT HIS OWN EYE AND SENT IT FORTH, INTO THE NUN, AND THERE IT SHONE ITS LIGHT UPON ALL HIDDEN THINGS."
"I CONTINUED TO WATCH THEM AS BEST I COULD. BY 1893 THEIR TEMPLE IN LONDON HAD CLOSED--DUE, I'M HAPPY TO SAY, LARGELY TO MY INFLUENCE--AND THE BROTHERHOOD HAD GONE UNDERGROUND. BY 1908 MOST OF THE MEMBERS I KNEW OF HAD FLED TO EUROPE. I CLOSED SHOP AND FOLLOWED...
"PARIS, GENEVA, AMSTERDAM...THEN TO AMERICA...RUMORS OF SECRET RITUALS AND BIZARRE SCIENTIFIC EXPERIMENTS, BUT I WAS ALWAYS A FEW STEPS BEHIND THEM, UNTIL..."
CHICAGO. MARCH 3, 1916.
HOLD ON! HOW DID YOU GET--?

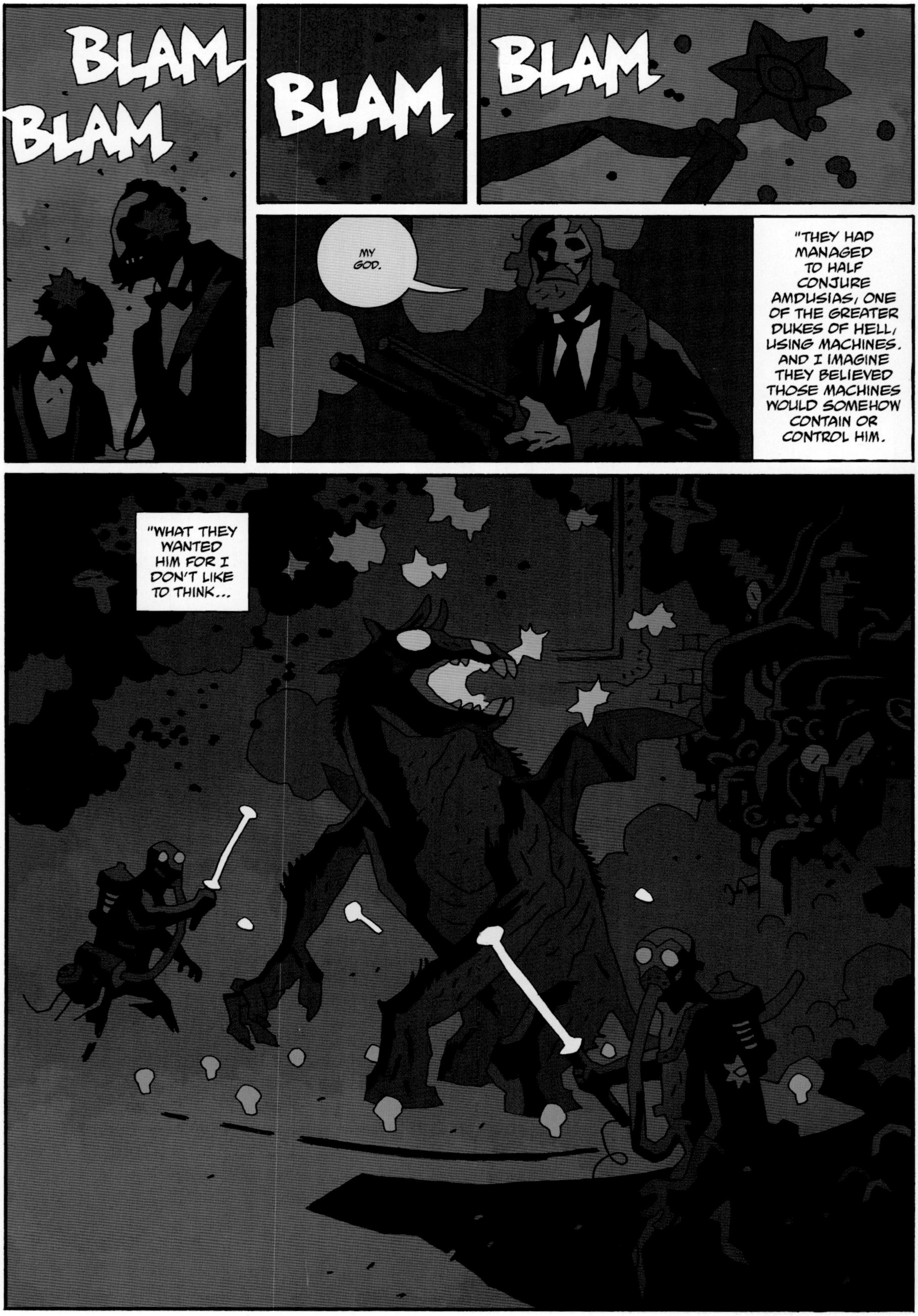

BLAM
BLAM
BLAM
BLAM
MY GOD.
"THEY HAD MANAGED TO HALF CONJURE AMDUSIAS, ONE OF THE GREATER DUKES OF HELL, USING MACHINES. AND I IMAGINE THEY BELIEVED THOSE MACHINES WOULD SOMEHOW CONTAIN OR CONTROL HIM.
"WHAT THEY WANTED HIM FOR I DON'T LIKE TO THINK...

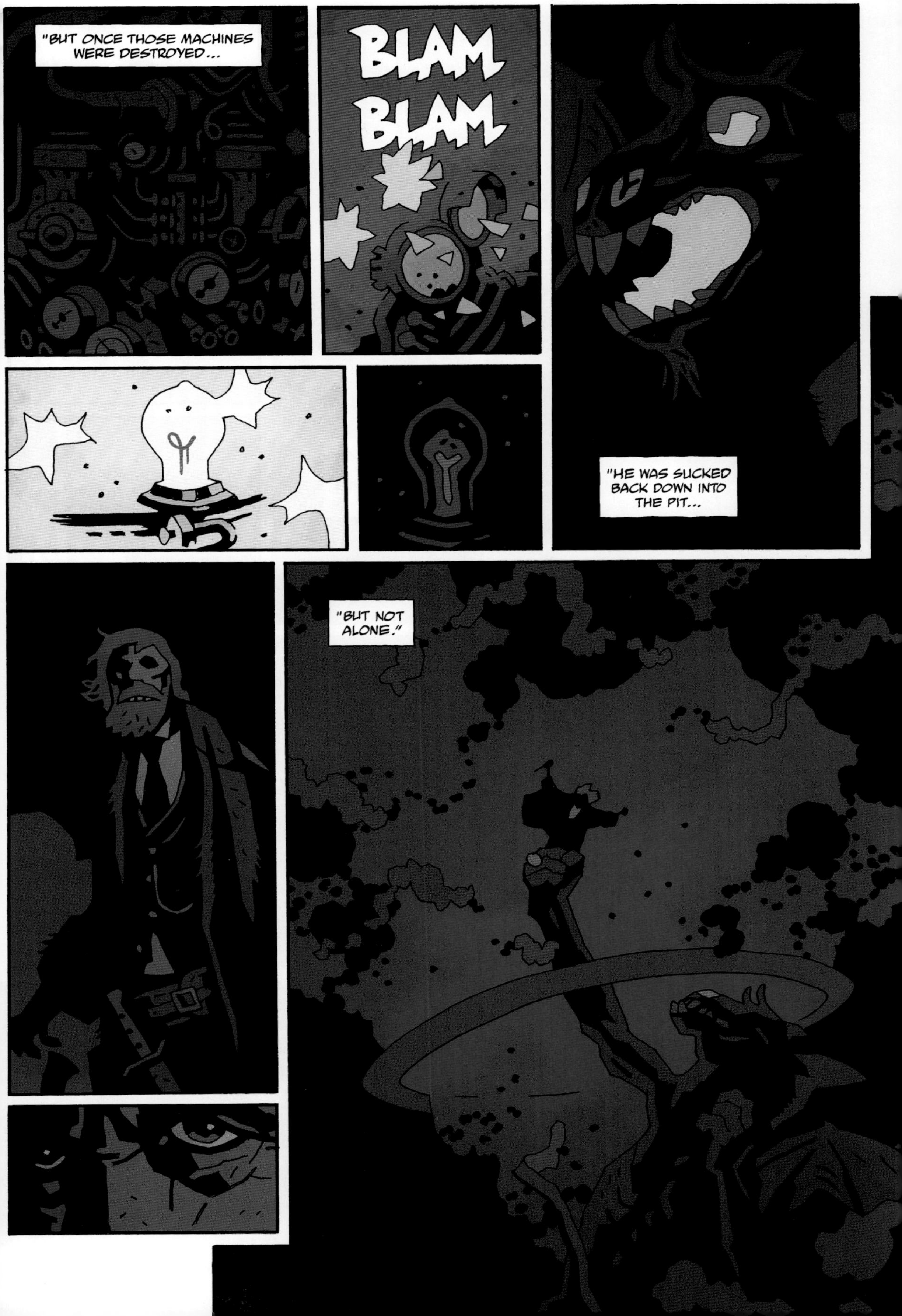
"BUT ONCE THOSE MACHINES WERE DESTROYED...
BLAM
BLAM
"HE WAS SUCKED BACK DOWN INTO THE PIT...
"BUT NOT ALONE."

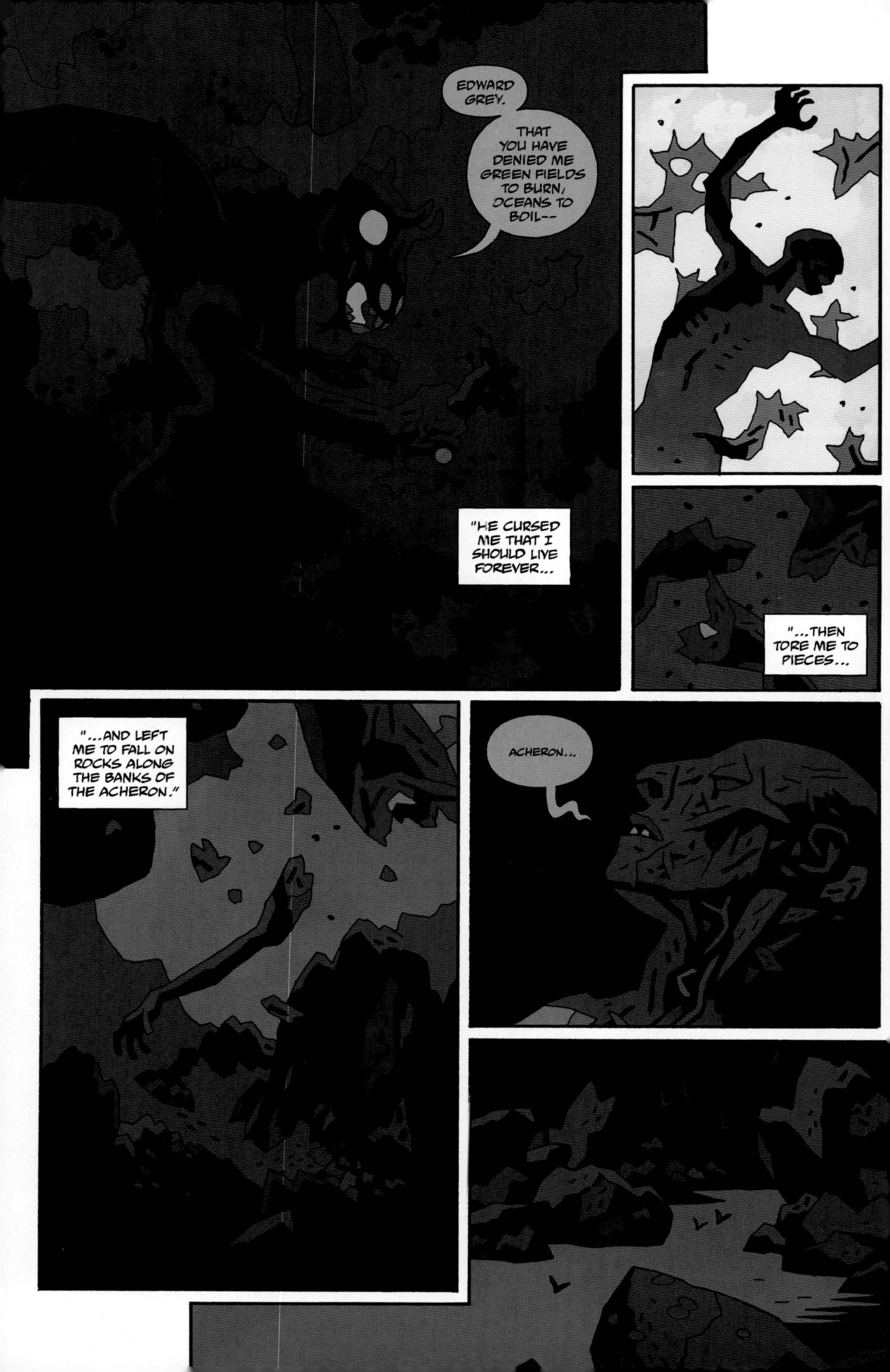

EDWARD GREY.
THAT YOU HAVE DENIED ME GREEN FIELDS TO BURN, OCEANS TO BOIL--
"HE CURSED ME THAT I SHOULD LIVE FOREVER...
"...THEN TORE ME TO PIECES...
"...AND LEFT ME TO FALL ON ROCKS ALONG THE BANKS OF THE ACHERON."
ACHERON...

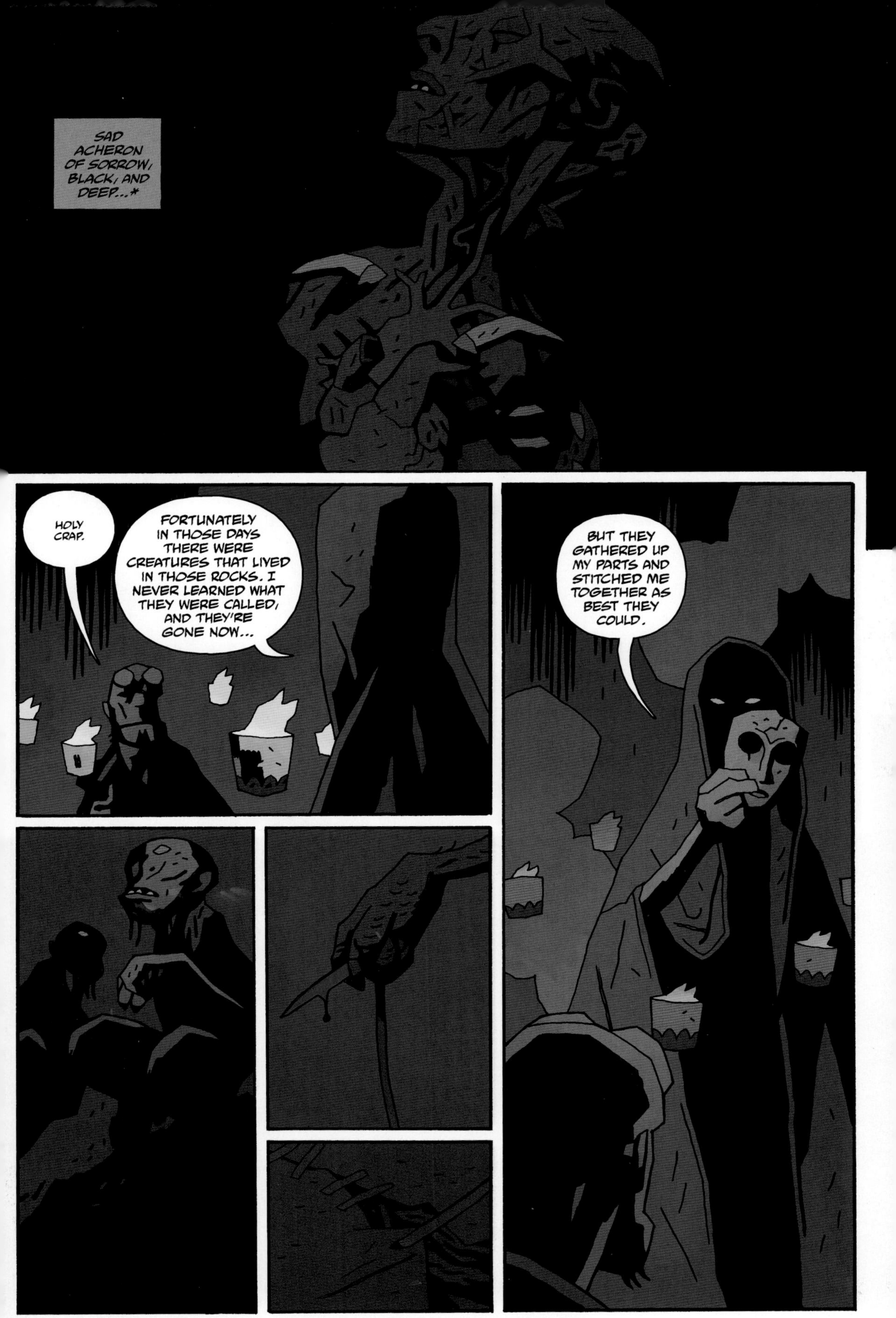
SAD ACHERON OF SORROW, BLACK, AND DEEP...*
HOLY CRAP.
FORTUNATELY IN THOSE DAYS THERE WERE CREATURES THAT LIVED IN THOSE ROCKS. I NEVER LEARNED WHAT THEY WERE CALLED, AND THEY'RE GONE NOW...
BUT THEY GATHERED UP MY PARTS AND STITCHED ME TOGETHER AS BEST THEY COULD.

*ONE OF THE FOUR RIVERS IN HELL. FROM **PARADISE LOST**, BY JOHN MILTON.

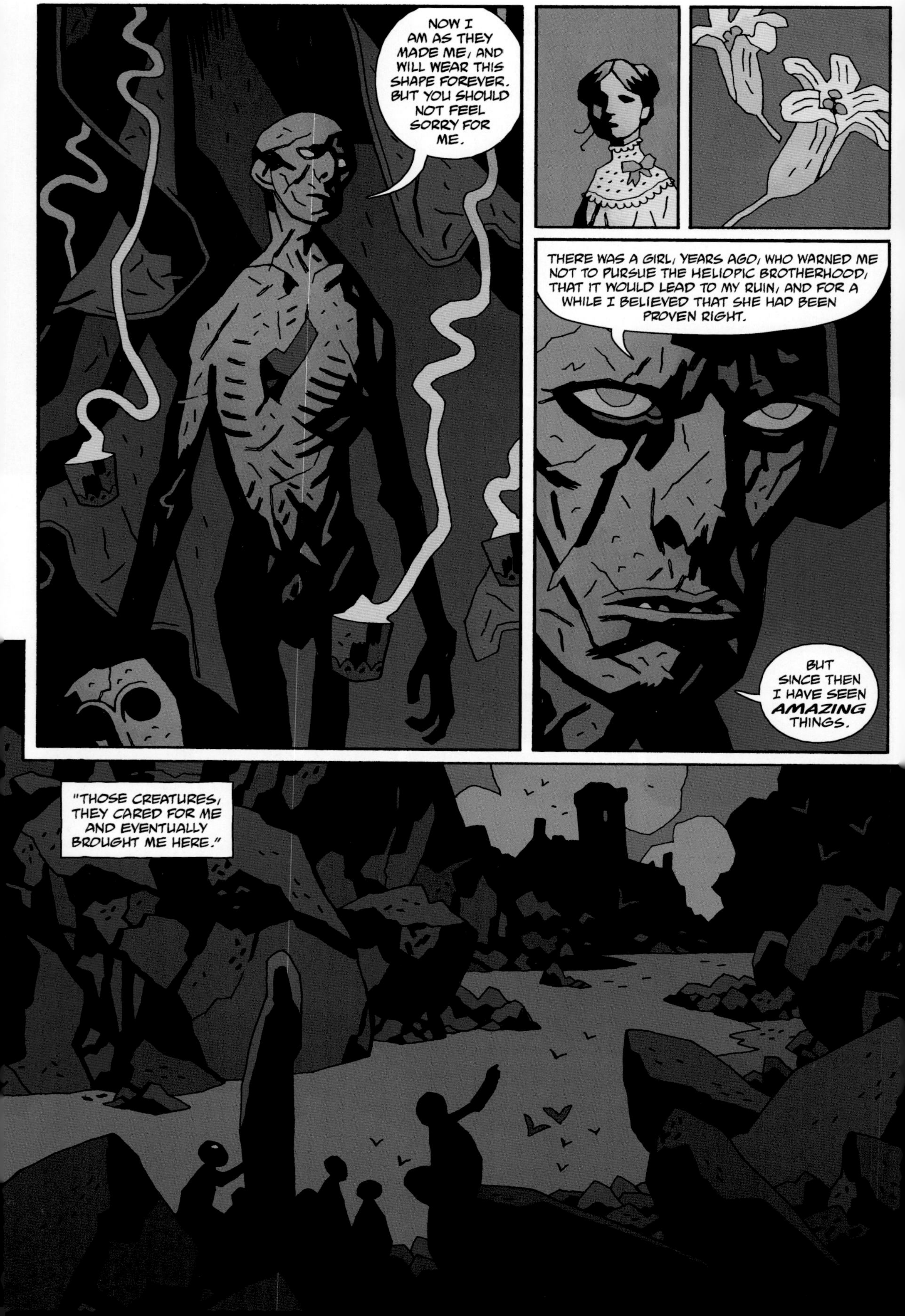

NOW I AM AS THEY MADE ME, AND WILL WEAR THIS SHAPE FOREVER. BUT YOU SHOULD NOT FEEL SORRY FOR ME.
THERE WAS A GIRL, YEARS AGO, WHO WARNED ME NOT TO PURSUE THE HELIOPIC BROTHERHOOD, THAT IT WOULD LEAD TO MY RUIN, AND FOR A WHILE I BELIEVED THAT SHE HAD BEEN PROVEN RIGHT.
BUT SINCE THEN I HAVE SEEN ***AMAZING*** THINGS.
"THOSE CREATURES, THEY CARED FOR ME AND EVENTUALLY BROUGHT ME HERE."

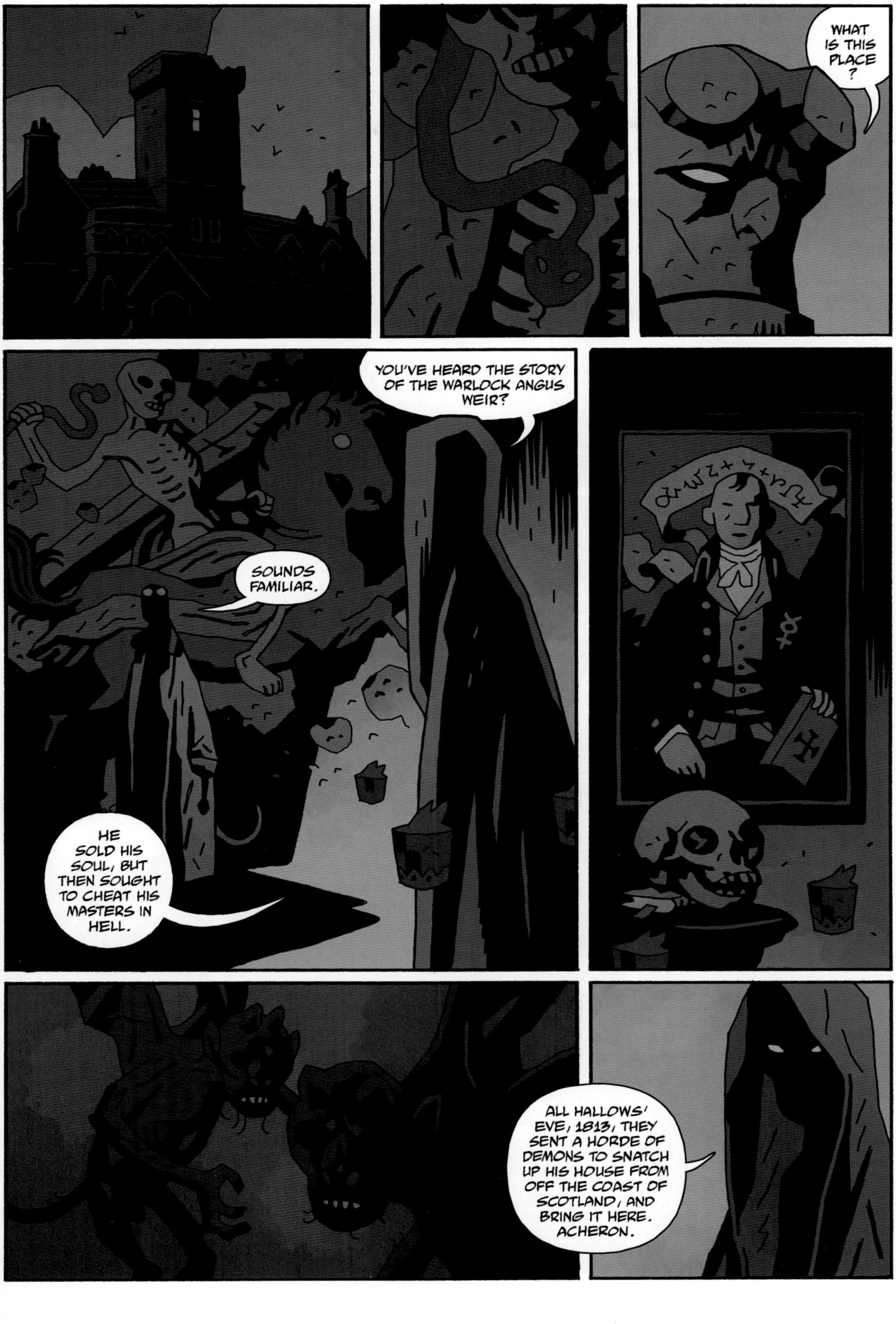
WHAT IS THIS PLACE ?
YOU'VE HEARD THE STORY OF THE WARLOCK ANGUS WEIR?
SOUNDS FAMILIAR.
HE SOLD HIS SOUL, BUT THEN SOUGHT TO CHEAT HIS MASTERS IN HELL.
ALL HALLOWS' EVE, 1813, THEY SENT A HORDE OF DEMONS TO SNATCH UP HIS HOUSE FROM OFF THE COAST OF SCOTLAND, AND BRING IT HERE. ACHERON.

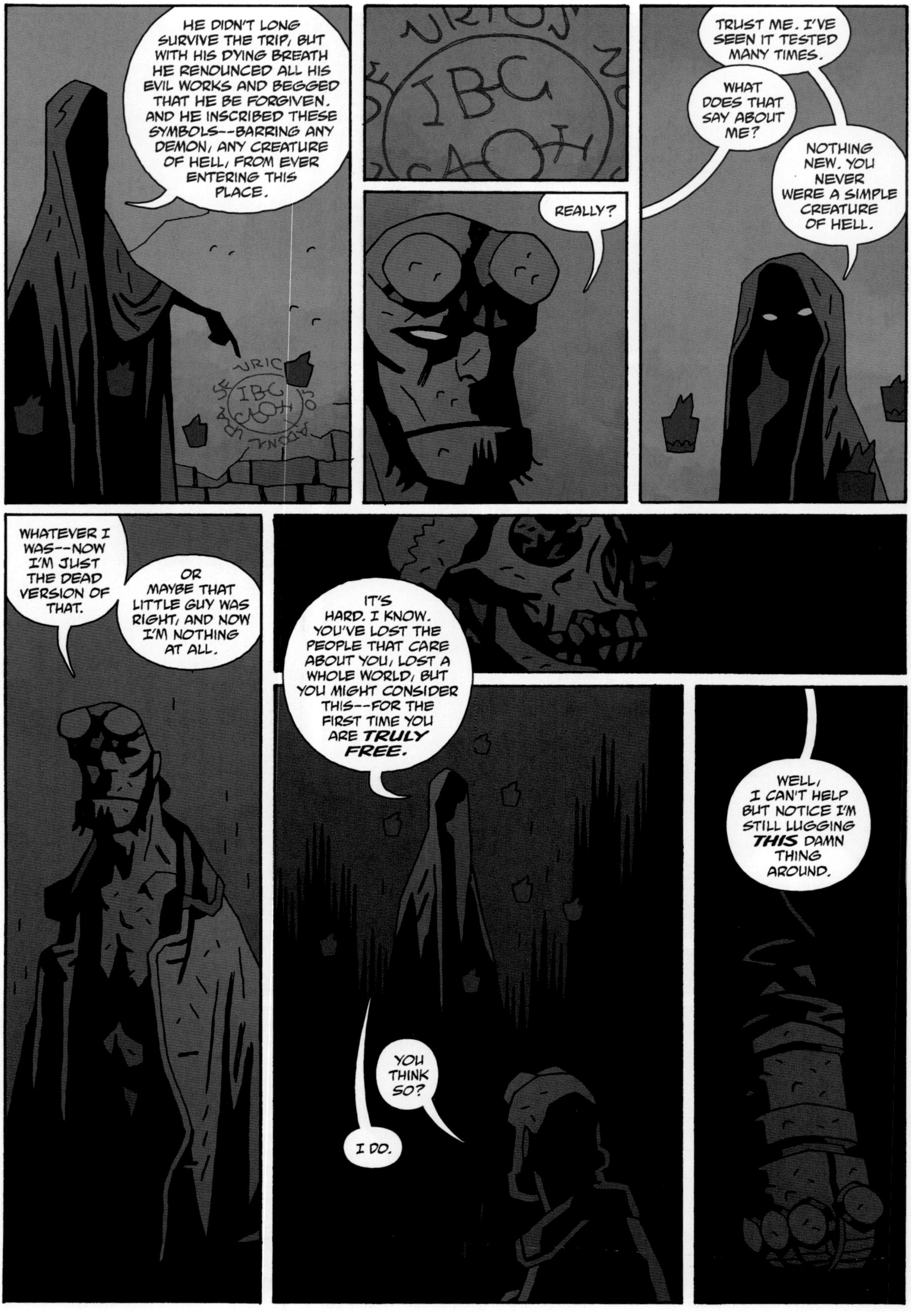
HE DIDN'T LONG SURVIVE THE TRIP, BUT WITH HIS DYING BREATH HE RENOUNCED ALL HIS EVIL WORKS AND BEGGED THAT HE BE FORGIVEN. AND HE INSCRIBED THESE SYMBOLS--BARRING ANY DEMON, ANY CREATURE OF HELL, FROM EVER ENTERING THIS PLACE.
REALLY?
TRUST ME. I'VE SEEN IT TESTED MANY TIMES.
WHAT DOES THAT SAY ABOUT ME?
NOTHING NEW. YOU NEVER WERE A SIMPLE CREATURE OF HELL.
WHATEVER I WAS--NOW I'M JUST THE DEAD VERSION OF THAT.
OR MAYBE THAT LITTLE GUY WAS RIGHT, AND NOW I'M NOTHING AT ALL.
IT'S HARD. I KNOW. YOU'VE LOST THE PEOPLE THAT CARE ABOUT YOU, LOST A WHOLE WORLD, BUT YOU MIGHT CONSIDER THIS--FOR THE FIRST TIME YOU ARE ***TRULY FREE.***
YOU THINK SO?
I DO.
WELL, I CAN'T HELP BUT NOTICE I'M STILL LUGGING ***THIS*** DAMN THING AROUND.

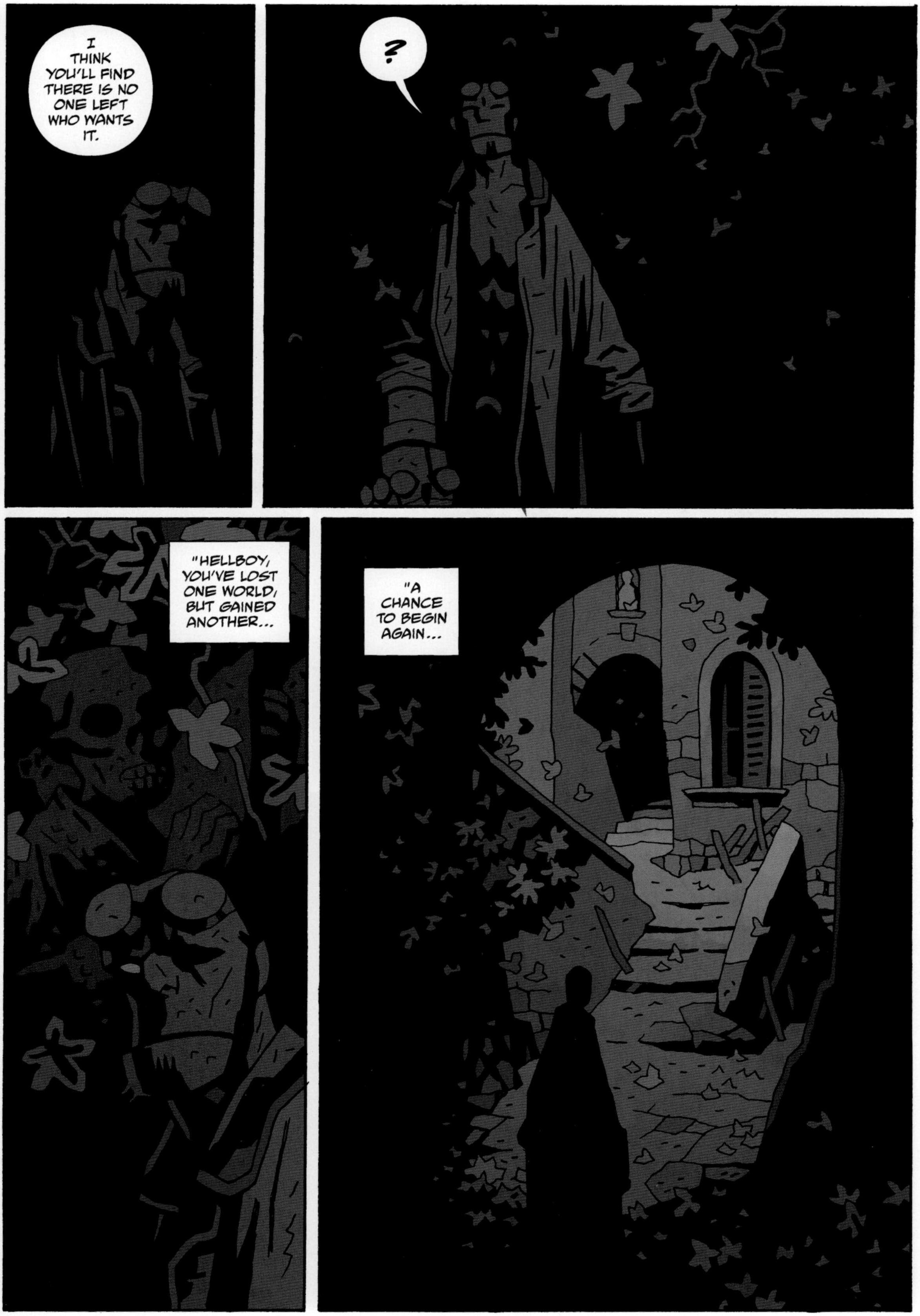
I THINK YOU'LL FIND THERE IS NO ONE LEFT WHO WANTS IT.
?
"HELLBOY, YOU'VE LOST ONE WORLD, BUT GAINED ANOTHER...
"A CHANCE TO BEGIN AGAIN...

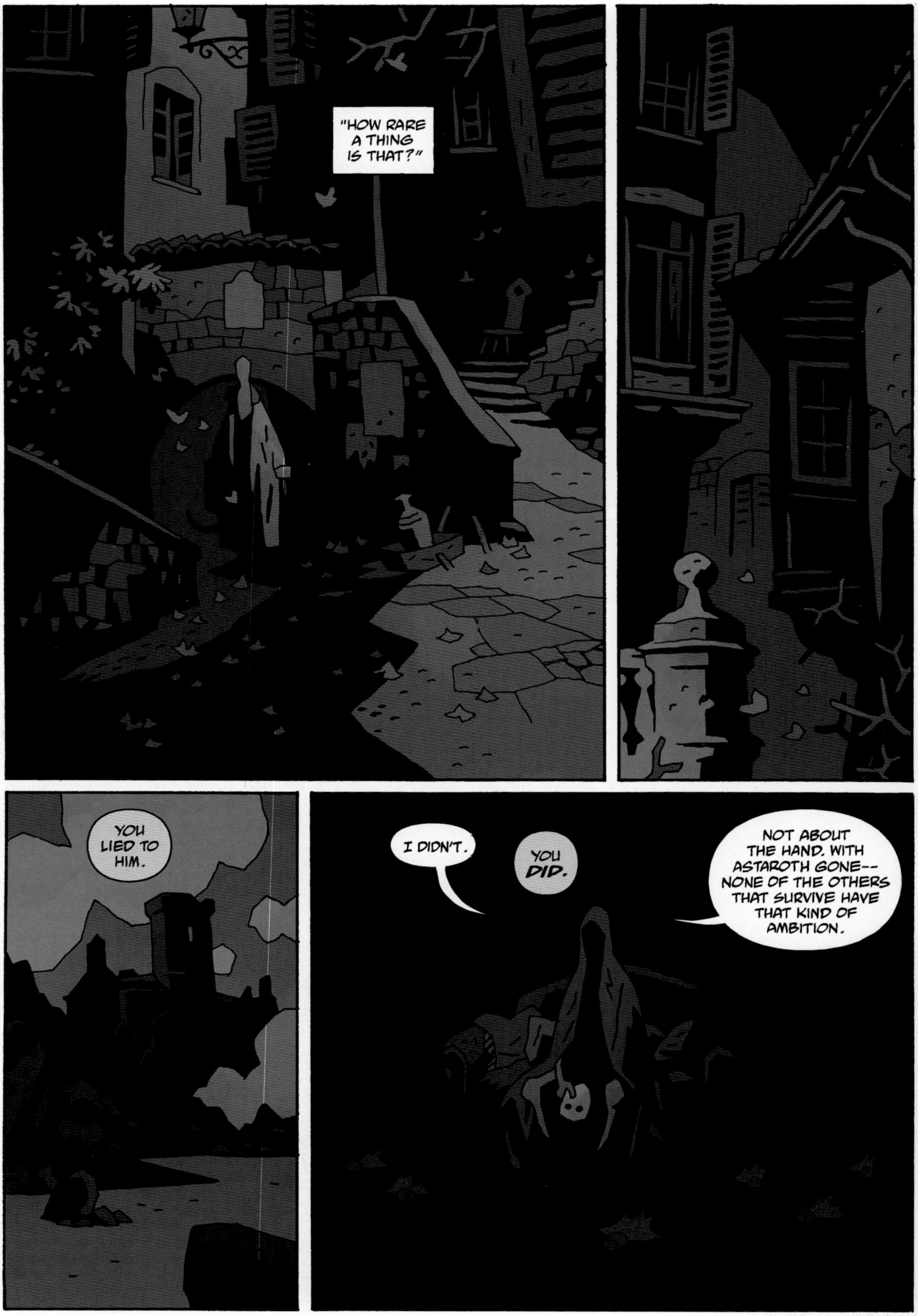
"HOW RARE A THING IS THAT?"
YOU LIED TO HIM.
I DIDN'T.
YOU DID.
NOT ABOUT THE HAND. WITH ASTAROTH GONE-- NONE OF THE OTHERS THAT SURVIVE HAVE THAT KIND OF AMBITION.

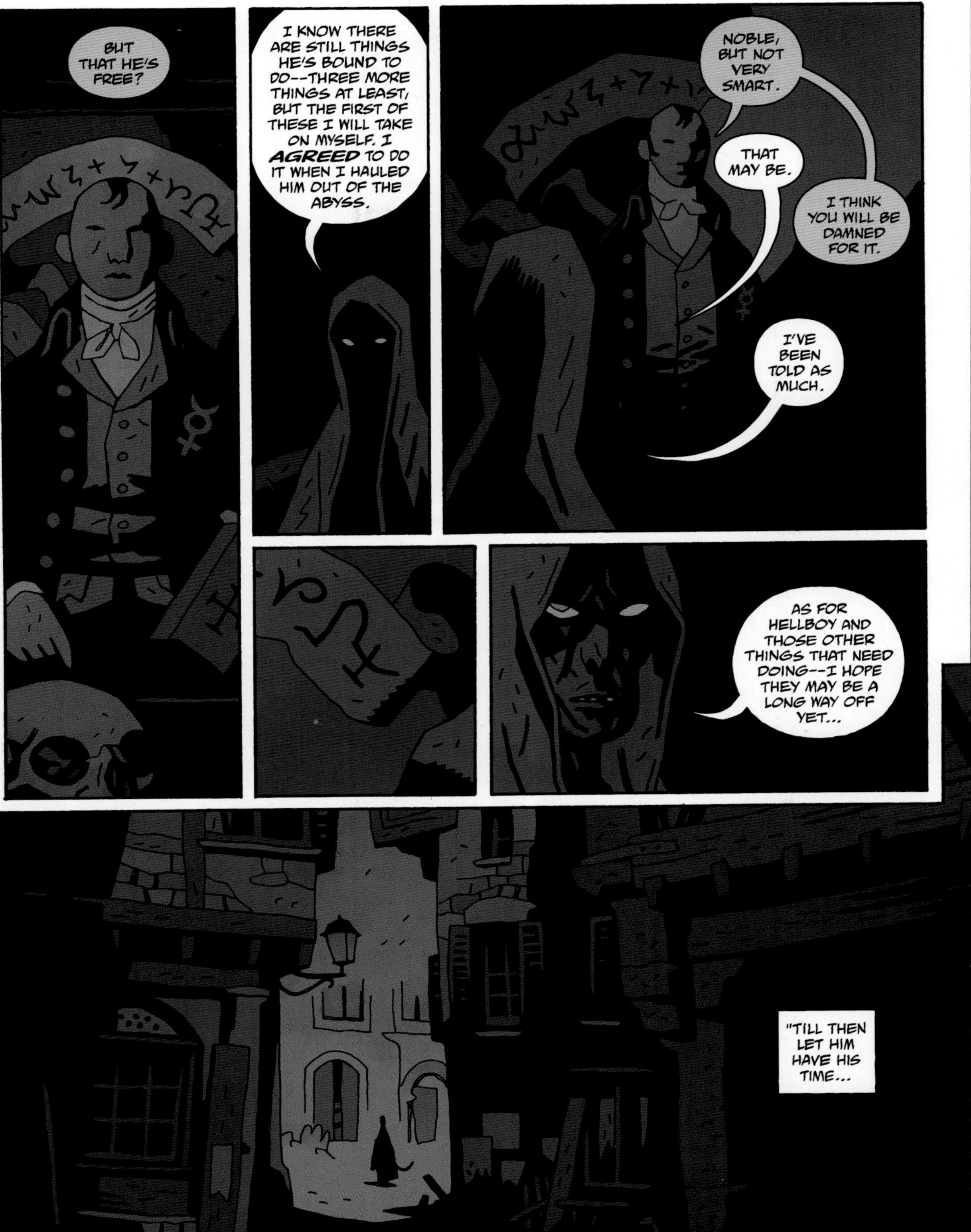

BUT THAT HE'S FREE?
I KNOW THERE ARE STILL THINGS HE'S BOUND TO DO--THREE MORE THINGS AT LEAST, BUT THE FIRST OF THESE I WILL TAKE ON MYSELF. I AGREED TO DO IT WHEN I HAULED HIM OUT OF THE ABYSS.
NOBLE, BUT NOT VERY SMART.
THAT MAY BE.
I THINK YOU WILL BE DAMNED FOR IT.
I'VE BEEN TOLD AS MUCH.
AS FOR HELLBOY AND THOSE OTHER THINGS THAT NEED DOING--I HOPE THEY MAY BE A LONG WAY OFF YET...
"TILL THEN LET HIM HAVE HIS TIME...

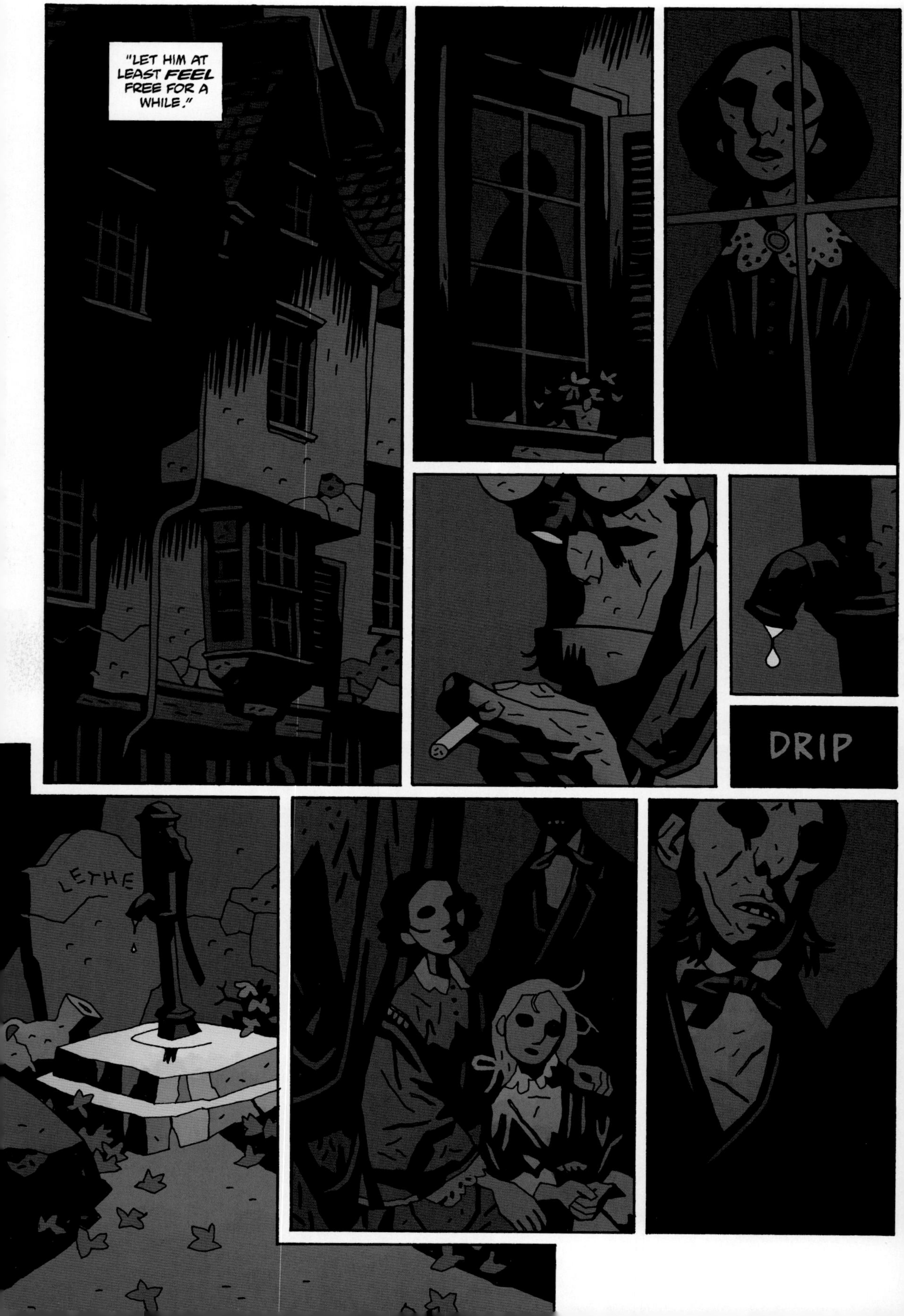
"LET HIM AT LEAST FEEL FREE FOR A WHILE."
DRIP
LETHE

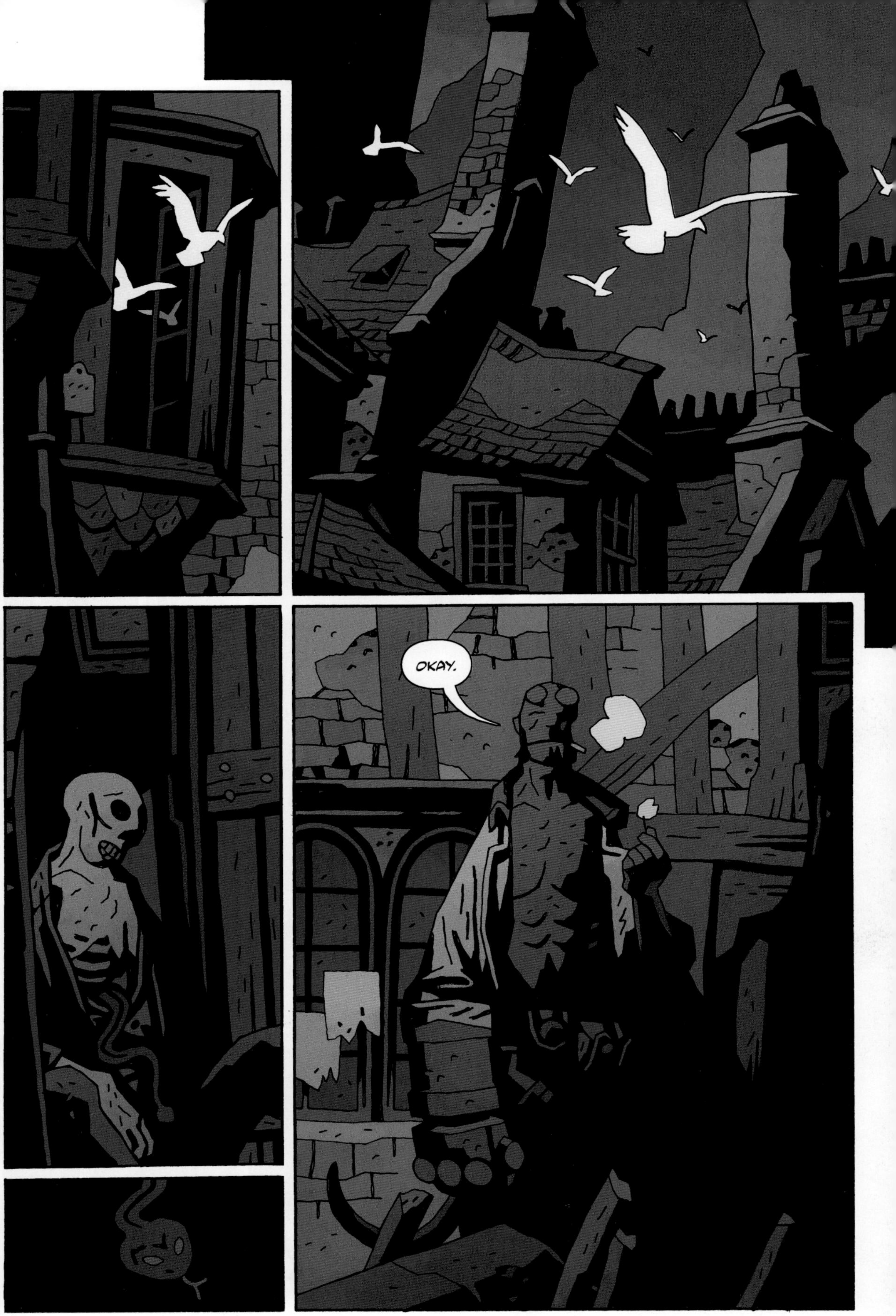
OKAY.

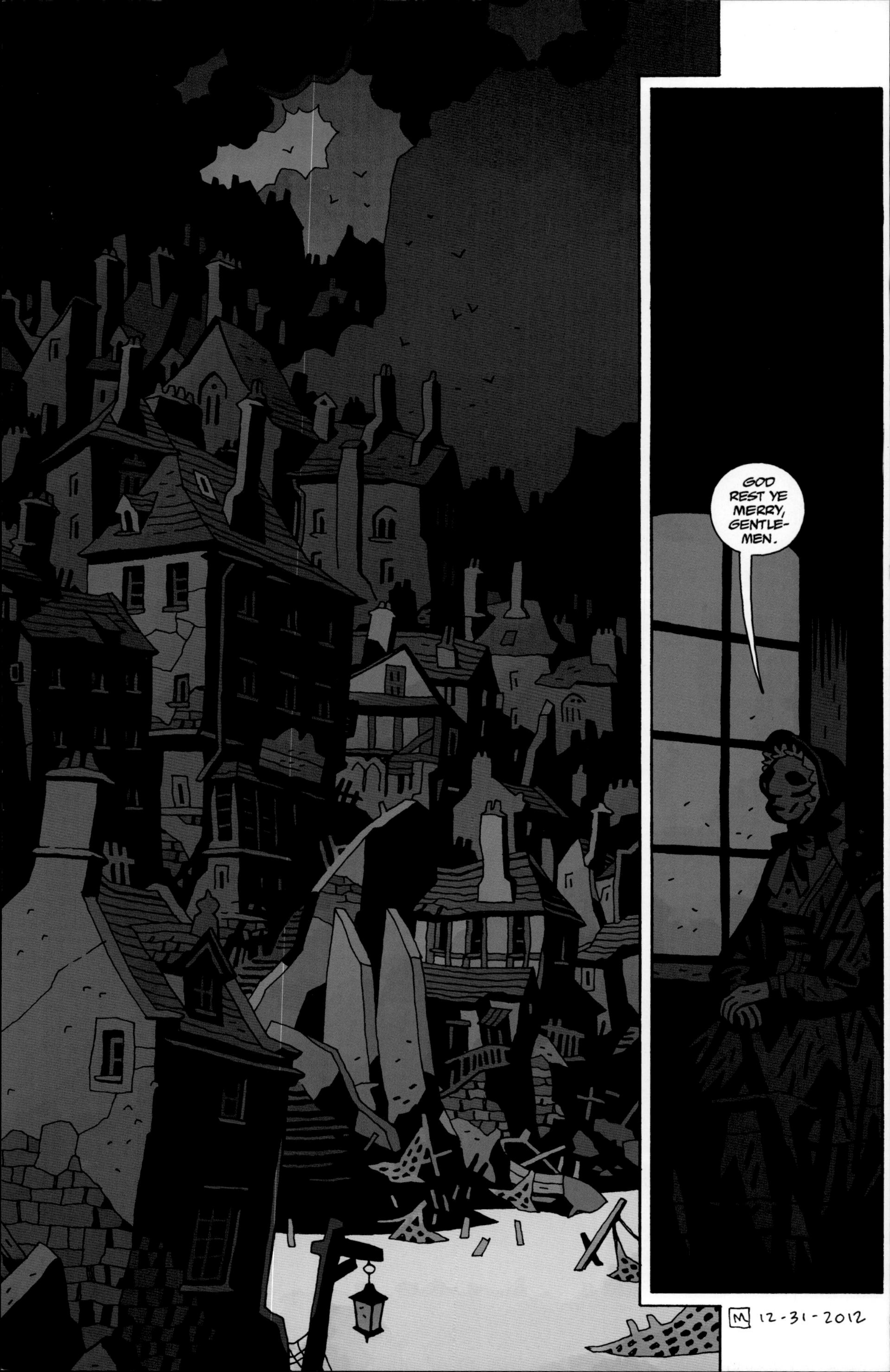
GOD REST YE MERRY, GENTLE-MEN.
M 12-31-2012

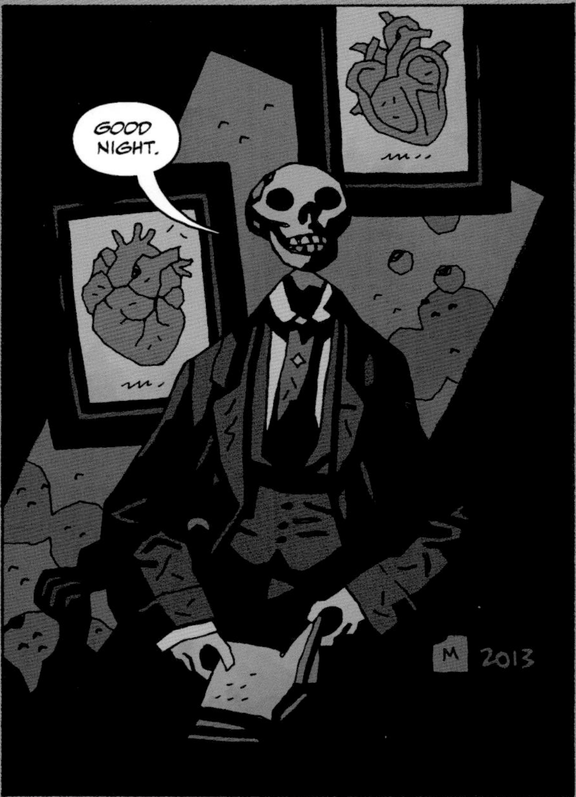
GOOD NIGHT.
M 2013

CHAPTER FIVE

THE THREE
GOLD WHIPS

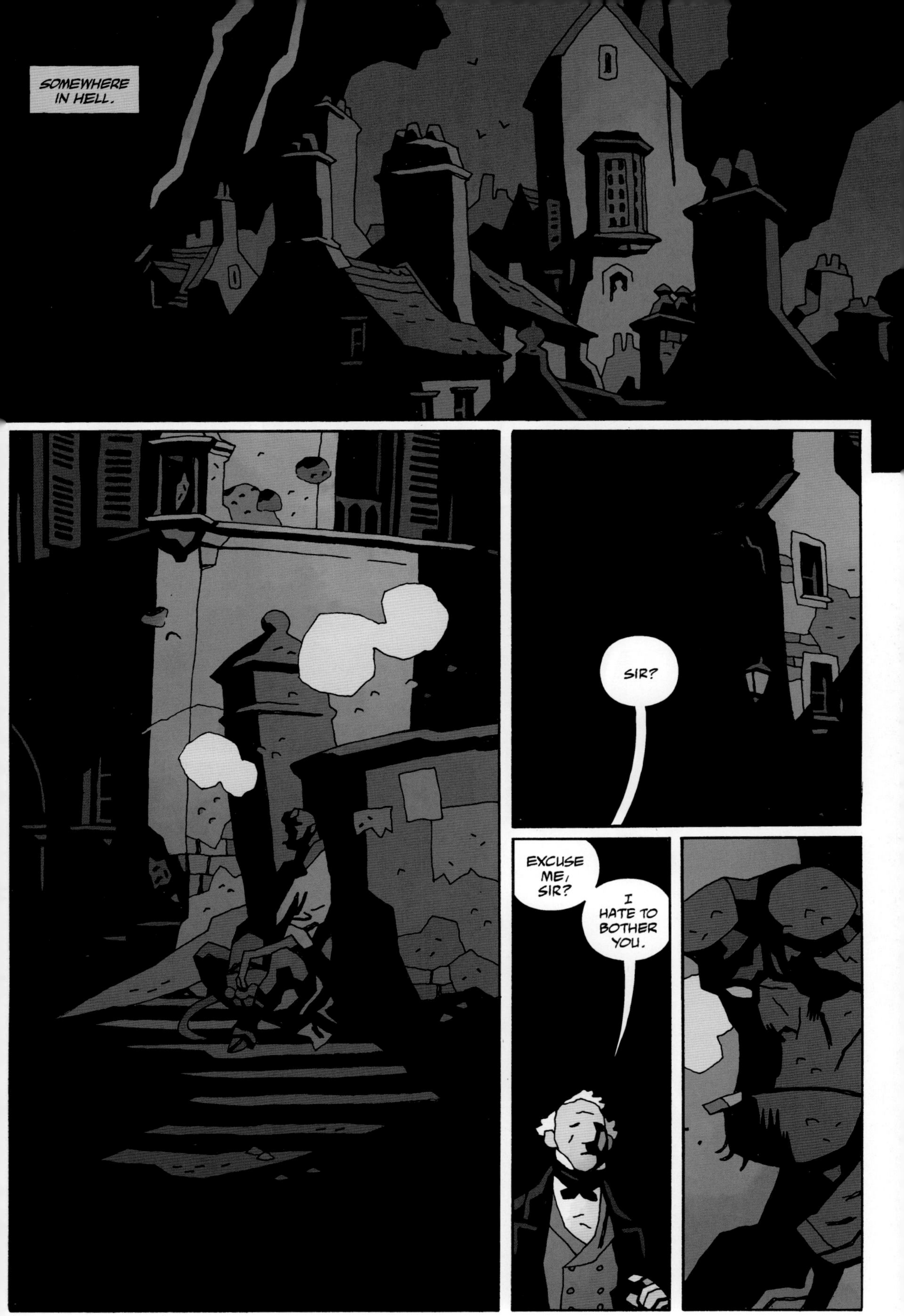
SOMEWHERE IN HELL.
SIR?
EXCUSE ME, SIR?
I HATE TO BOTHER YOU.

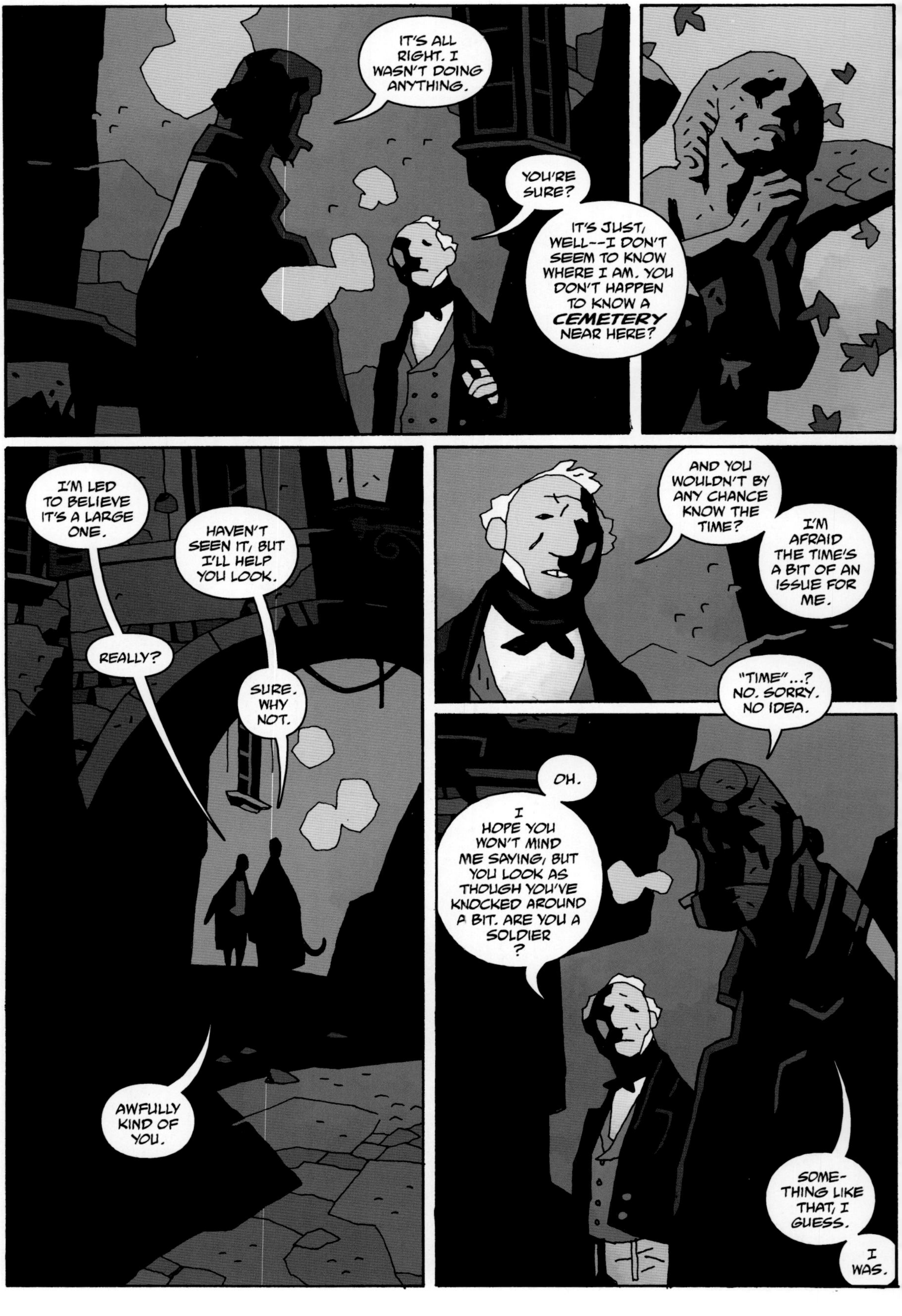
IT'S ALL RIGHT. I WASN'T DOING ANYTHING.
YOU'RE SURE?
IT'S JUST, WELL--I DON'T SEEM TO KNOW WHERE I AM. YOU DON'T HAPPEN TO KNOW A CEMETERY NEAR HERE?
I'M LED TO BELIEVE IT'S A LARGE ONE.
HAVEN'T SEEN IT, BUT I'LL HELP YOU LOOK.
REALLY?
SURE. WHY NOT.
AWFULLY KIND OF YOU.
AND YOU WOULDN'T BY ANY CHANCE KNOW THE TIME?
I'M AFRAID THE TIME'S A BIT OF AN ISSUE FOR ME.
"TIME"...? NO. SORRY. NO IDEA.
OH.
I HOPE YOU WON'T MIND ME SAYING, BUT YOU LOOK AS THOUGH YOU'VE KNOCKED AROUND A BIT. ARE YOU A SOLDIER ?
SOME-THING LIKE THAT, I GUESS.
I WAS.

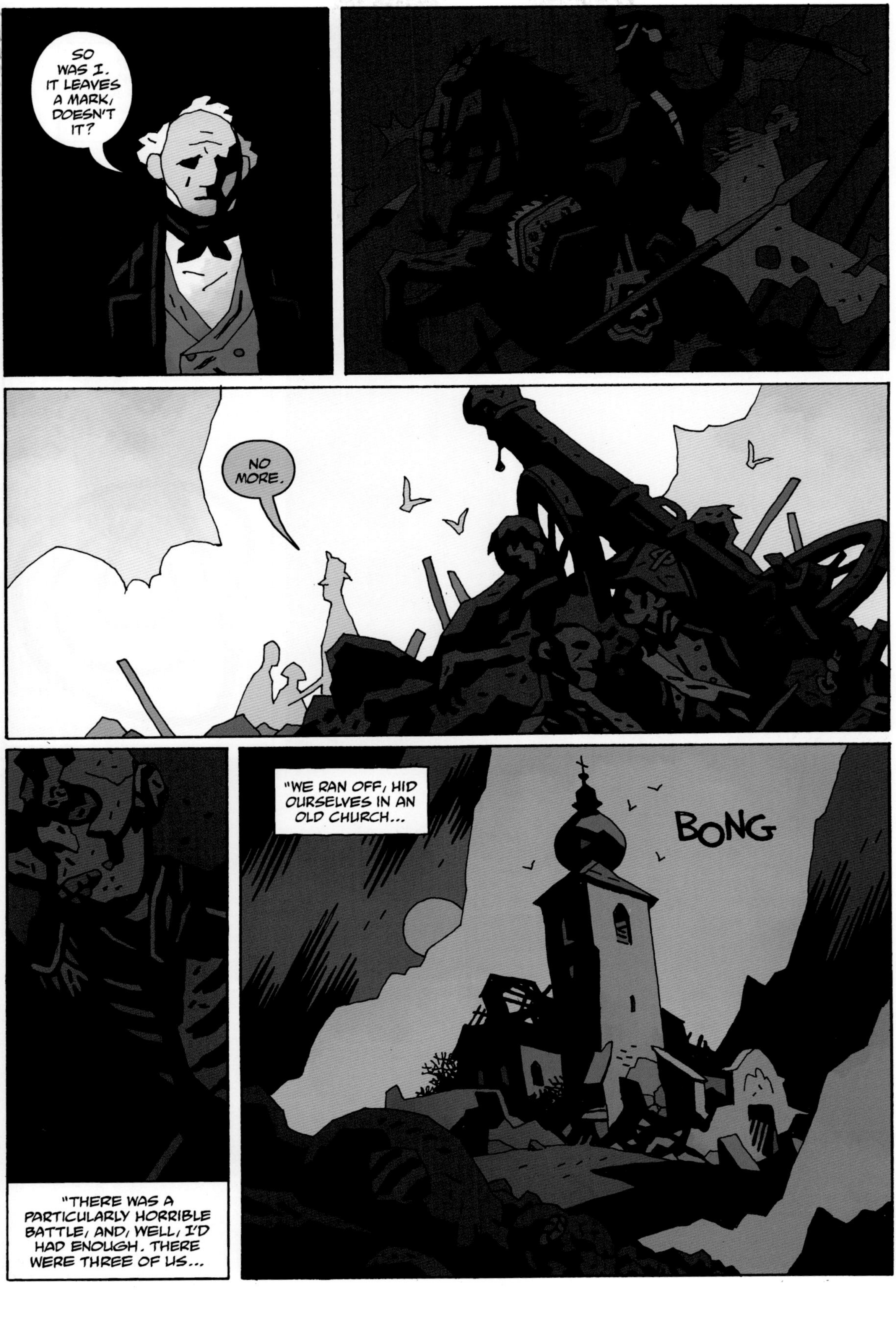
SO WAS I. IT LEAVES A MARK, DOESN'T IT?
NO MORE.
"THERE WAS A PARTICULARLY HORRIBLE BATTLE, AND, WELL, I'D HAD ENOUGH. THERE WERE THREE OF US...
"WE RAN OFF, HID OURSELVES IN AN OLD CHURCH...
BONG

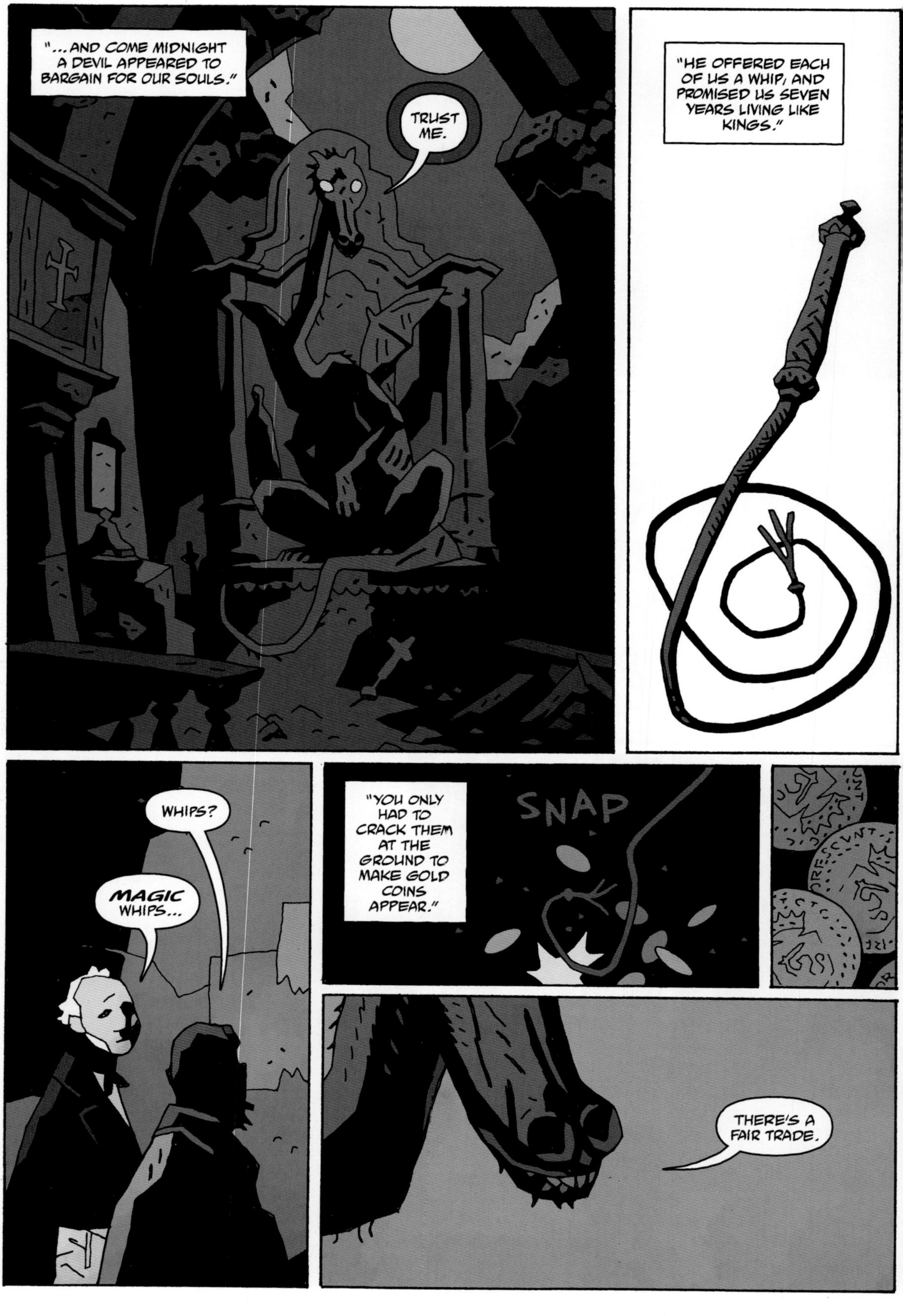
"...AND COME MIDNIGHT A DEVIL APPEARED TO BARGAIN FOR OUR SOULS."
TRUST ME.
"HE OFFERED EACH OF US A WHIP, AND PROMISED US SEVEN YEARS LIVING LIKE KINGS."
WHIPS?
MAGIC WHIPS...
"YOU ONLY HAD TO CRACK THEM AT THE GROUND TO MAKE GOLD COINS APPEAR."
SNAP
THERE'S A FAIR TRADE.

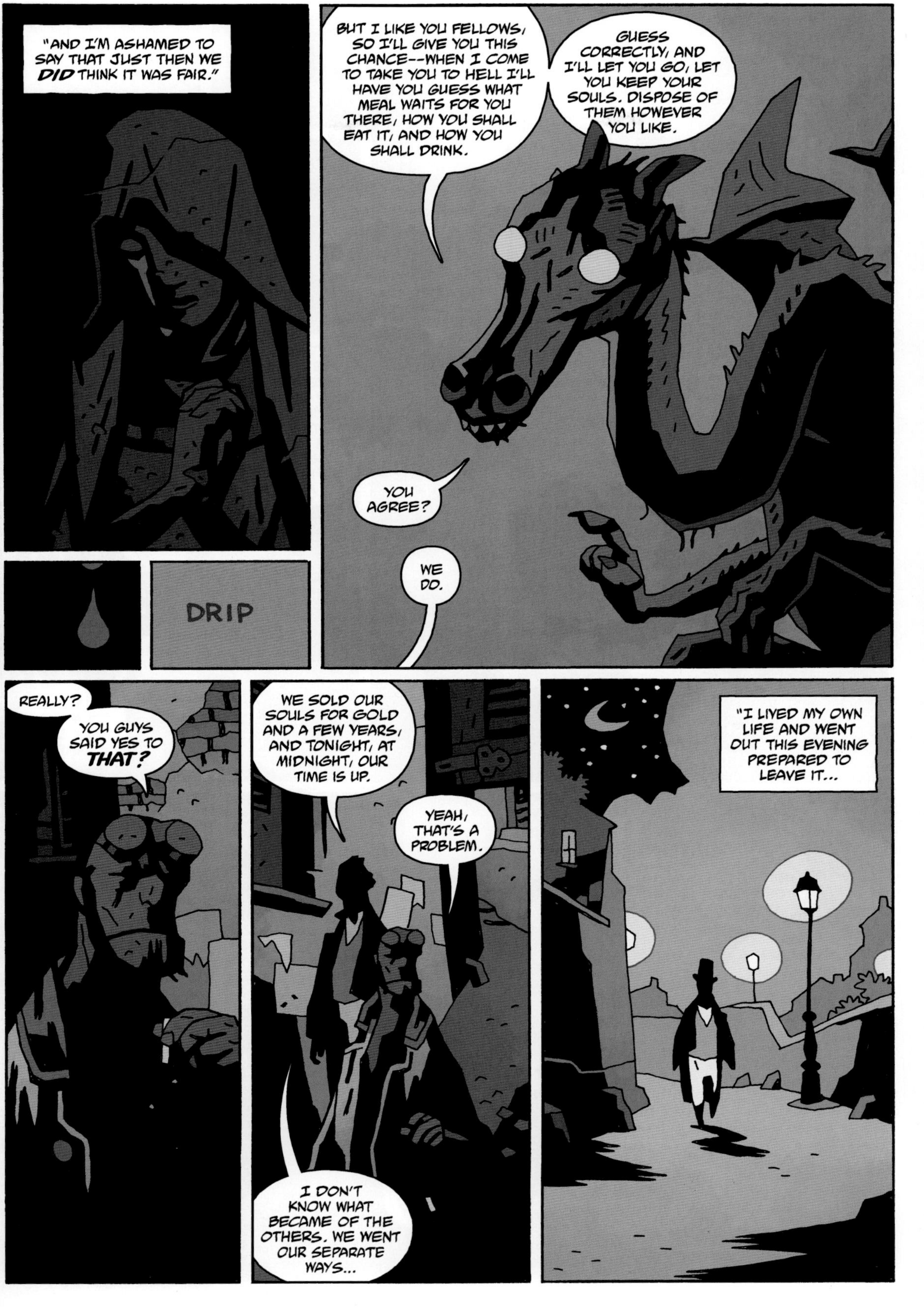
"AND I'M ASHAMED TO SAY THAT JUST THEN WE DID THINK IT WAS FAIR."
BUT I LIKE YOU FELLOWS, SO I'LL GIVE YOU THIS CHANCE--WHEN I COME TO TAKE YOU TO HELL I'LL HAVE YOU GUESS WHAT MEAL WAITS FOR YOU THERE, HOW YOU SHALL EAT IT, AND HOW YOU SHALL DRINK.
GUESS CORRECTLY, AND I'LL LET YOU GO, LET YOU KEEP YOUR SOULS. DISPOSE OF THEM HOWEVER YOU LIKE.
YOU AGREE?
WE DO.
DRIP
REALLY?
YOU GUYS SAID YES TO THAT?
WE SOLD OUR SOULS FOR GOLD AND A FEW YEARS, AND TONIGHT, AT MIDNIGHT, OUR TIME IS UP.
YEAH, THAT'S A PROBLEM.
I DON'T KNOW WHAT BECAME OF THE OTHERS. WE WENT OUR SEPARATE WAYS...
"I LIVED MY OWN LIFE AND WENT OUT THIS EVENING PREPARED TO LEAVE IT...

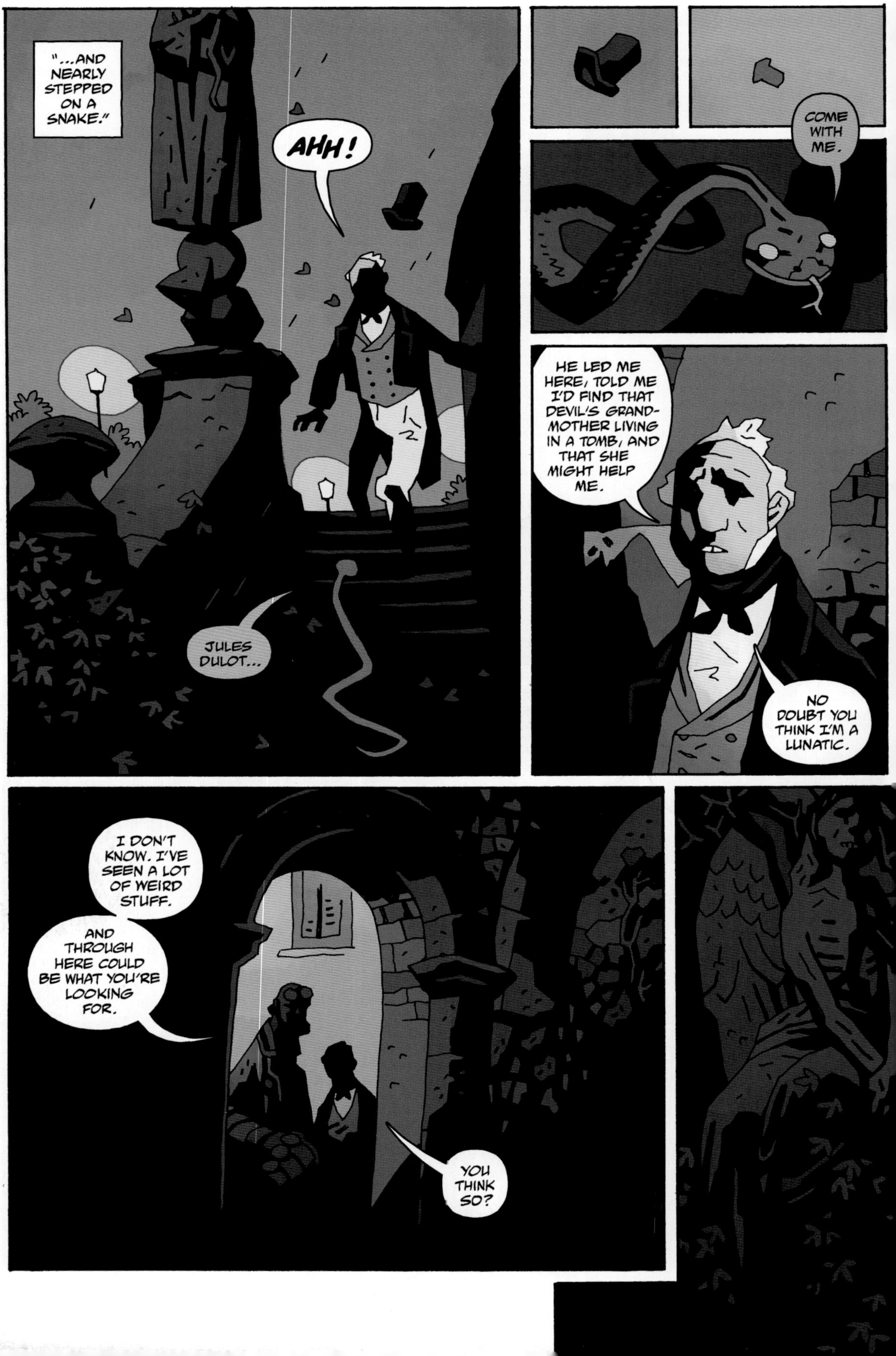
"...AND NEARLY STEPPED ON A SNAKE."
AHH!
JULES DULOT...
COME WITH ME.
HE LED ME HERE, TOLD ME I'D FIND THAT DEVIL'S GRAND-MOTHER LIVING IN A TOMB, AND THAT SHE MIGHT HELP ME.
NO DOUBT YOU THINK I'M A LUNATIC.
I DON'T KNOW. I'VE SEEN A LOT OF WEIRD STUFF.
AND THROUGH HERE COULD BE WHAT YOU'RE LOOKING FOR.
YOU THINK SO?

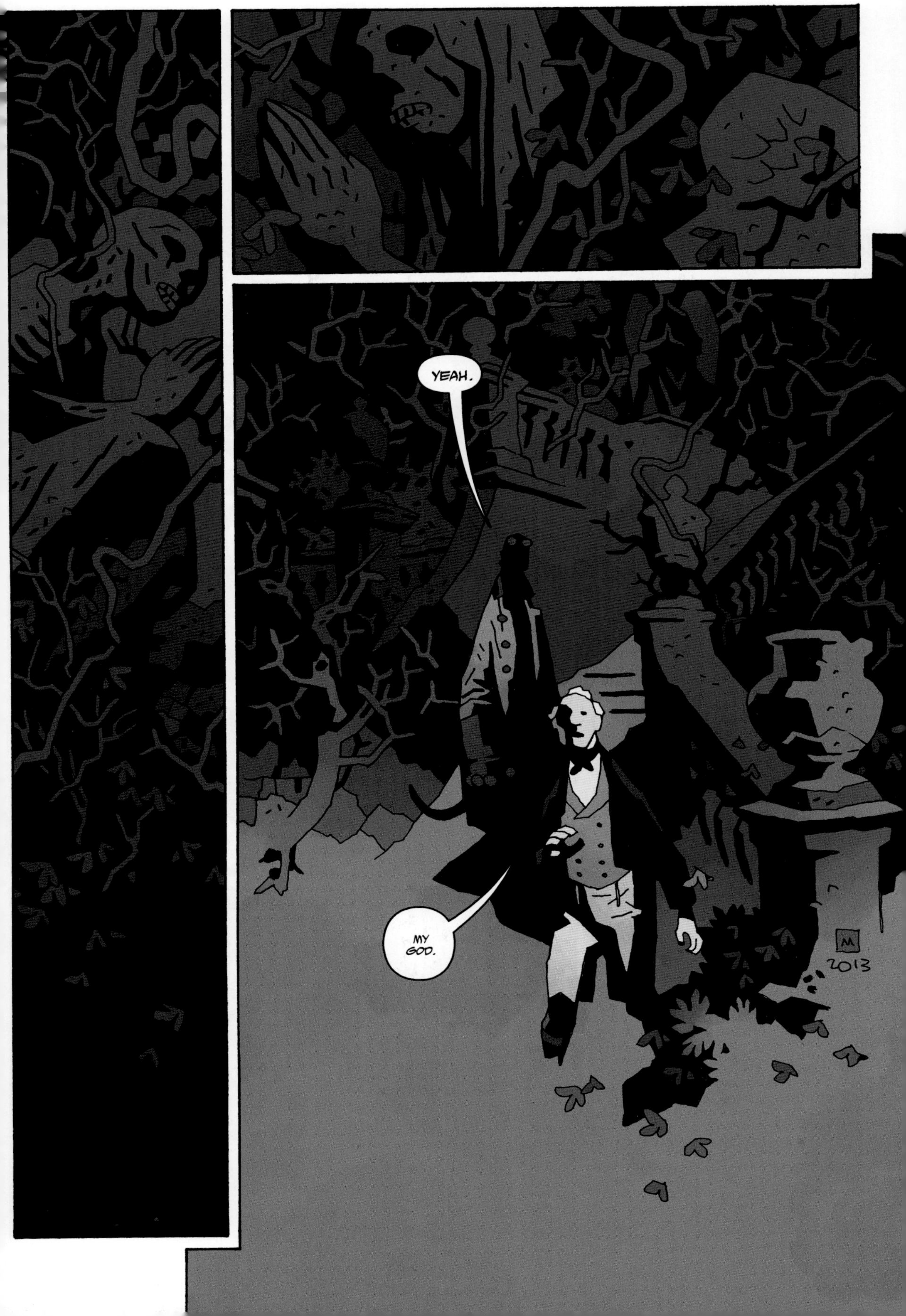
YEAH.
MY GOD.
M 2013

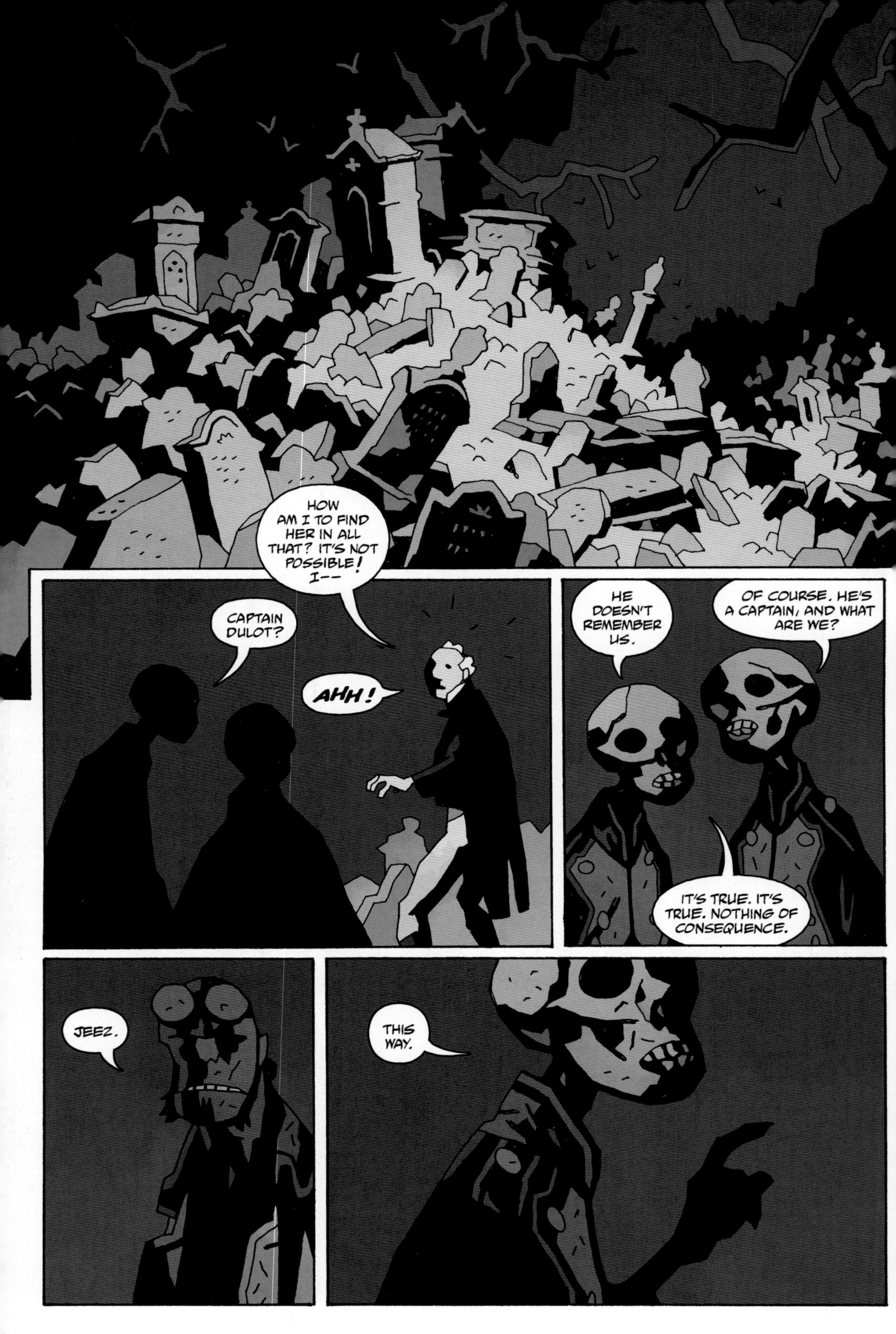
HOW AM I TO FIND HER IN ALL THAT? IT'S NOT POSSIBLE! I--
CAPTAIN DULOT?
AHH!
HE DOESN'T REMEMBER US.
OF COURSE. HE'S A CAPTAIN, AND WHAT ARE WE?
IT'S TRUE. IT'S TRUE. NOTHING OF CONSEQUENCE.
JEEZ.
THIS WAY.

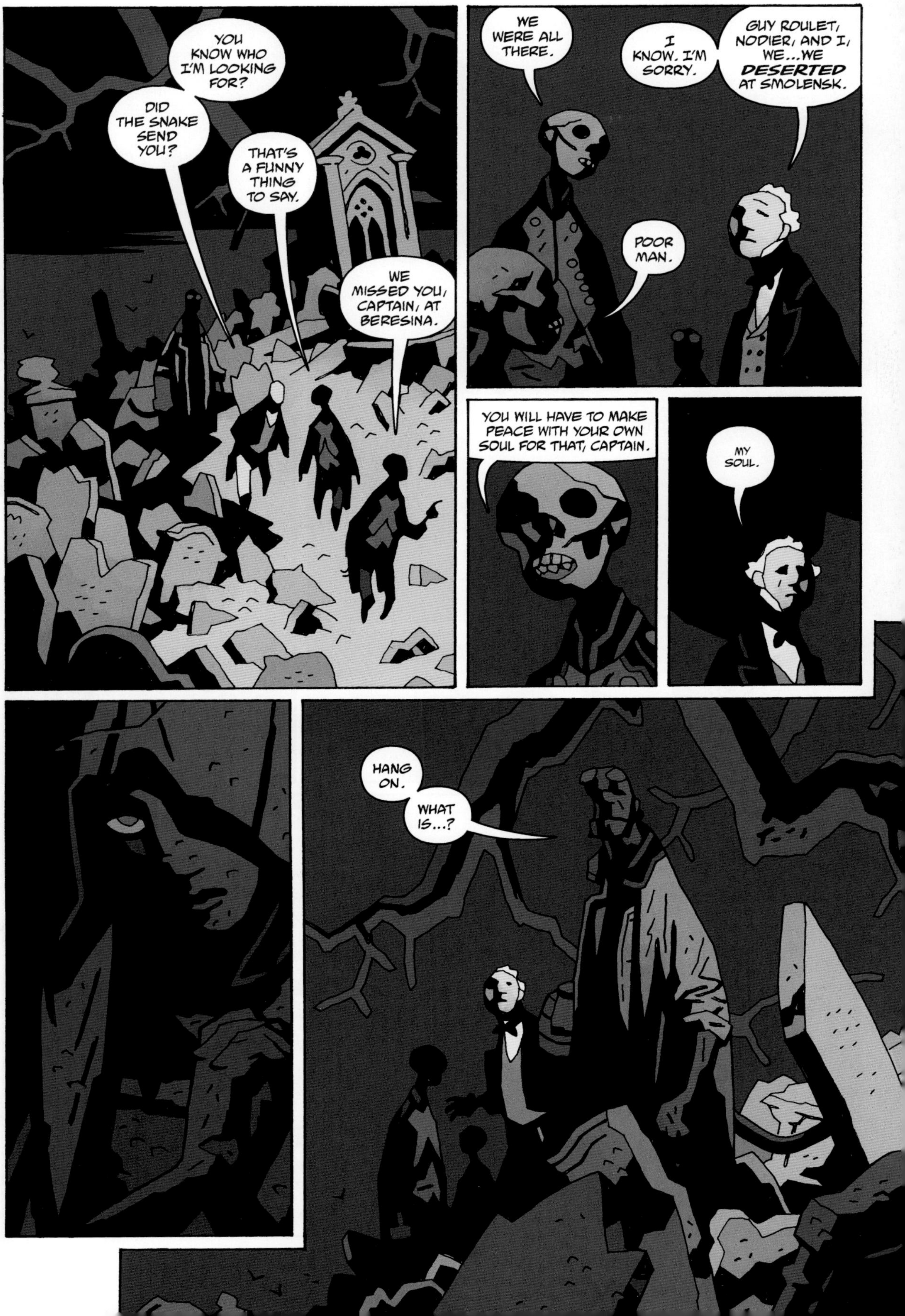
YOU KNOW WHO I'M LOOKING FOR?
DID THE SNAKE SEND YOU?
THAT'S A FUNNY THING TO SAY.
WE MISSED YOU, CAPTAIN, AT BERESINA.
WE WERE ALL THERE.
I KNOW. I'M SORRY.
GUY ROULET, NODIER, AND I, WE...WE **DESERTED** AT SMOLENSK.
POOR MAN.
YOU WILL HAVE TO MAKE PEACE WITH YOUR OWN SOUL FOR THAT, CAPTAIN.
MY SOUL.
HANG ON.
WHAT IS...?

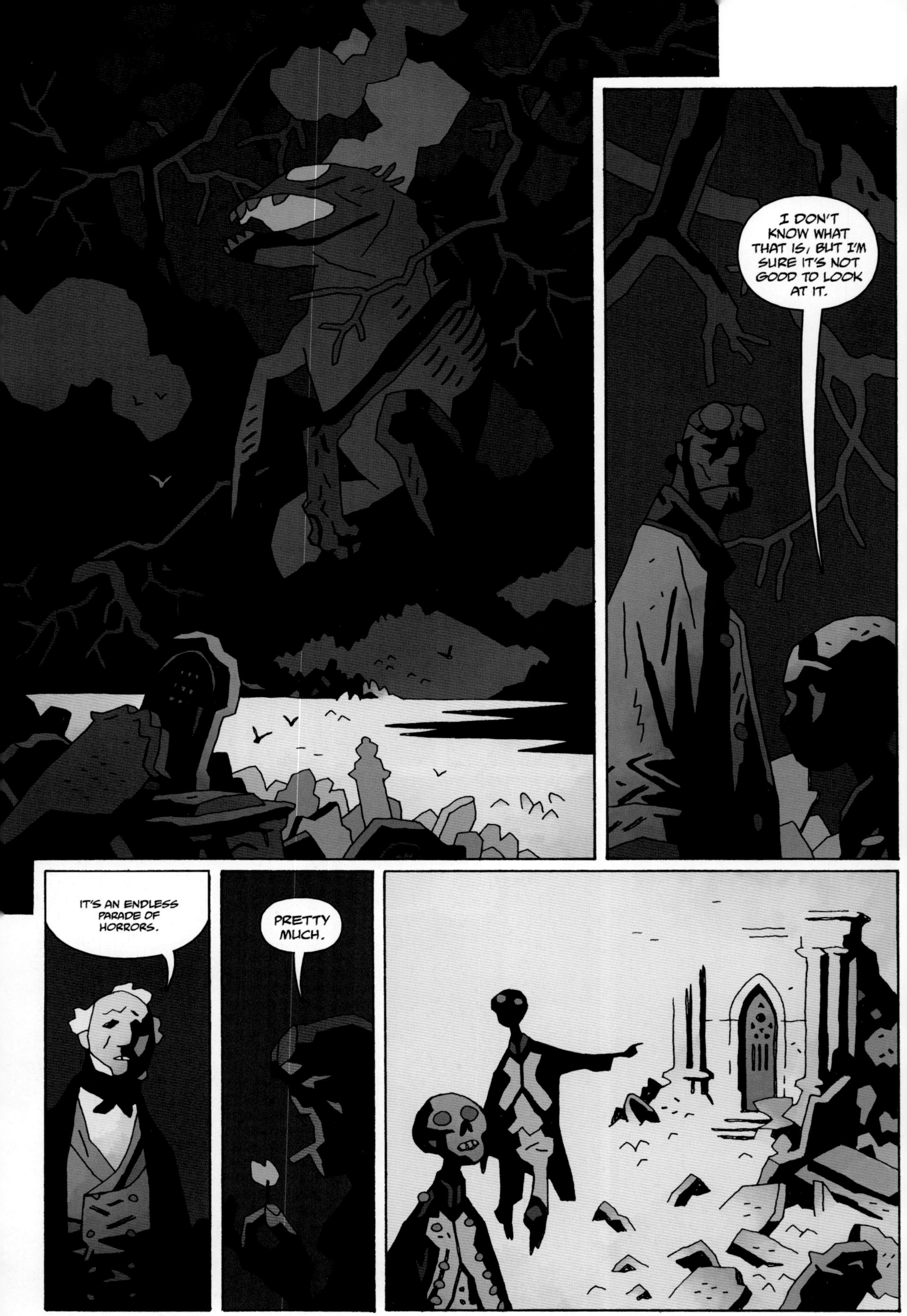

I DON'T KNOW WHAT THAT IS, BUT I'M SURE IT'S NOT GOOD TO LOOK AT IT.
IT'S AN ENDLESS PARADE OF HORRORS.
PRETTY MUCH.

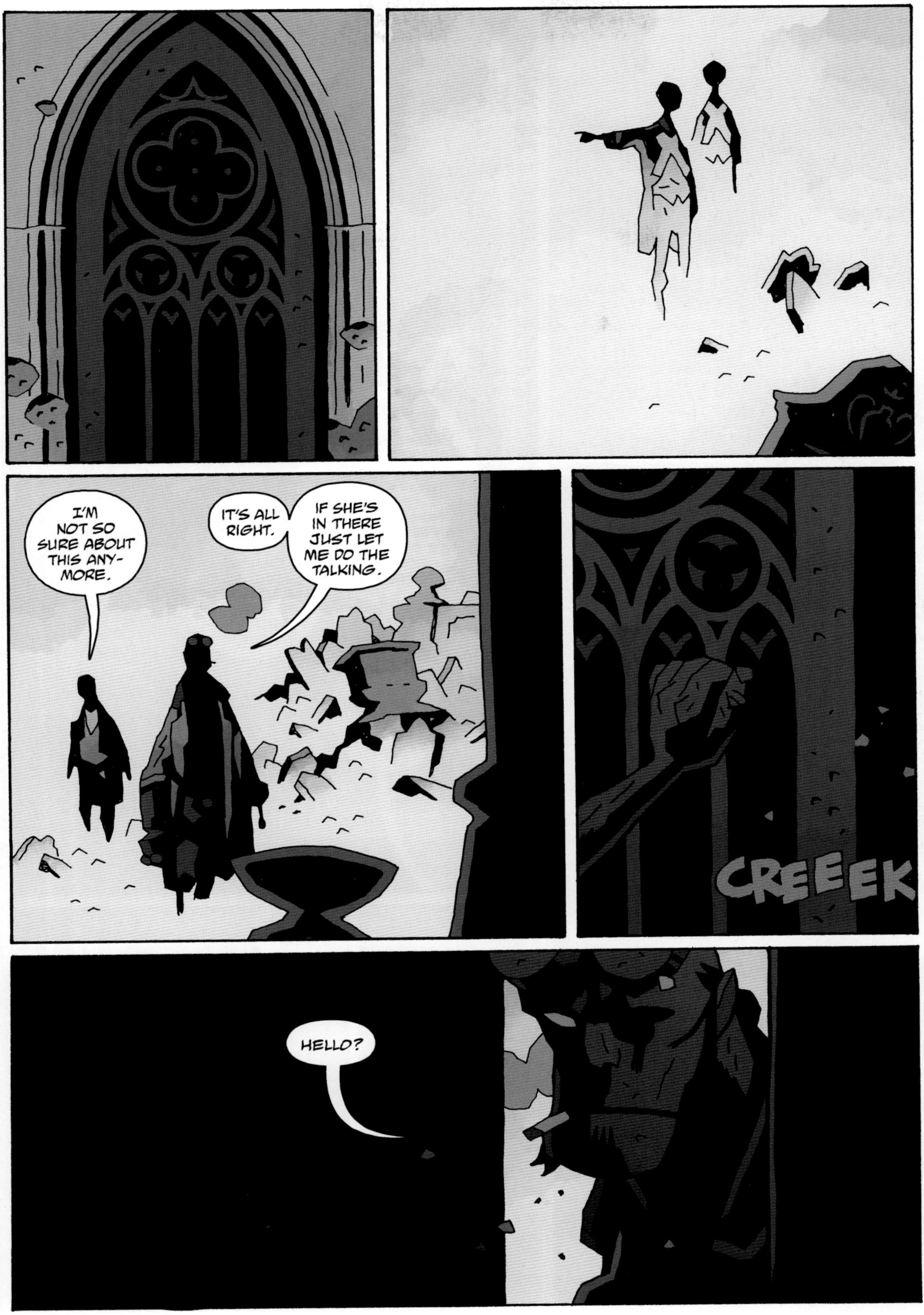
I'M NOT SO SURE ABOUT THIS ANY-MORE.
IT'S ALL RIGHT.
IF SHE'S IN THERE JUST LET ME DO THE TALKING.
CREEEK
HELLO?

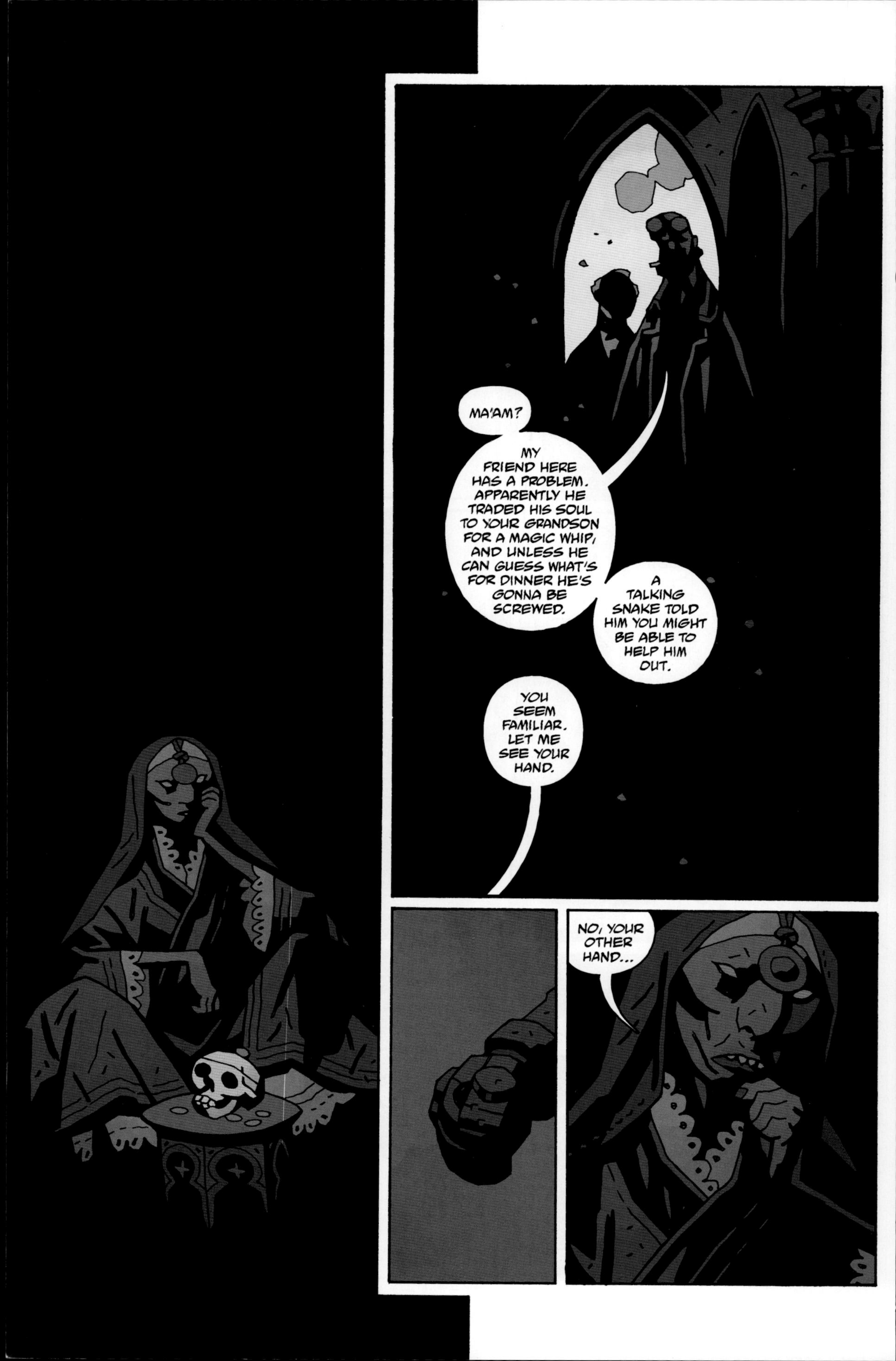
MA'AM?
MY FRIEND HERE HAS A PROBLEM. APPARENTLY HE TRADED HIS SOUL TO YOUR GRANDSON FOR A MAGIC WHIP, AND UNLESS HE CAN GUESS WHAT'S FOR DINNER HE'S GONNA BE SCREWED.
A TALKING SNAKE TOLD HIM YOU MIGHT BE ABLE TO HELP HIM OUT.
YOU SEEM FAMILIAR. LET ME SEE YOUR HAND.
NO, YOUR OTHER HAND...

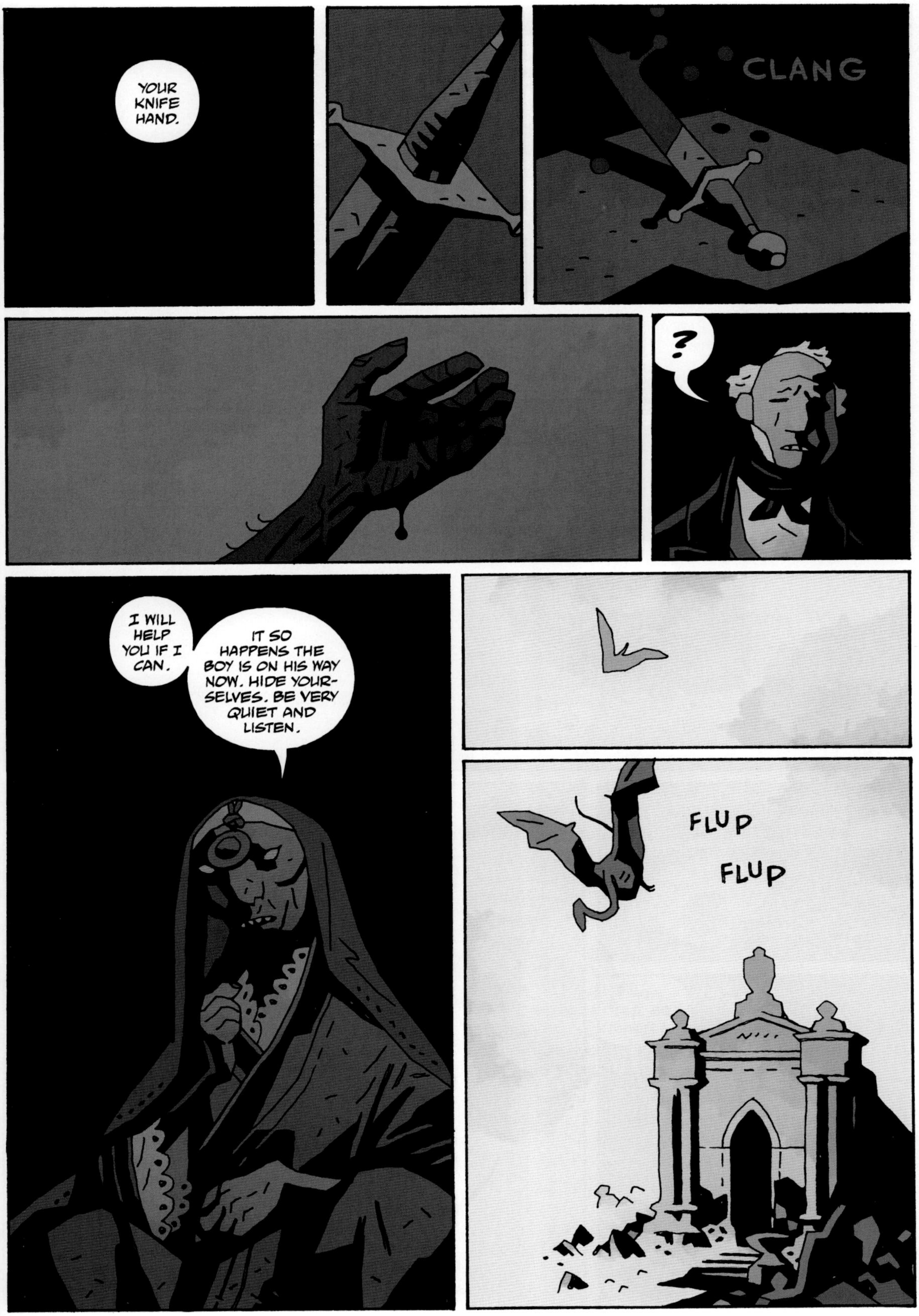
YOUR KNIFE HAND.
CLANG
?
I WILL HELP YOU IF I CAN.
IT SO HAPPENS THE BOY IS ON HIS WAY NOW. HIDE YOURSELVES. BE VERY QUIET AND LISTEN.
FLUP
FLUP

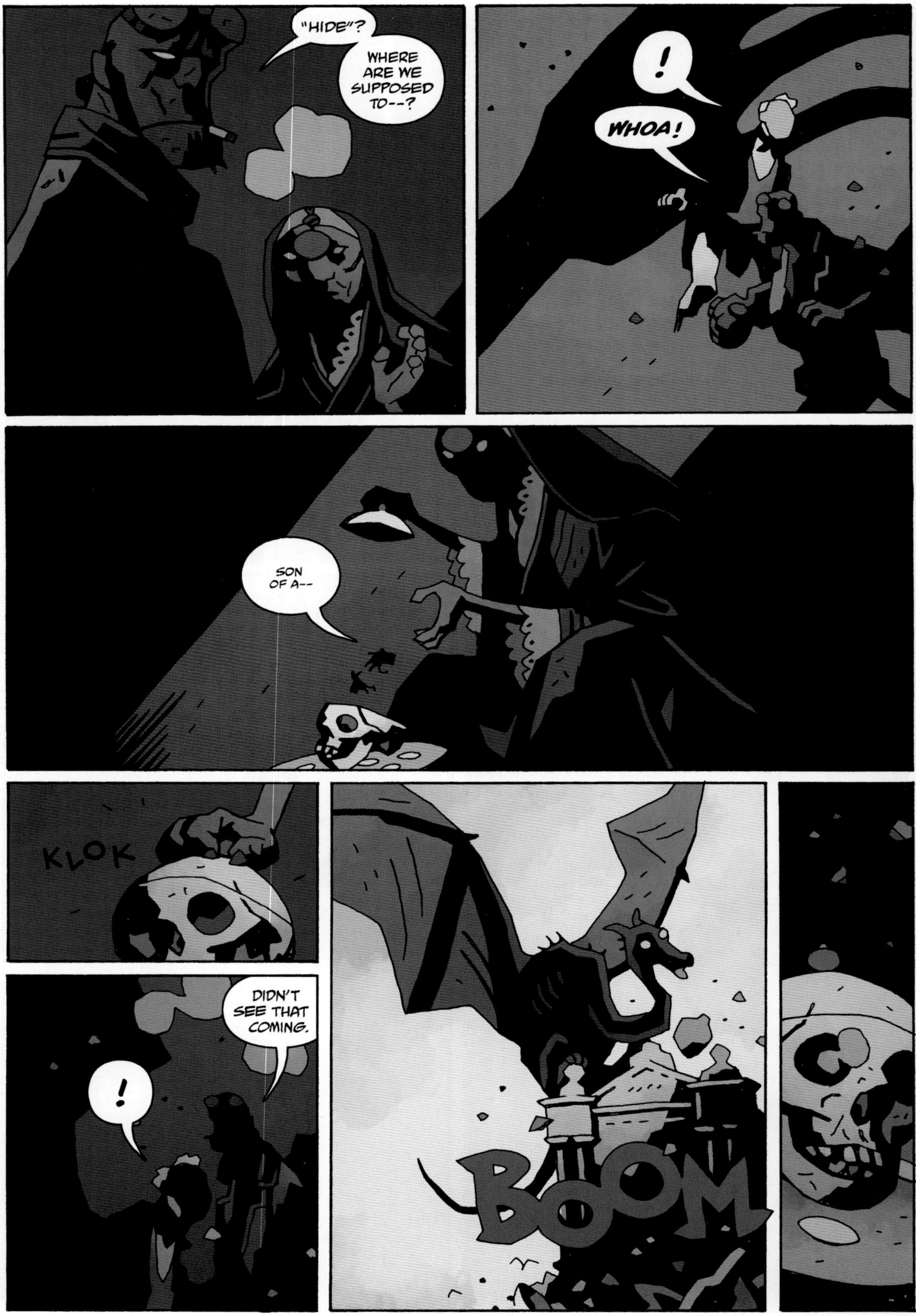
"HIDE"?
WHERE ARE WE SUPPOSED TO--?
!
WHOA!
SON OF A--
KLOK
!
DIDN'T SEE THAT COMING.
BOOM

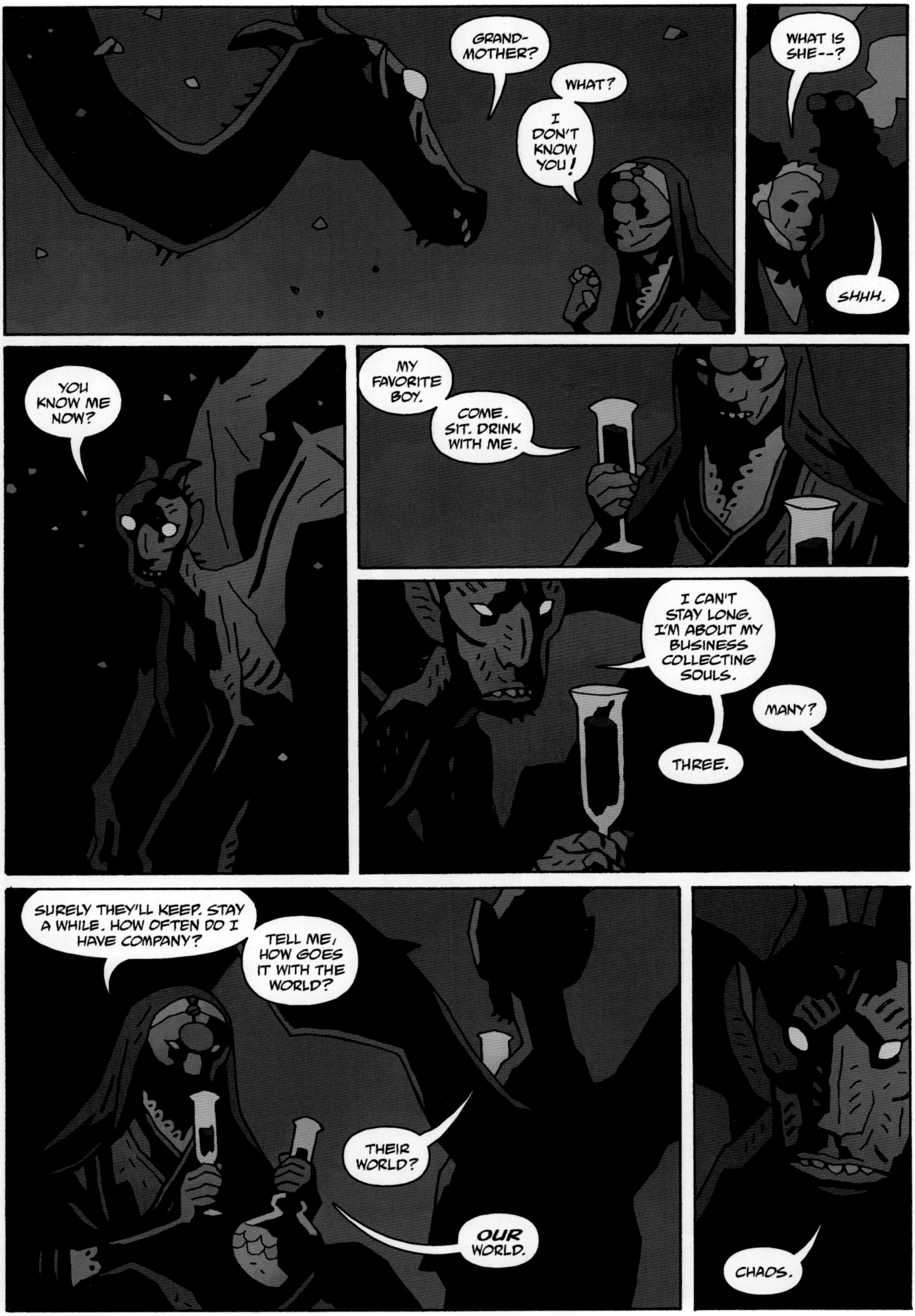
GRAND-MOTHER?
WHAT?
I DON'T KNOW YOU!
WHAT IS SHE--?
SHHH.
YOU KNOW ME NOW?
MY FAVORITE BOY.
COME. SIT. DRINK WITH ME.
I CAN'T STAY LONG. I'M ABOUT MY BUSINESS COLLECTING SOULS.
MANY?
THREE.
SURELY THEY'LL KEEP. STAY A WHILE. HOW OFTEN DO I HAVE COMPANY?
TELL ME, HOW GOES IT WITH THE WORLD?
THEIR WORLD?
OUR WORLD.
CHAOS.

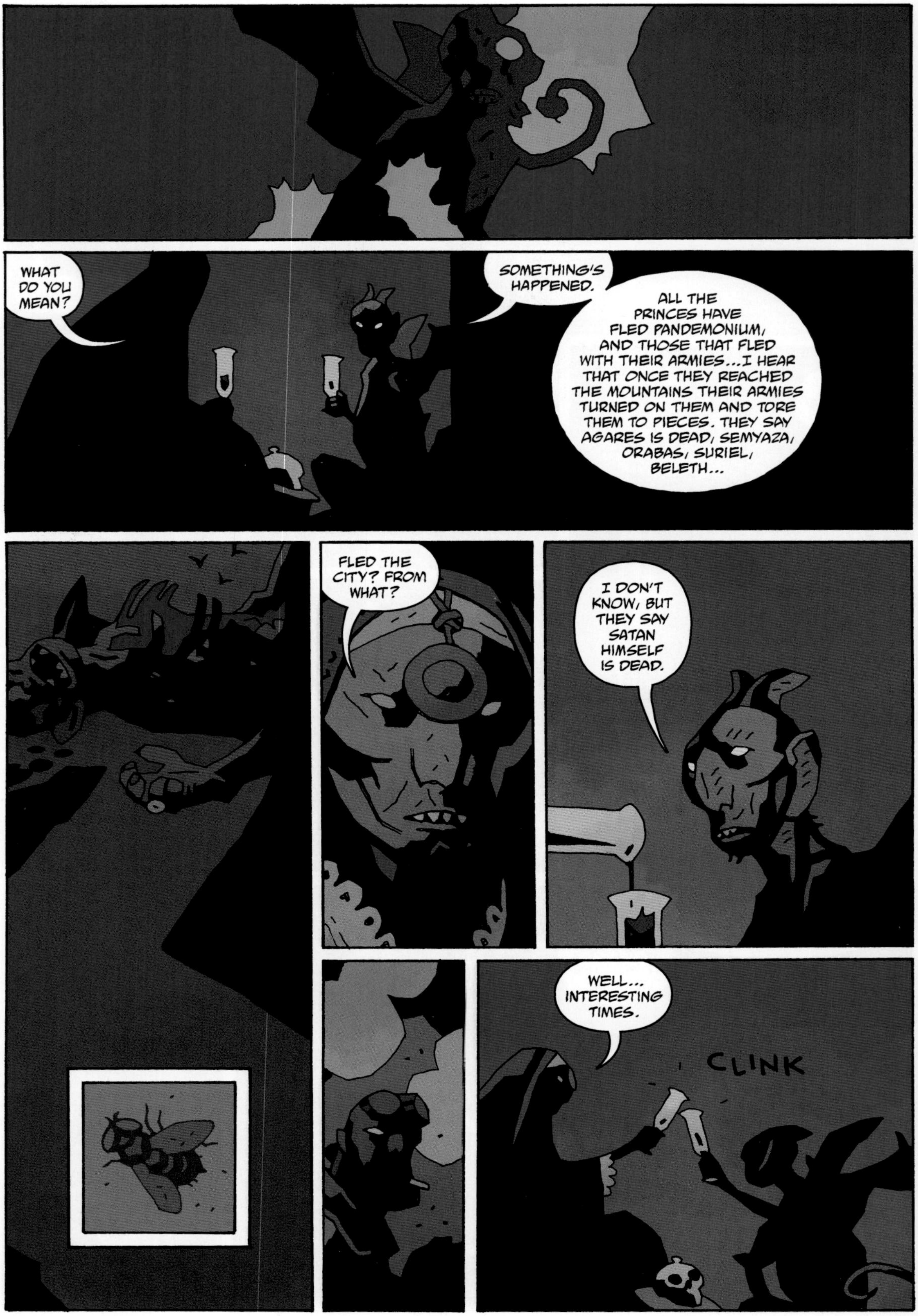
WHAT DO YOU MEAN?
SOMETHING'S HAPPENED.
ALL THE PRINCES HAVE FLED PANDEMONIUM, AND THOSE THAT FLED WITH THEIR ARMIES... I HEAR THAT ONCE THEY REACHED THE MOUNTAINS THEIR ARMIES TURNED ON THEM AND TORE THEM TO PIECES. THEY SAY AGARES IS DEAD, SEMYAZA, ORABAS, SURIEL, BELETH...
FLED THE CITY? FROM WHAT?
I DON'T KNOW, BUT THEY SAY SATAN HIMSELF IS DEAD.
WELL... INTERESTING TIMES.
CLINK

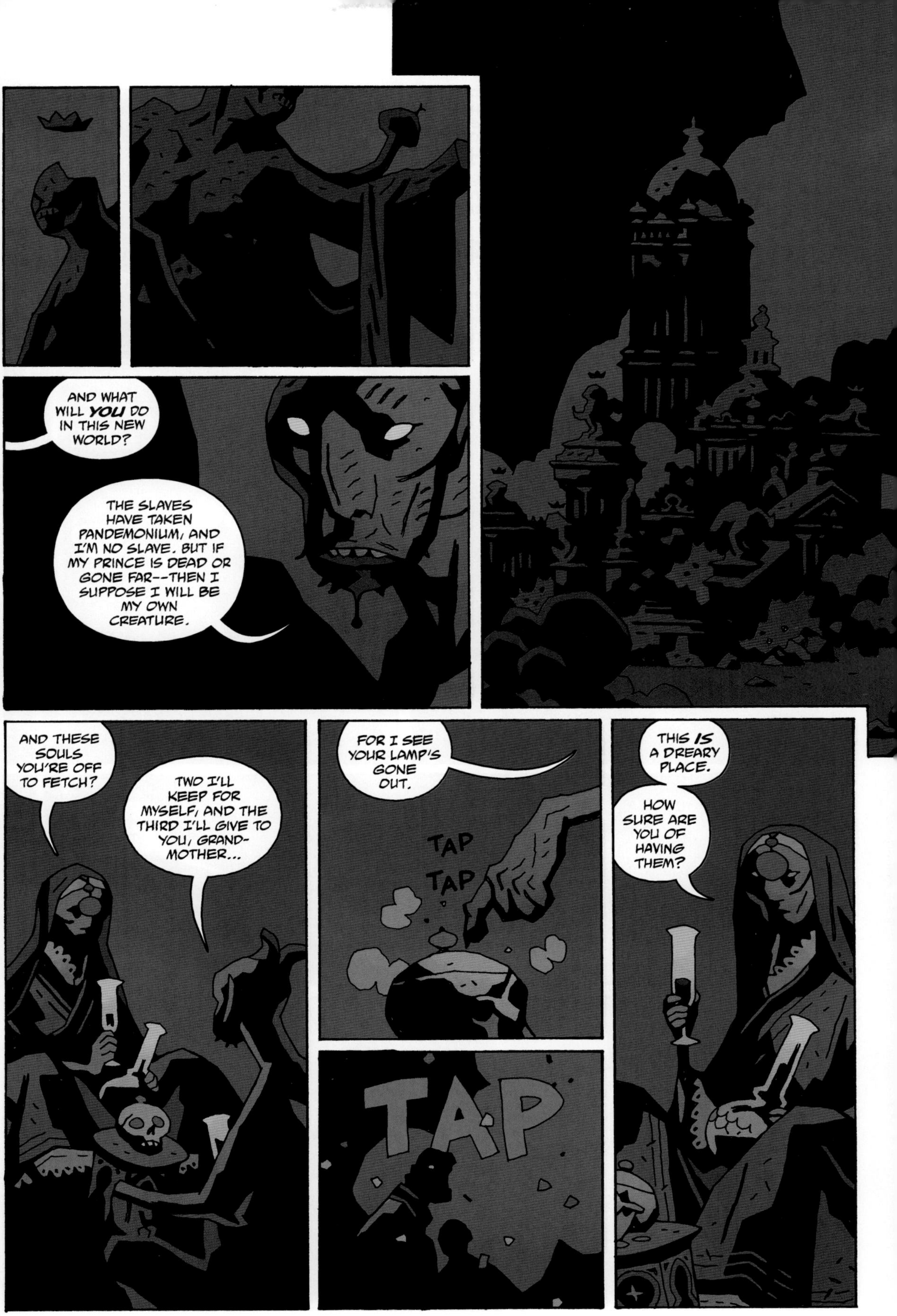

AND WHAT WILL YOU DO IN THIS NEW WORLD?
THE SLAVES HAVE TAKEN PANDEMONIUM, AND I'M NO SLAVE. BUT IF MY PRINCE IS DEAD OR GONE FAR--THEN I SUPPOSE I WILL BE MY OWN CREATURE.
AND THESE SOULS YOU'RE OFF TO FETCH?
TWO I'LL KEEP FOR MYSELF, AND THE THIRD I'LL GIVE TO YOU, GRAND-MOTHER...
FOR I SEE YOUR LAMP'S GONE OUT.
TAP
TAP
TAP
THIS IS A DREARY PLACE.
HOW SURE ARE YOU OF HAVING THEM?

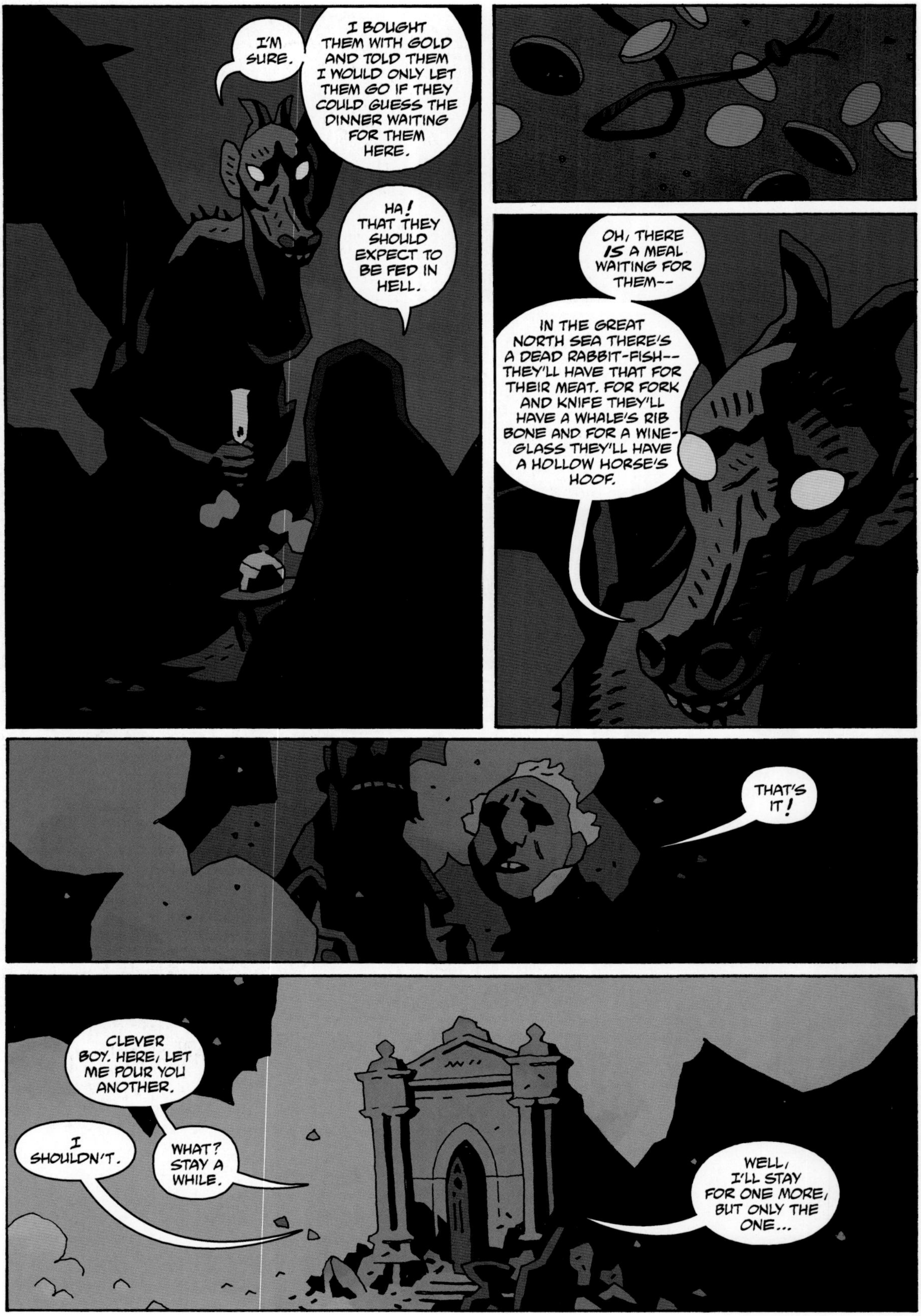
I'M SURE.
I BOUGHT THEM WITH GOLD AND TOLD THEM I WOULD ONLY LET THEM GO IF THEY COULD GUESS THE DINNER WAITING FOR THEM HERE.
HA! THAT THEY SHOULD EXPECT TO BE FED IN HELL.
OH, THERE IS A MEAL WAITING FOR THEM--
IN THE GREAT NORTH SEA THERE'S A DEAD RABBIT-FISH-- THEY'LL HAVE THAT FOR THEIR MEAT. FOR FORK AND KNIFE THEY'LL HAVE A WHALE'S RIB BONE AND FOR A WINE-GLASS THEY'LL HAVE A HOLLOW HORSE'S HOOF.
THAT'S IT!
CLEVER BOY. HERE, LET ME POUR YOU ANOTHER.
I SHOULDN'T.
WHAT? STAY A WHILE.
WELL, I'LL STAY FOR ONE MORE, BUT ONLY THE ONE...

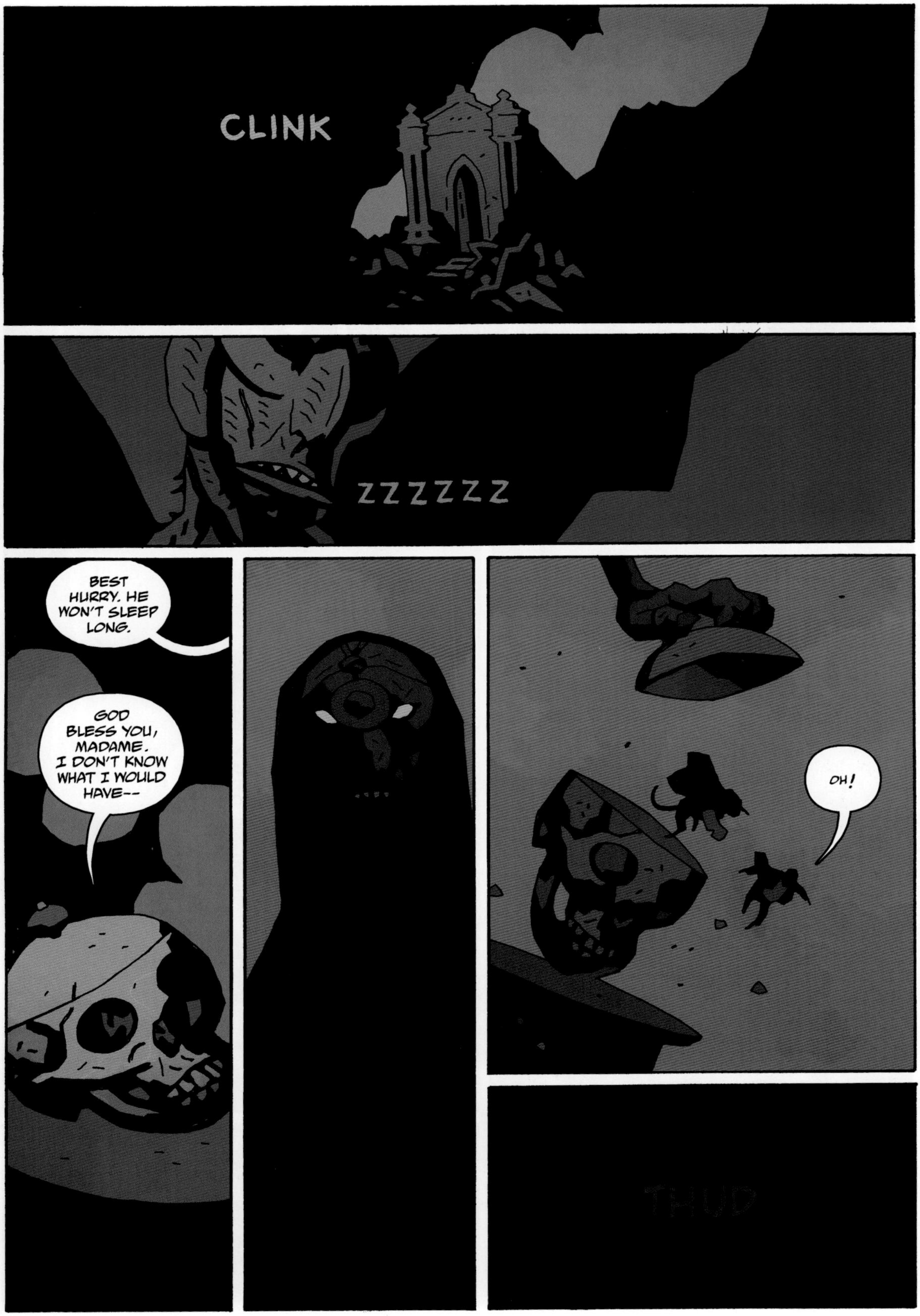
CLINK
ZZZZZZ
BEST HURRY. HE WON'T SLEEP LONG.
GOD BLESS YOU, MADAME. I DON'T KNOW WHAT I WOULD HAVE--
OH!
THUD

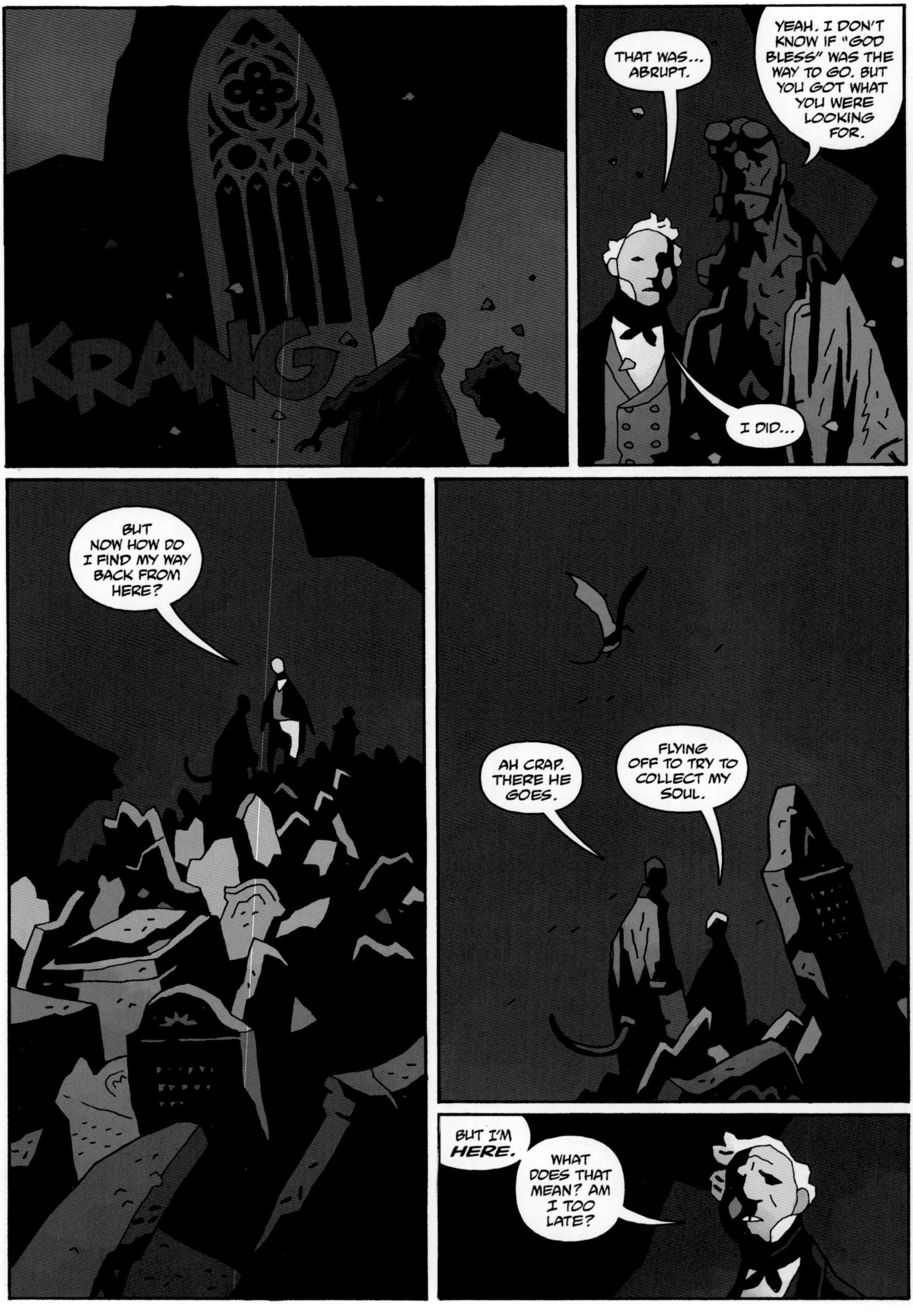
KRANG
THAT WAS... ABRUPT.
YEAH. I DON'T KNOW IF "GOD BLESS" WAS THE WAY TO GO. BUT YOU GOT WHAT YOU WERE LOOKING FOR.
I DID...
BUT NOW HOW DO I FIND MY WAY BACK FROM HERE?
AH CRAP. THERE HE GOES.
FLYING OFF TO TRY TO COLLECT MY SOUL.
BUT I'M *HERE.*
WHAT DOES THAT MEAN? AM I TOO LATE?

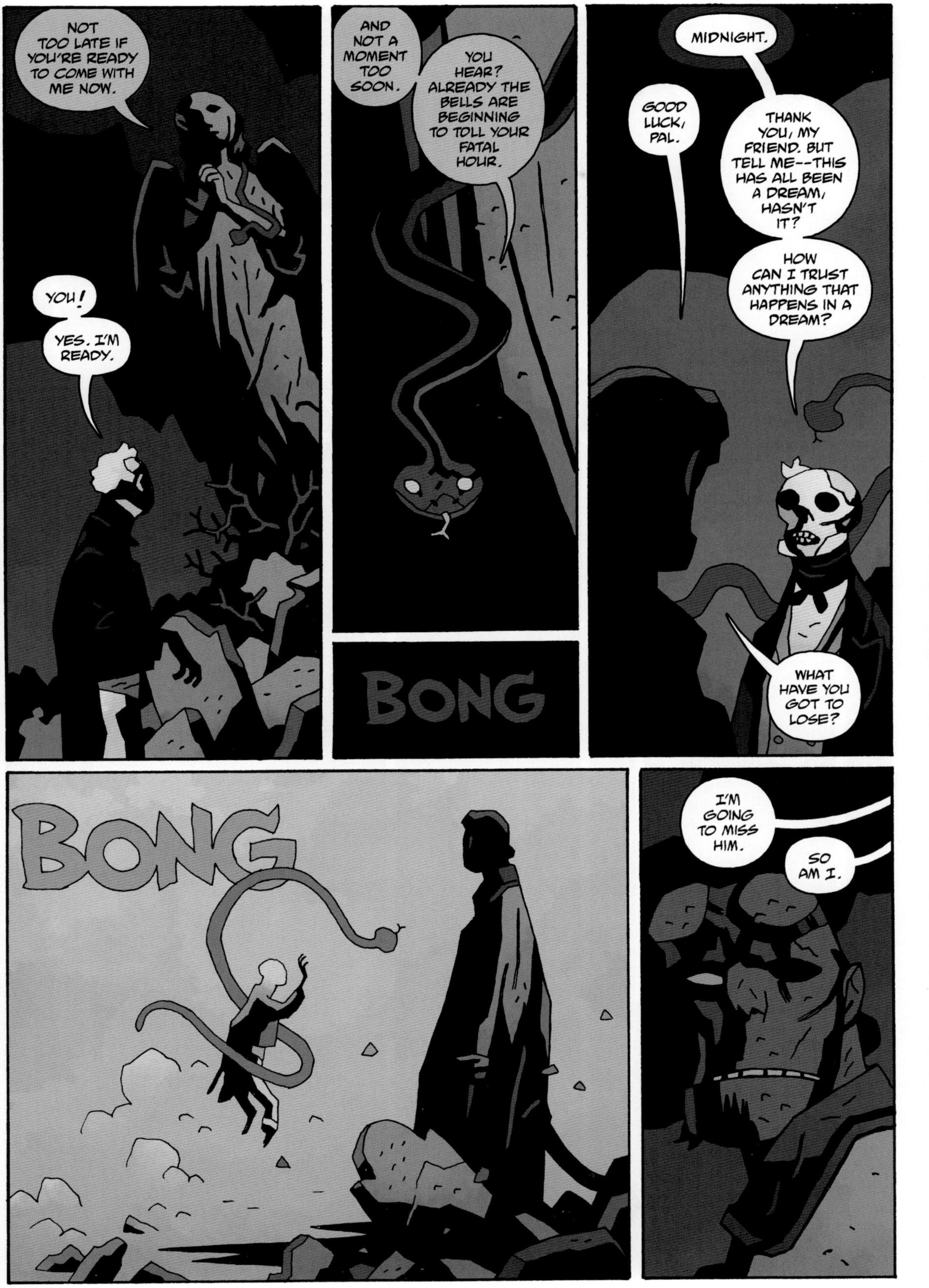
NOT TOO LATE IF YOU'RE READY TO COME WITH ME NOW.
YOU!
YES. I'M READY.
AND NOT A MOMENT TOO SOON.
YOU HEAR? ALREADY THE BELLS ARE BEGINNING TO TOLL YOUR FATAL HOUR.
BONG
MIDNIGHT.
GOOD LUCK, PAL.
THANK YOU, MY FRIEND. BUT TELL ME--THIS HAS ALL BEEN A DREAM, HASN'T IT?
HOW CAN I TRUST ANYTHING THAT HAPPENS IN A DREAM?
WHAT HAVE YOU GOT TO LOSE?
BONG
I'M GOING TO MISS HIM.
SO AM I.

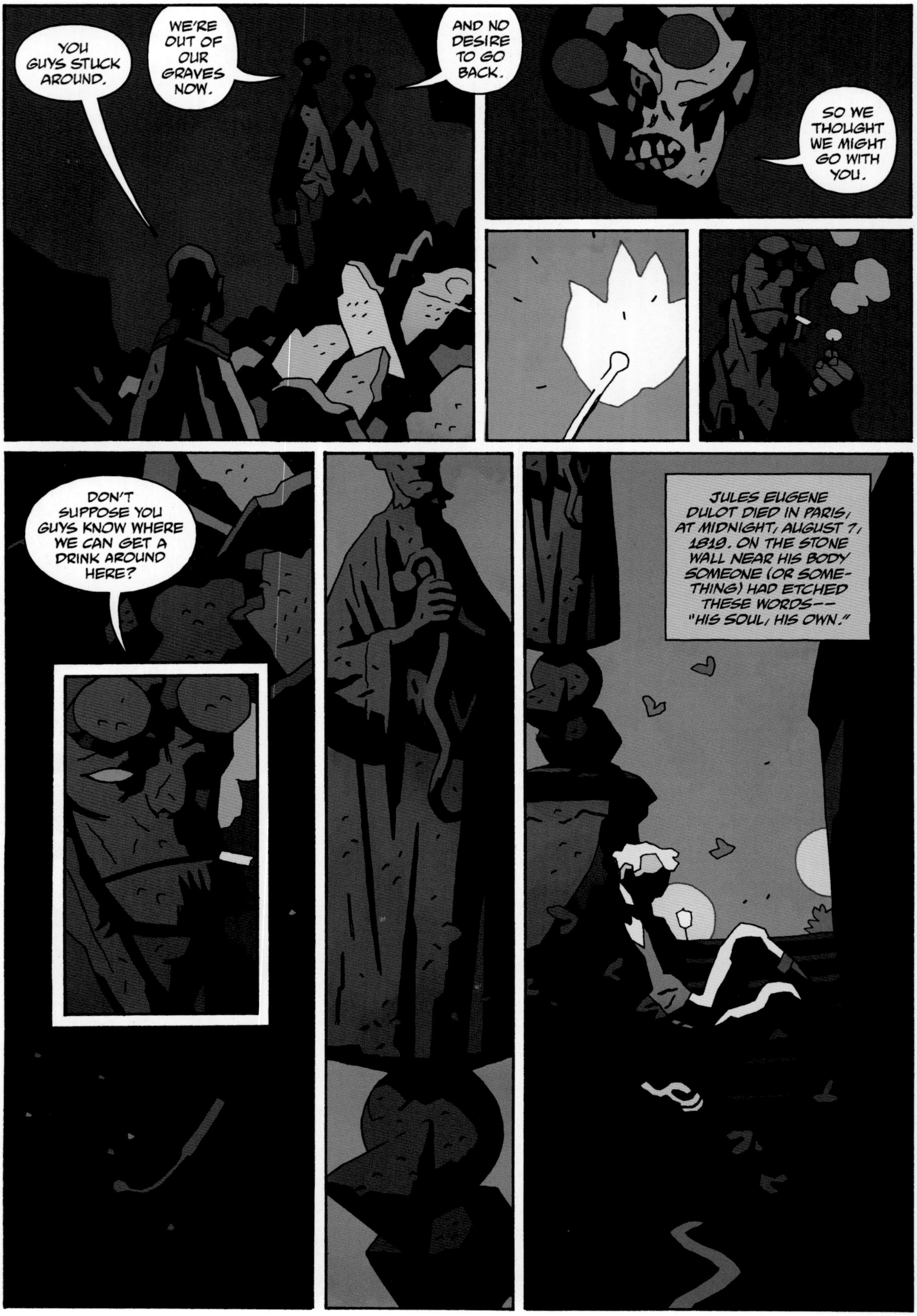
YOU GUYS STUCK AROUND.
WE'RE OUT OF OUR GRAVES NOW.
AND NO DESIRE TO GO BACK.
SO WE THOUGHT WE MIGHT GO WITH YOU.
DON'T SUPPOSE YOU GUYS KNOW WHERE WE CAN GET A DRINK AROUND HERE?
JULES EUGENE DULOT DIED IN PARIS, AT MIDNIGHT, AUGUST 7, 1819. ON THE STONE WALL NEAR HIS BODY SOMEONE (OR SOMETHING) HAD ETCHED THESE WORDS-- "HIS SOUL, HIS OWN."

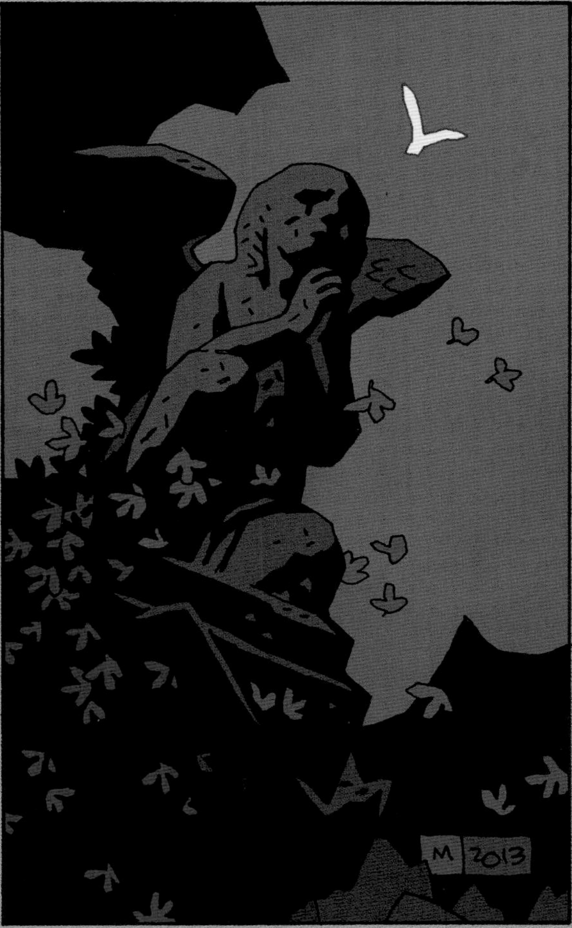
M 2013

THE END

WALTER EDMOND HEAP

Heap never achieved any real success as a painter. He is better
remembered as the author of *The Incredible Adventures of a Small
Mechanical Head* (1899) and its sequels, *The Mechanical Head
Returns* (1900) and *The Mechanical Head Returns Again* (1902). In
1911, while traveling in India, he was injured in a railway accident
and shortly thereafter eaten by a tiger.

SKETCHBOOK

Notes by Mike Mignola

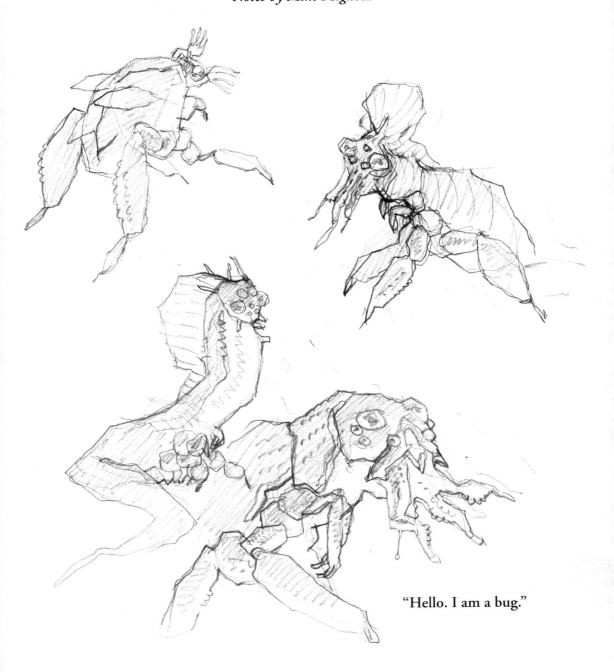

"Hello. I am a bug."

More bugs. The abyss is apparently full of giant, semitransparent bugs. These guys were a lot of fun to do, and I drew a ton of them before starting the book.

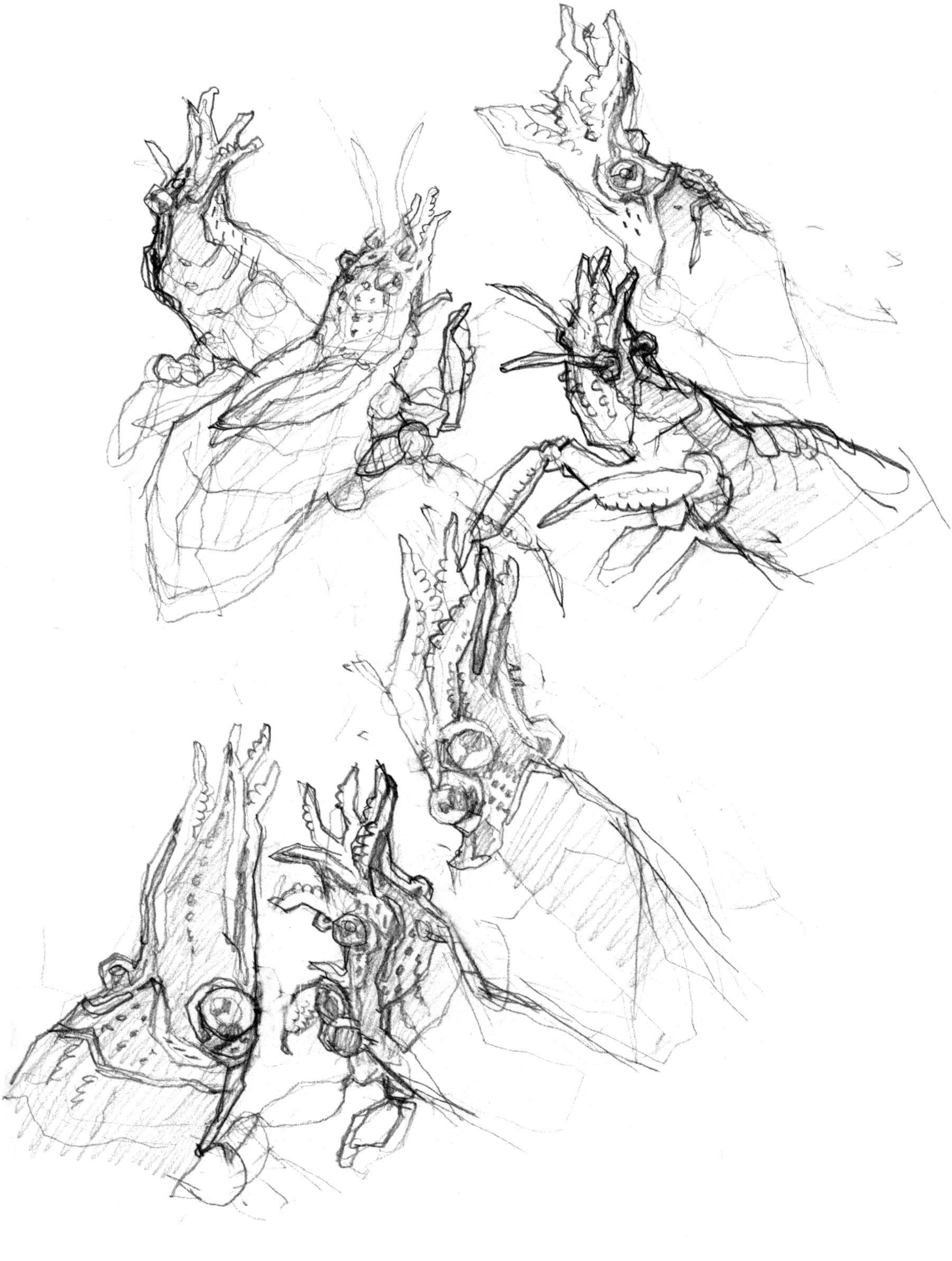

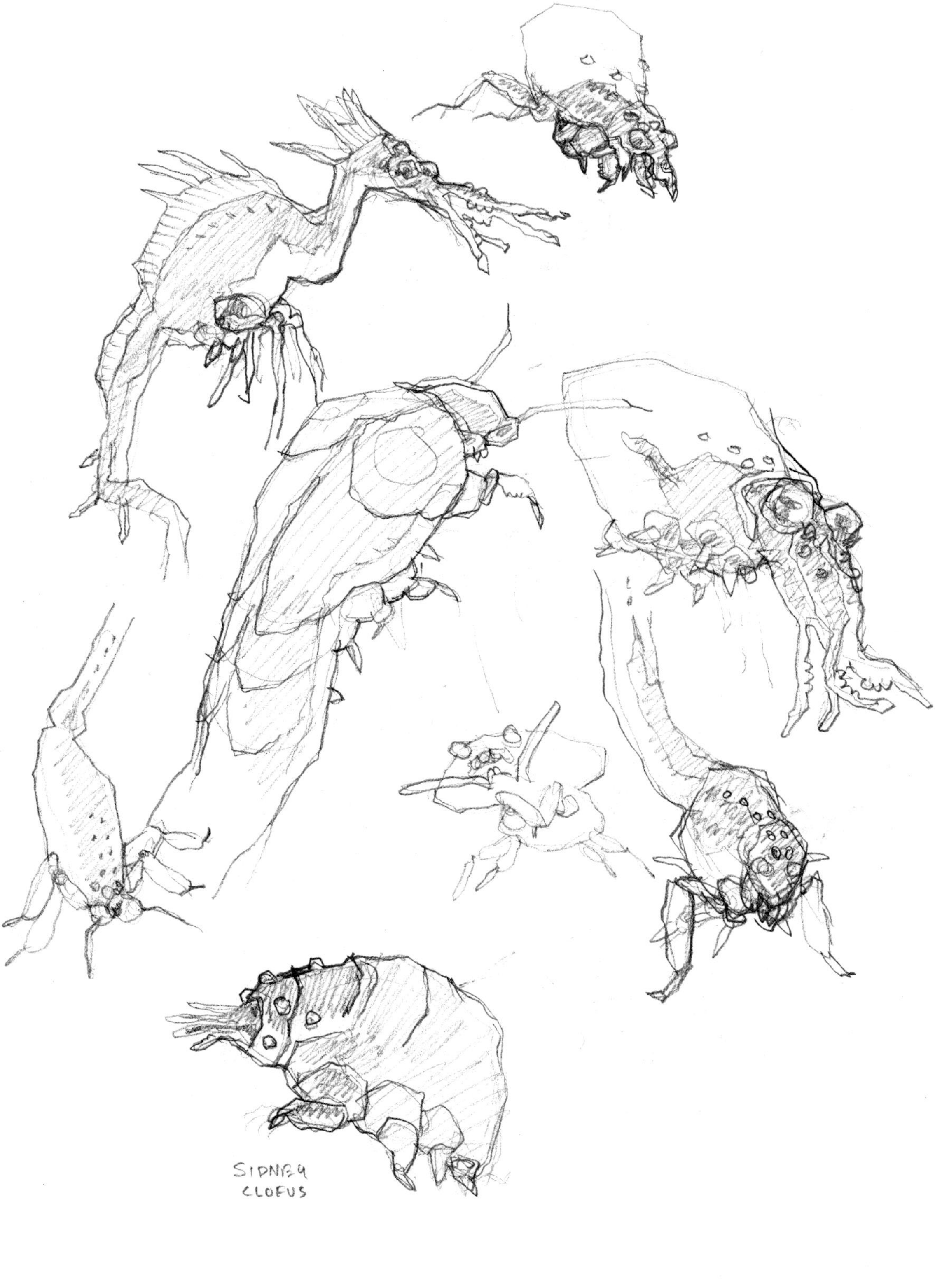
SIDNEY
CLOFUS

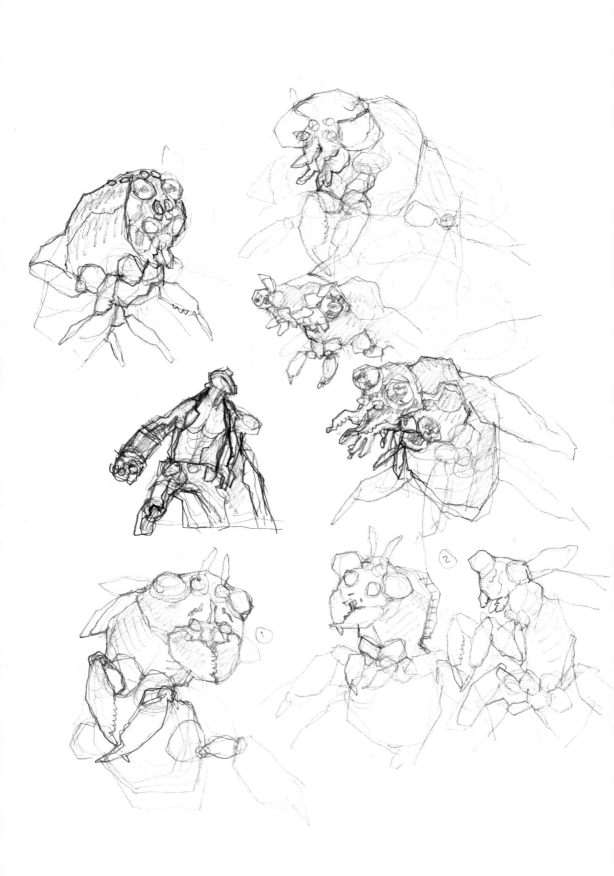

Also to be found in the abyss—Duke
Eligos. I originally intended to remove the
armor from his head, so we could see his
evil, burning skull. I like the big crack in
his face much better.

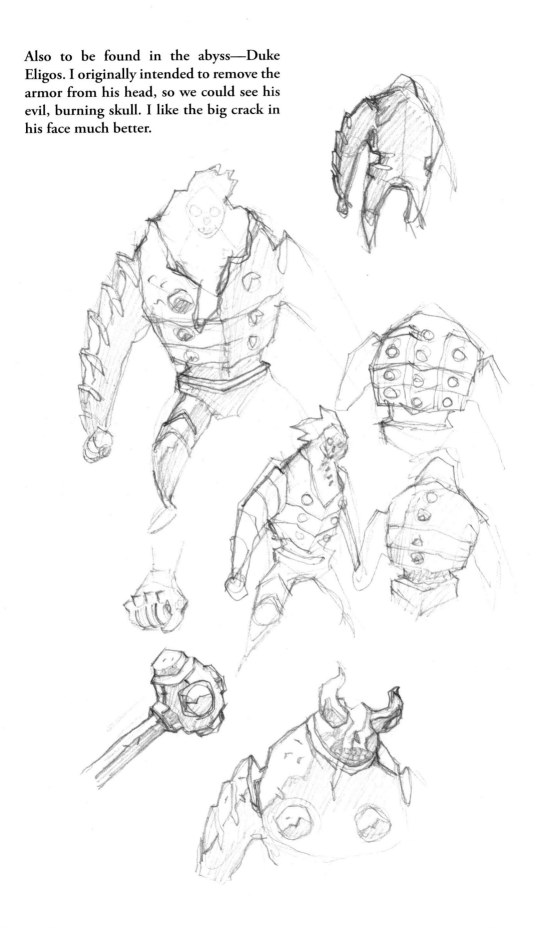

Sir Edward Grey.

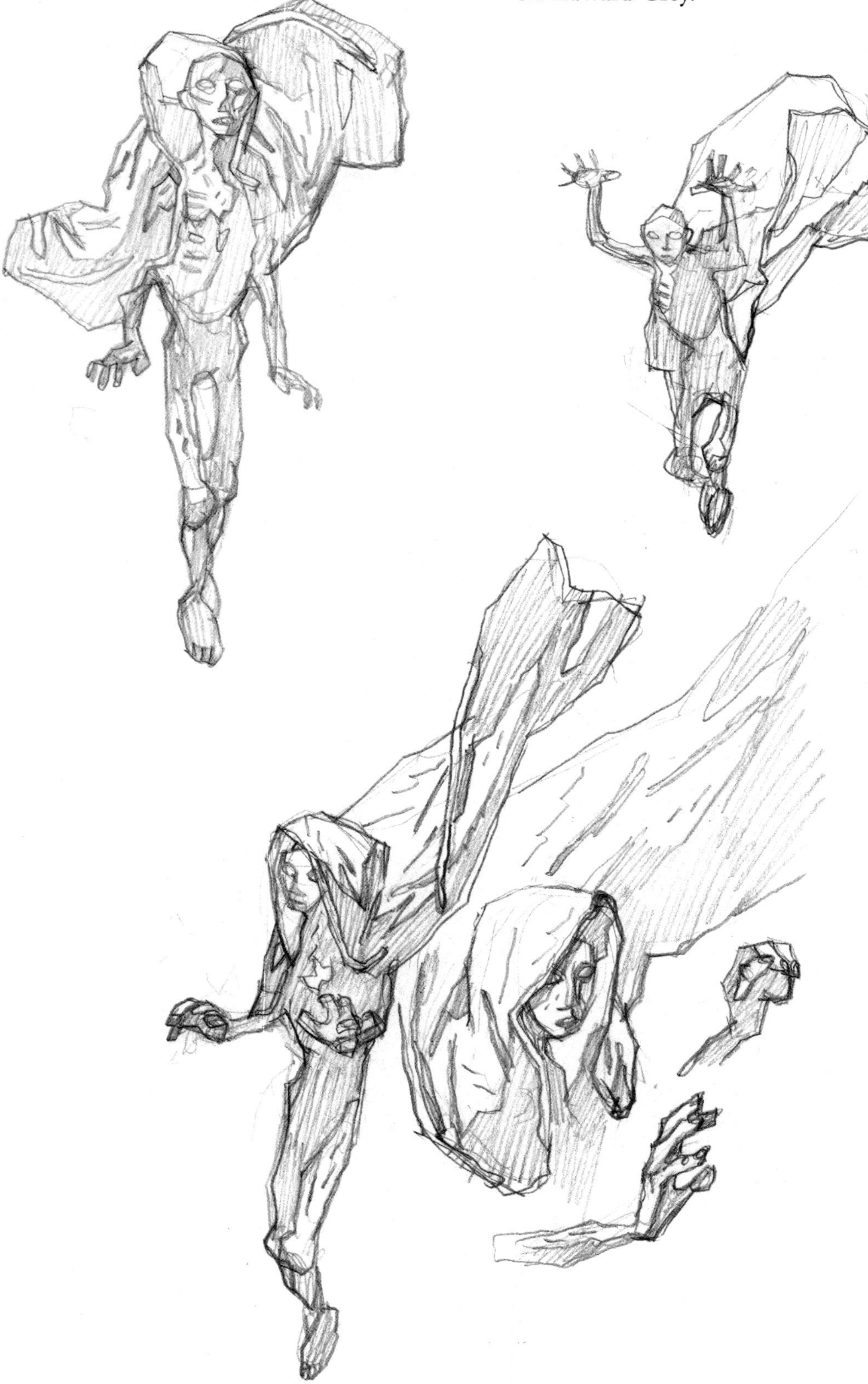

These sketches were actually done years before starting this book. I like that they include a diagram for how to *build* him.

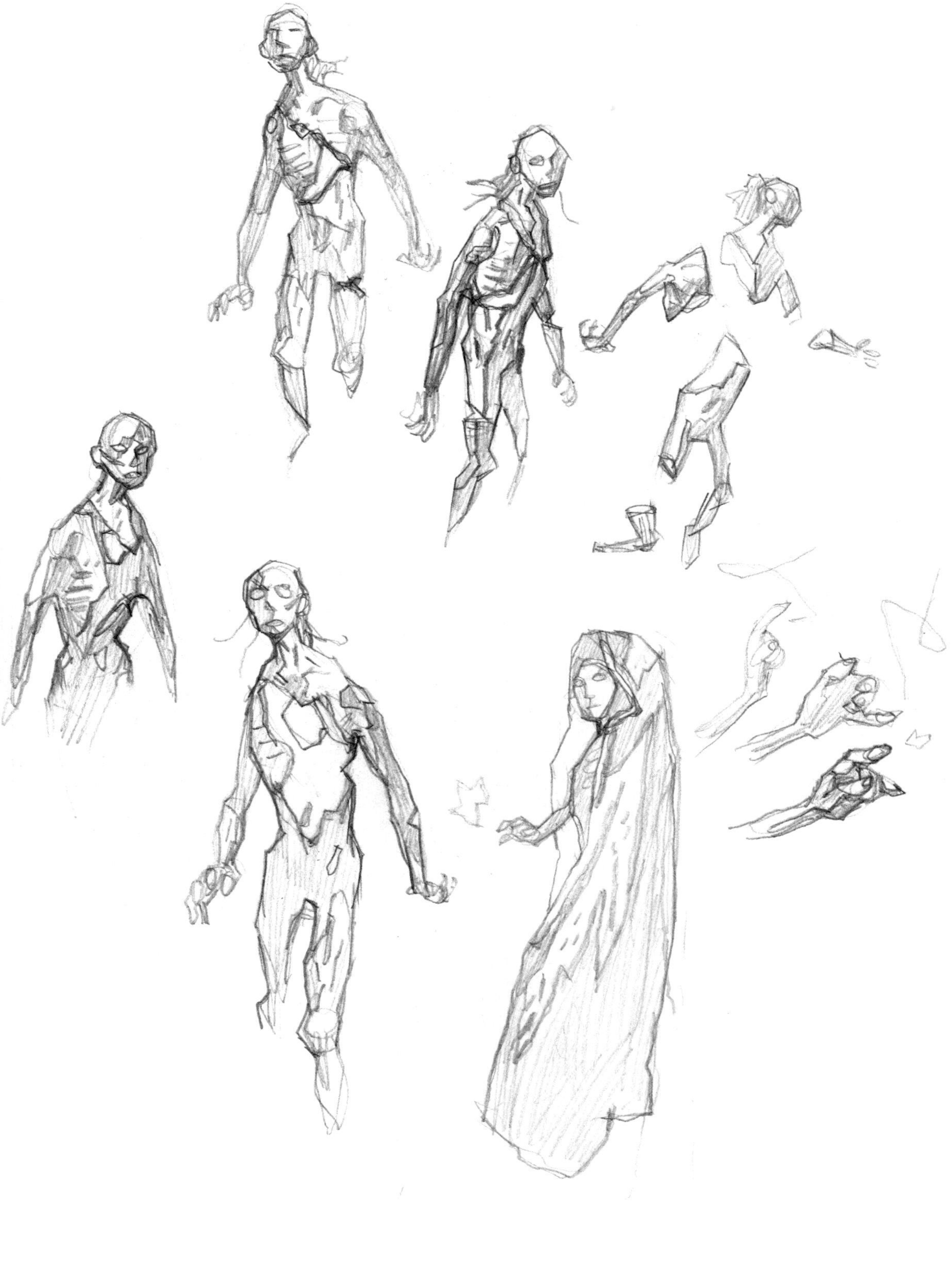

Statues.

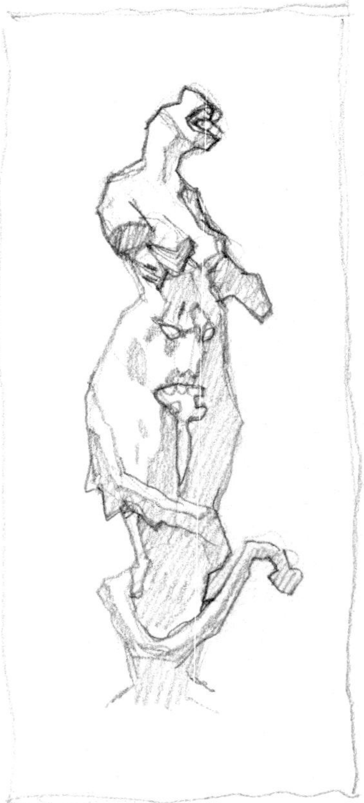

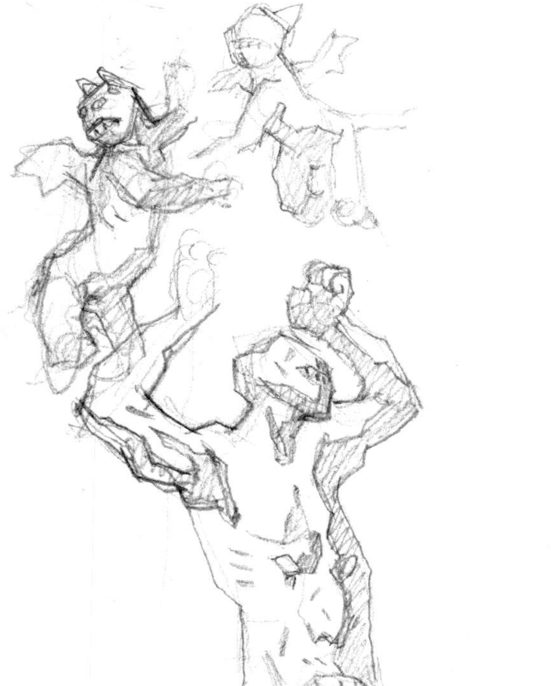

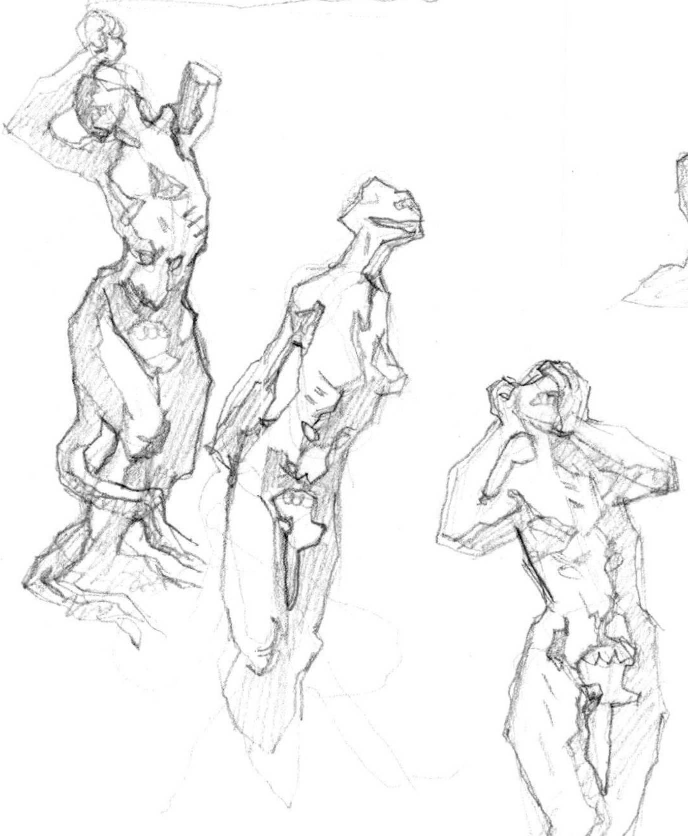

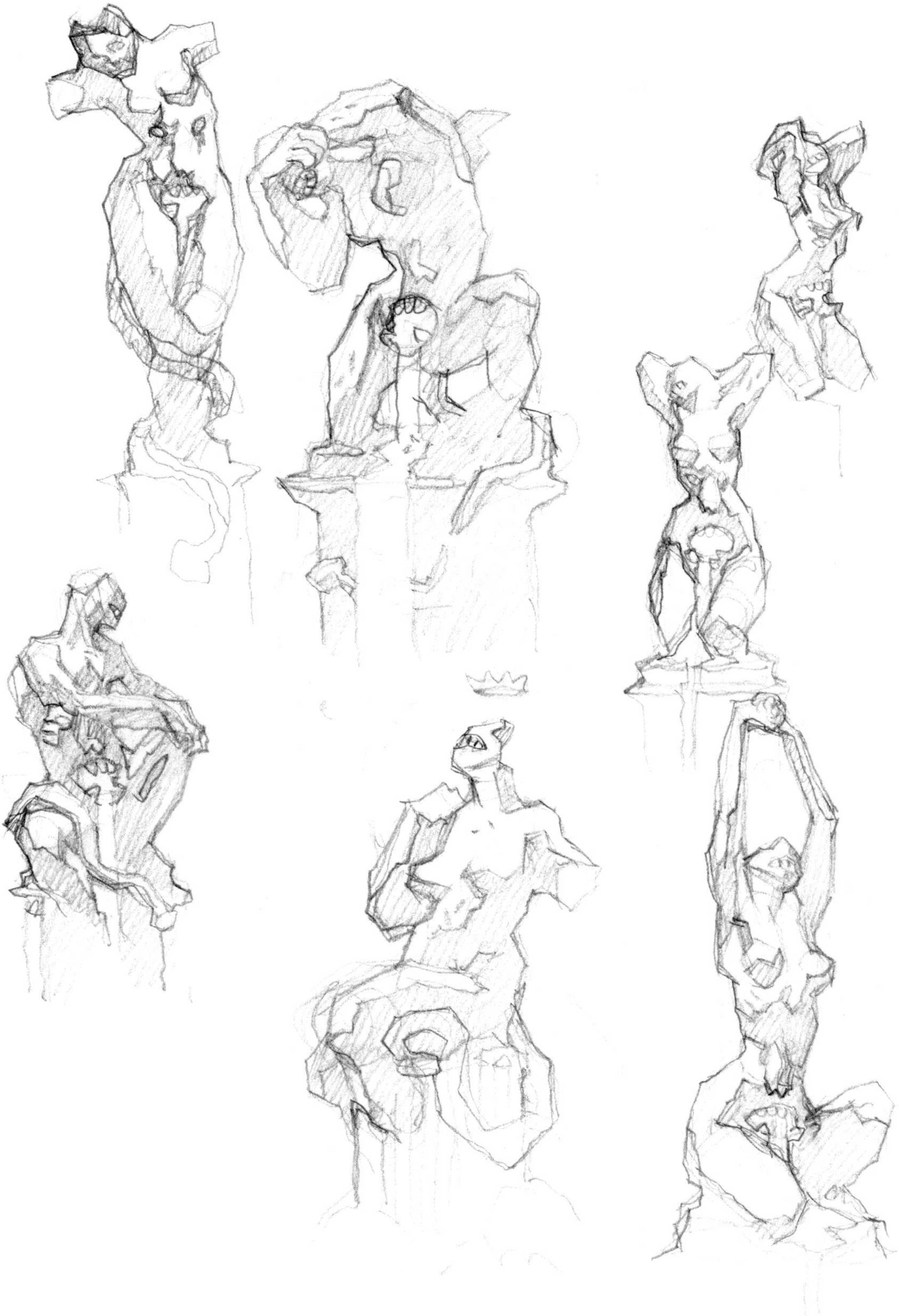

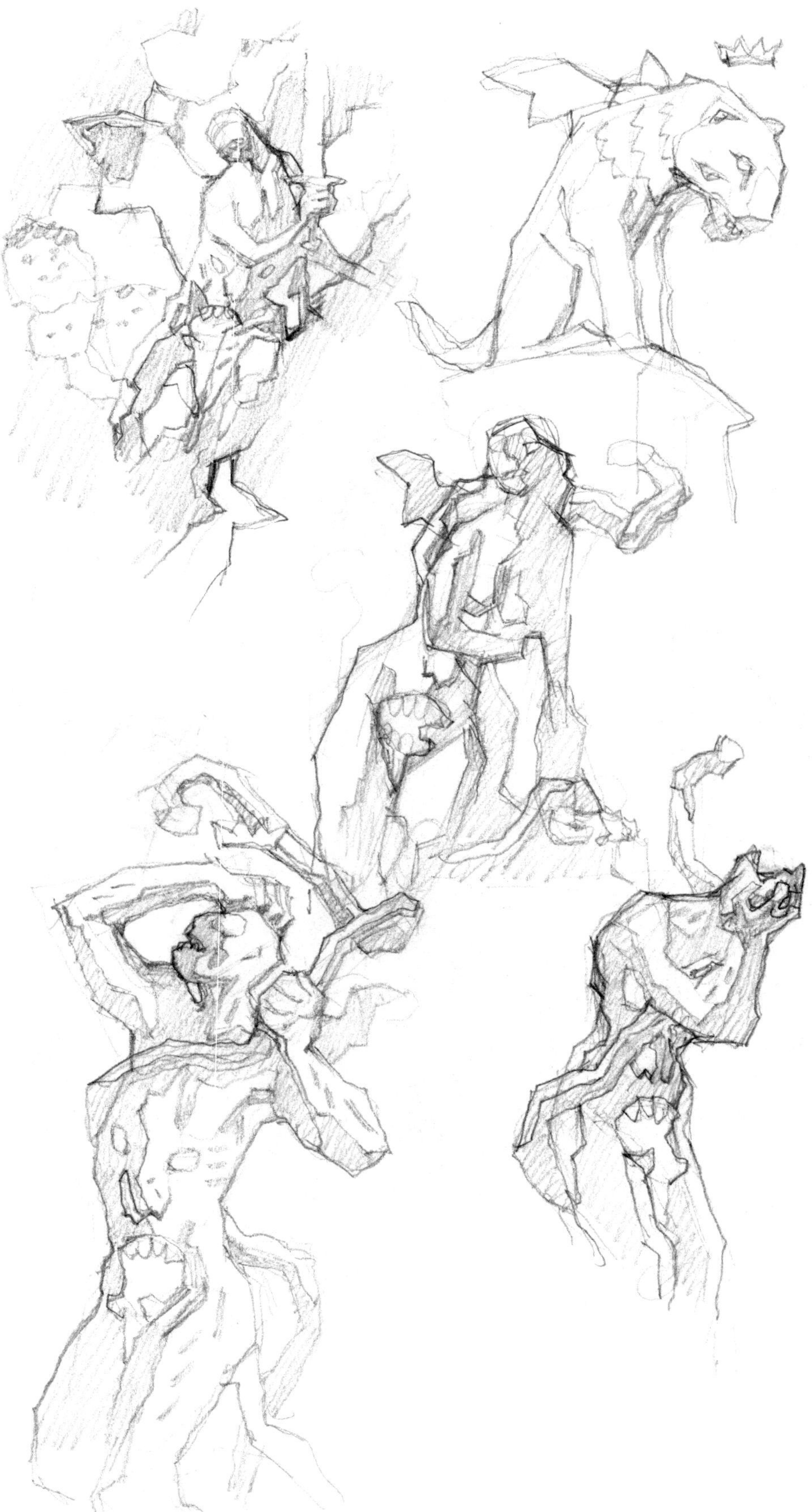

More statues.

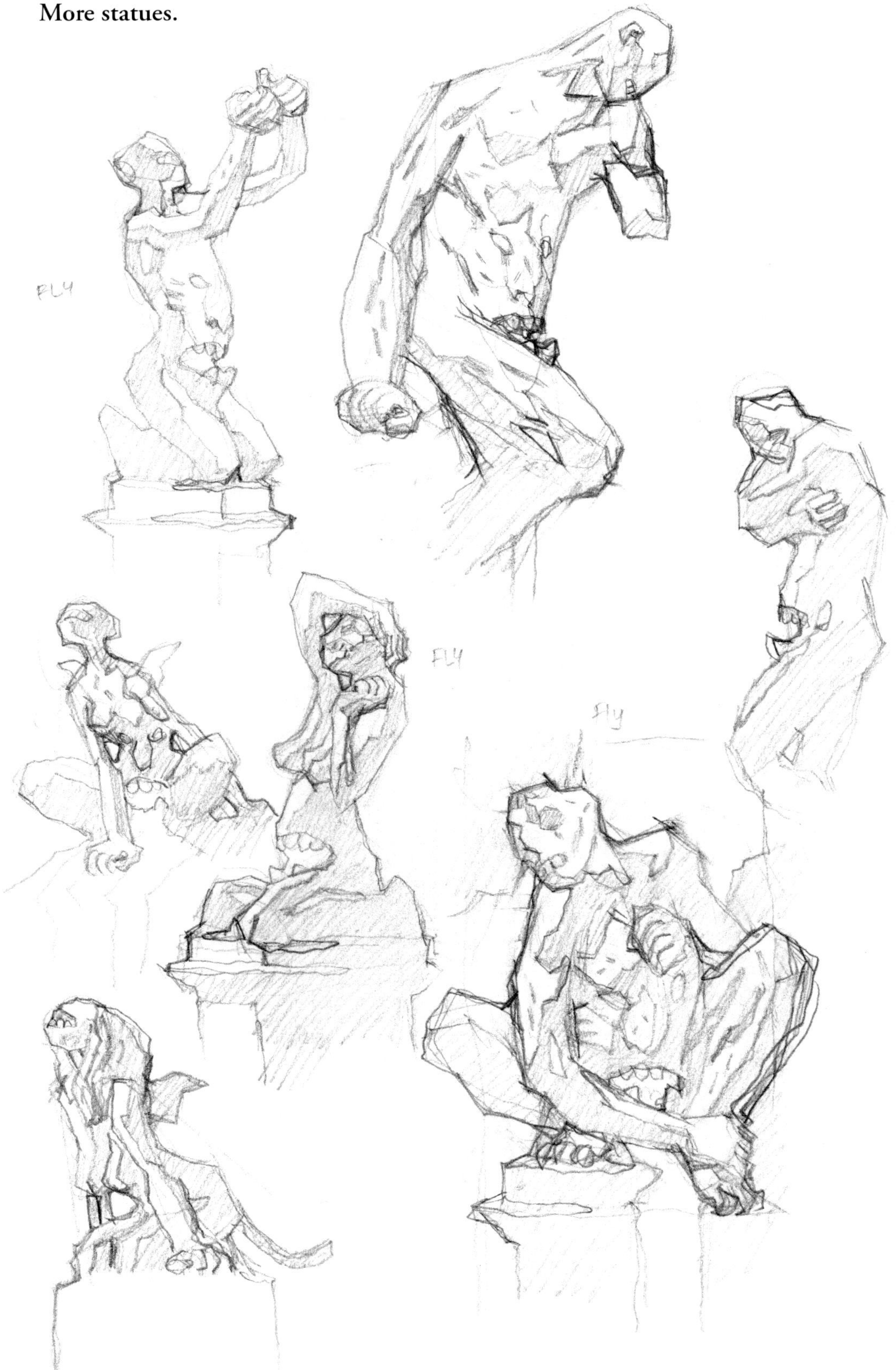
FLY
FLY
Fly

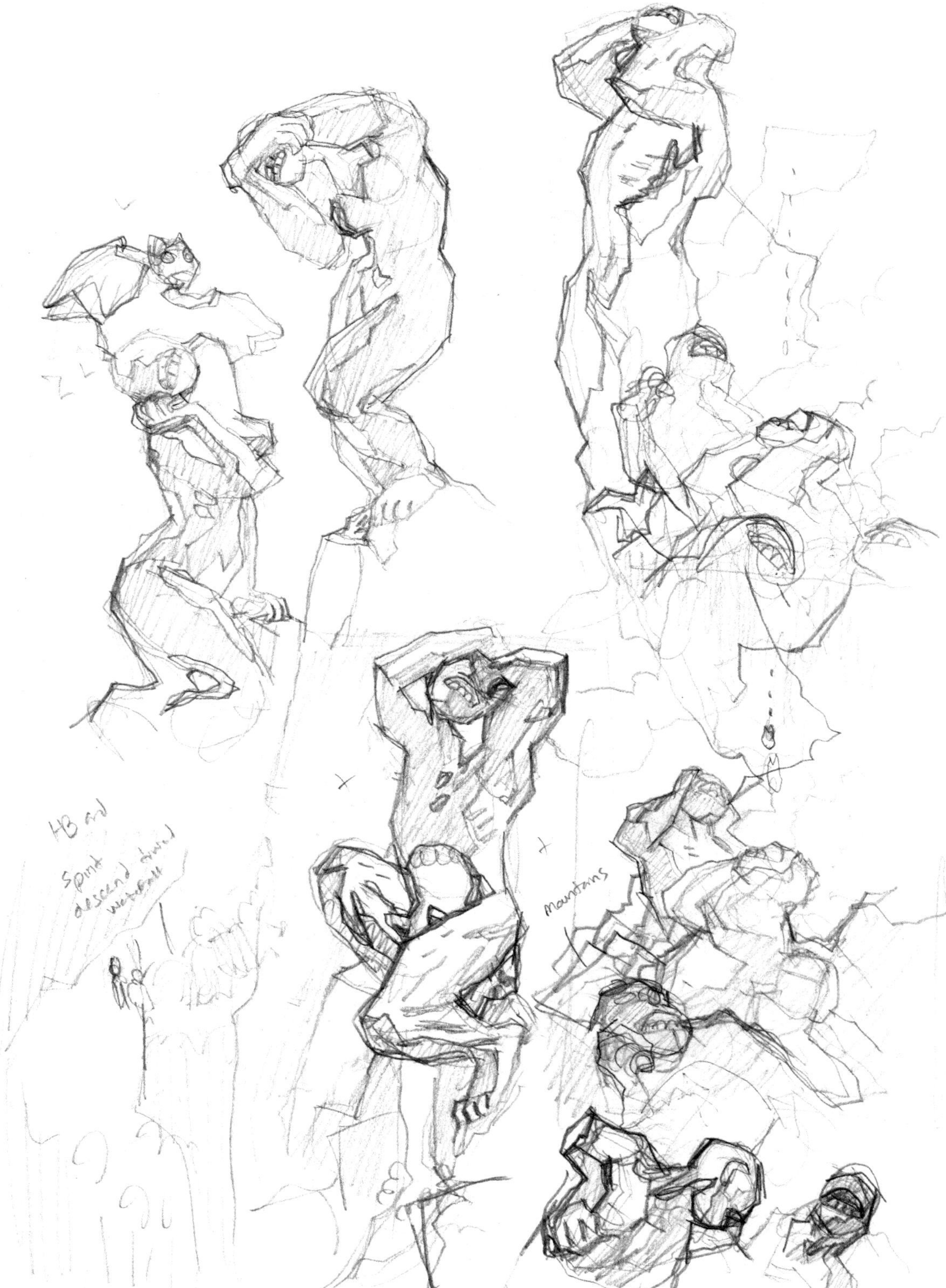
HB and
Spirit
descend toward
waterfall
mountains

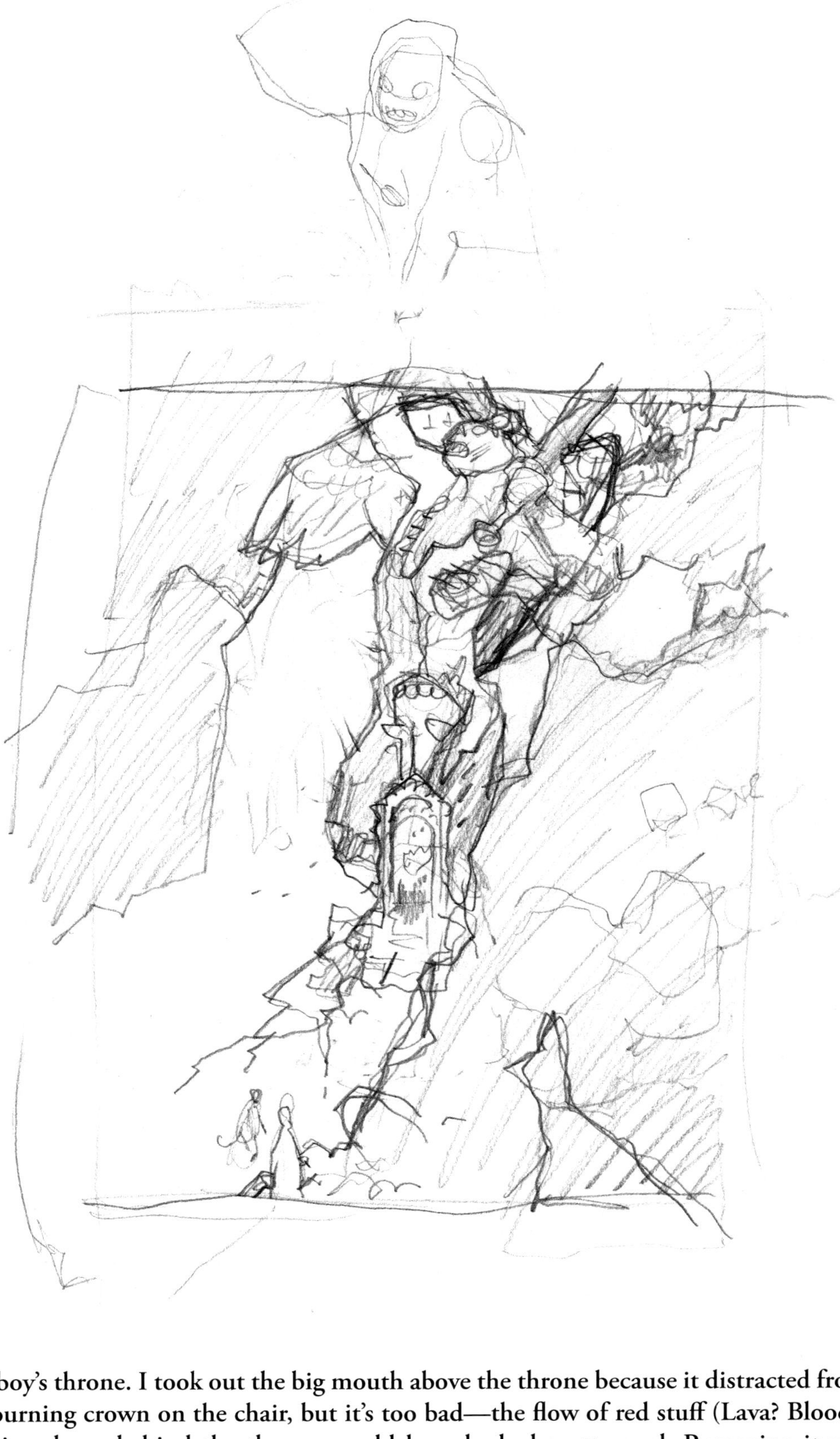

Hellboy's throne. I took out the big mouth above the throne because it distracted from the burning crown on the chair, but it's too bad—the flow of red stuff (Lava? Blood?) running down behind the throne would have looked pretty cool. Removing it was probably a mistake.

Leviathan.

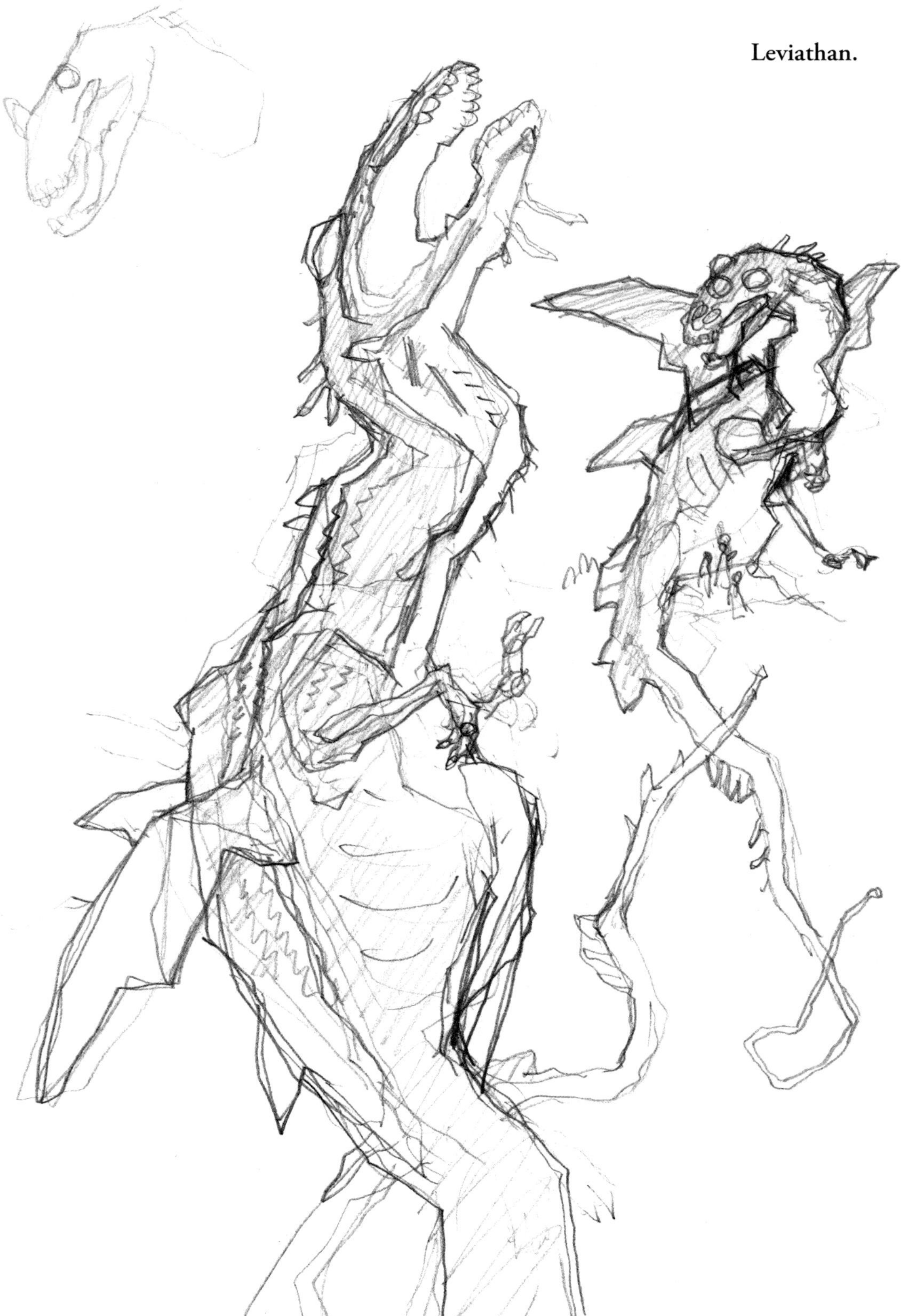

I did dozens of city studies like this before starting this series. Almost all the buildings are at least partially based on real buildings, and cobbling all the bits and pieces together was fun, but it took forever.

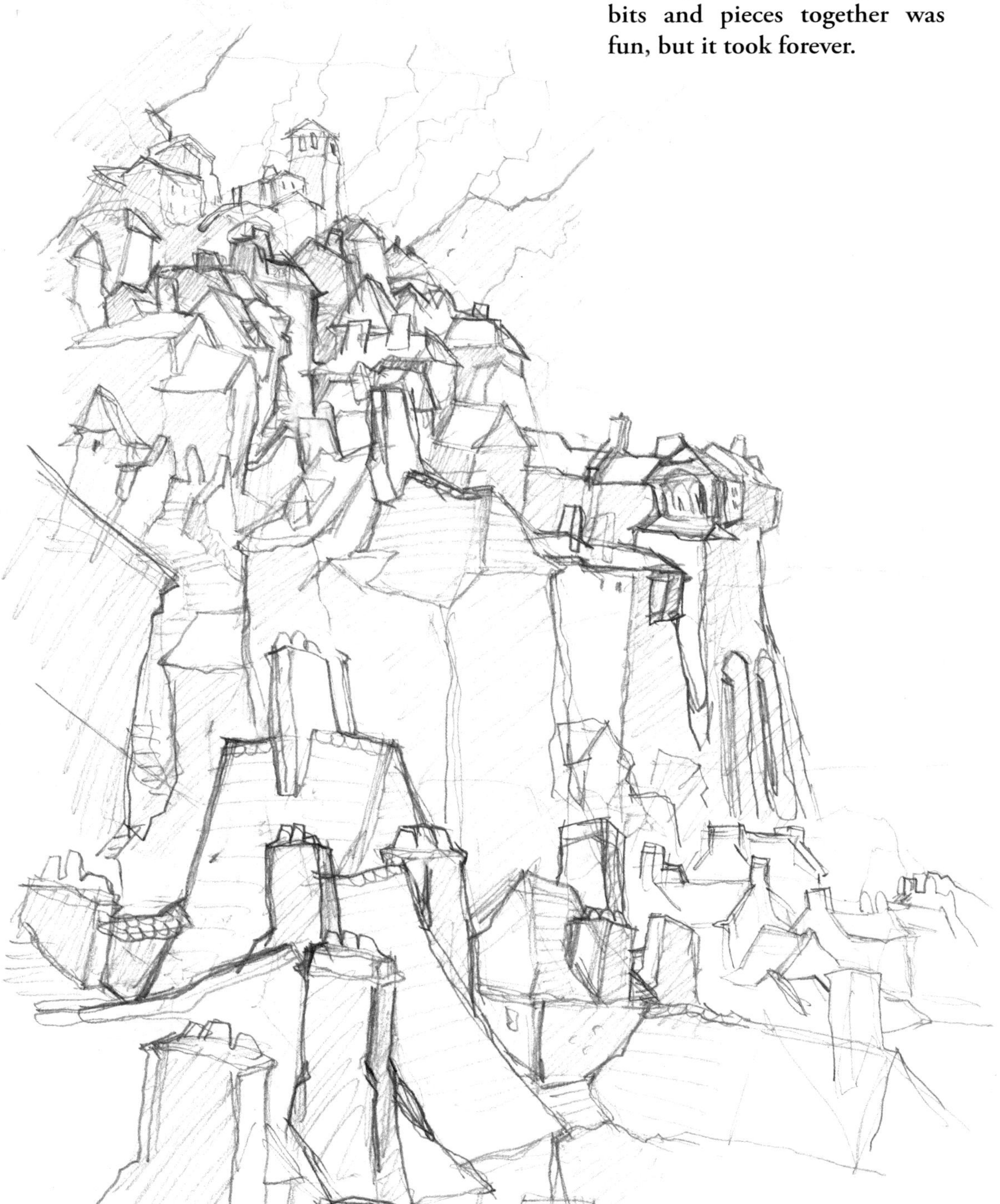

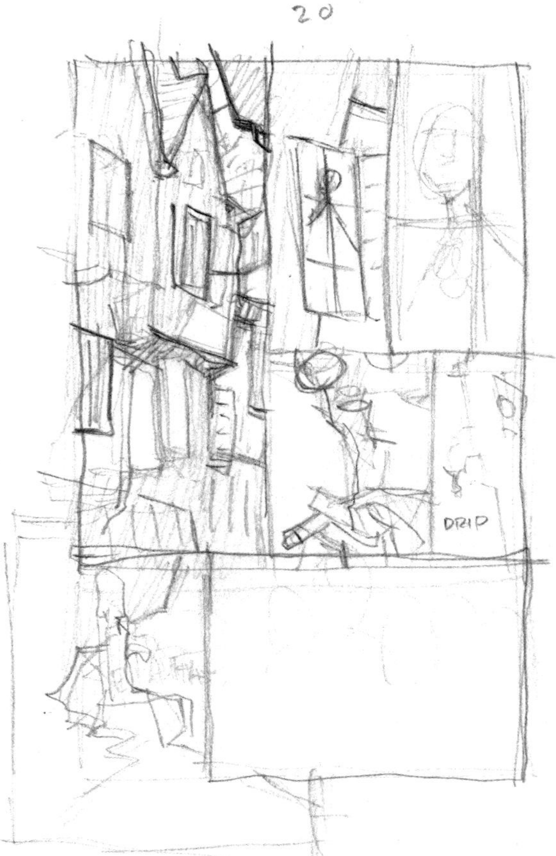
20
DRIP

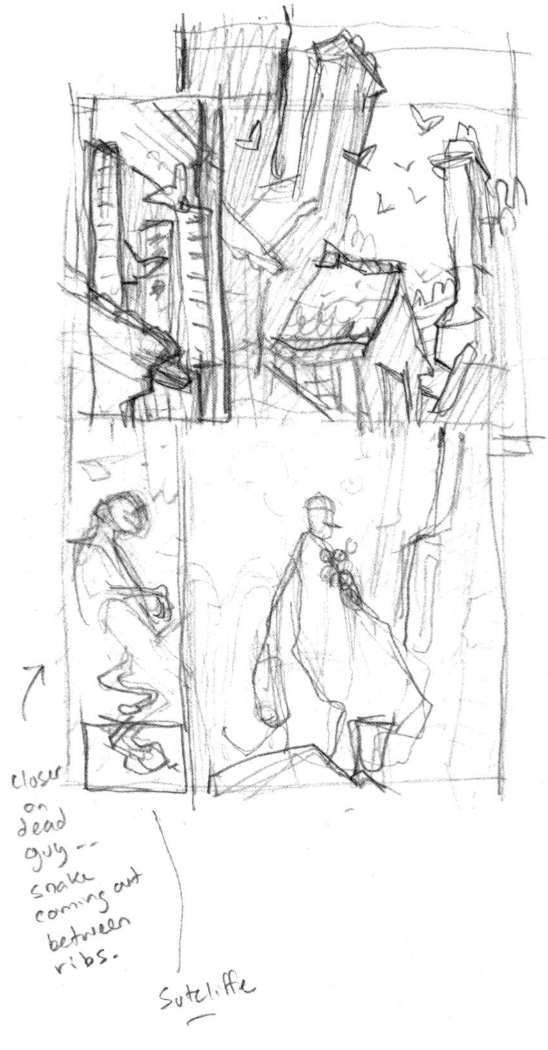
closer on dead guy -- snake coming out between ribs.
Sutcliffe

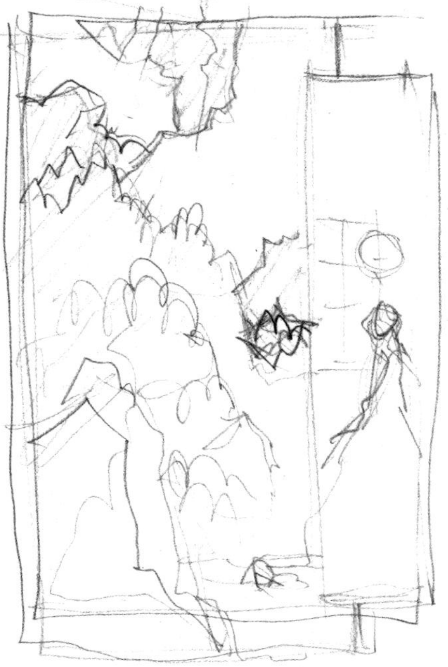

Studies for the last couple of pages of chapter 4. My thumbnails for most of the series were pretty loose and primitive—these drawings were done as I got close to drawing the actual pages.

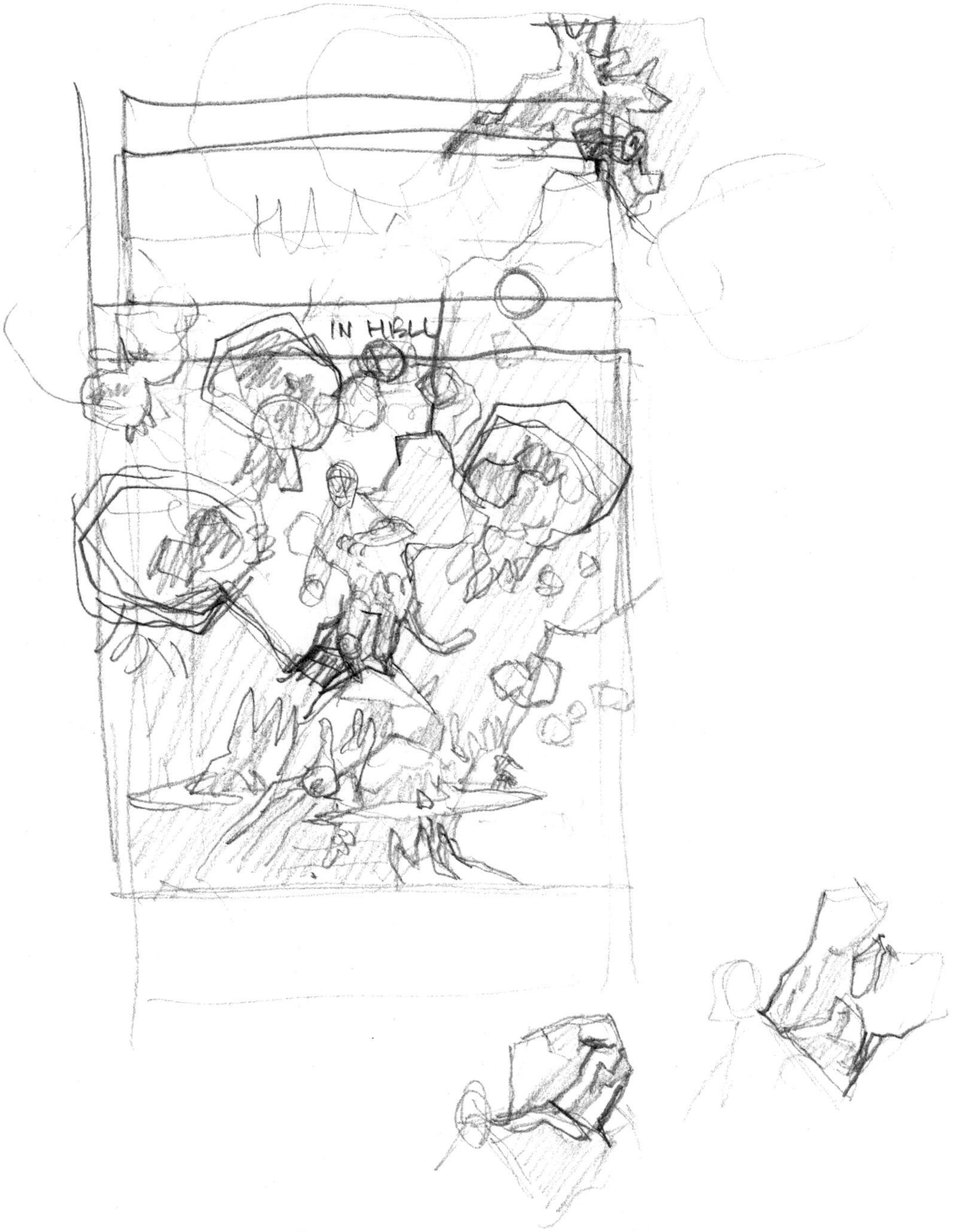

Study for the cover of issue one.

Following pages: Covers for issues one through four and the Year of Monsters variant cover for issue one.

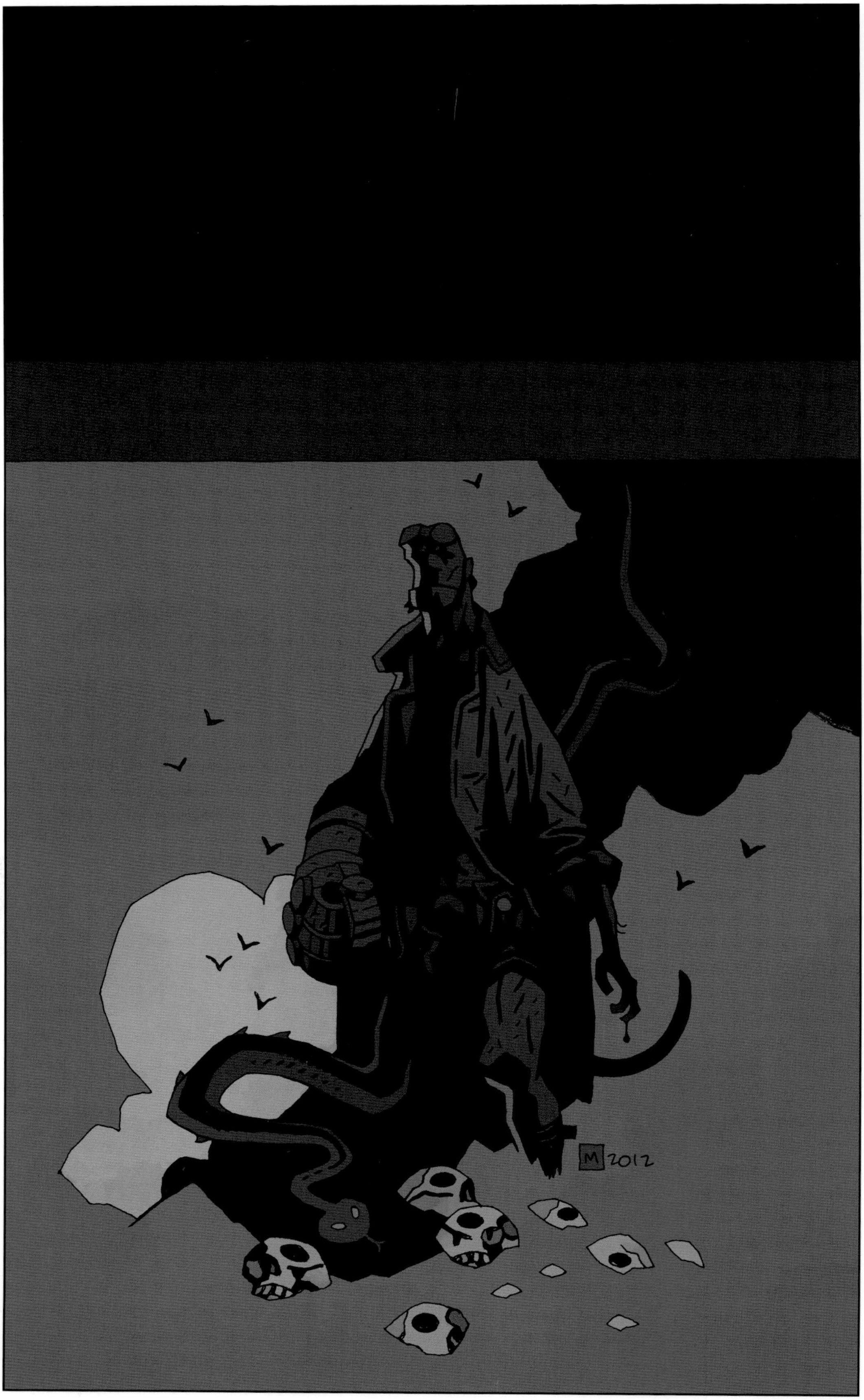
M 2012

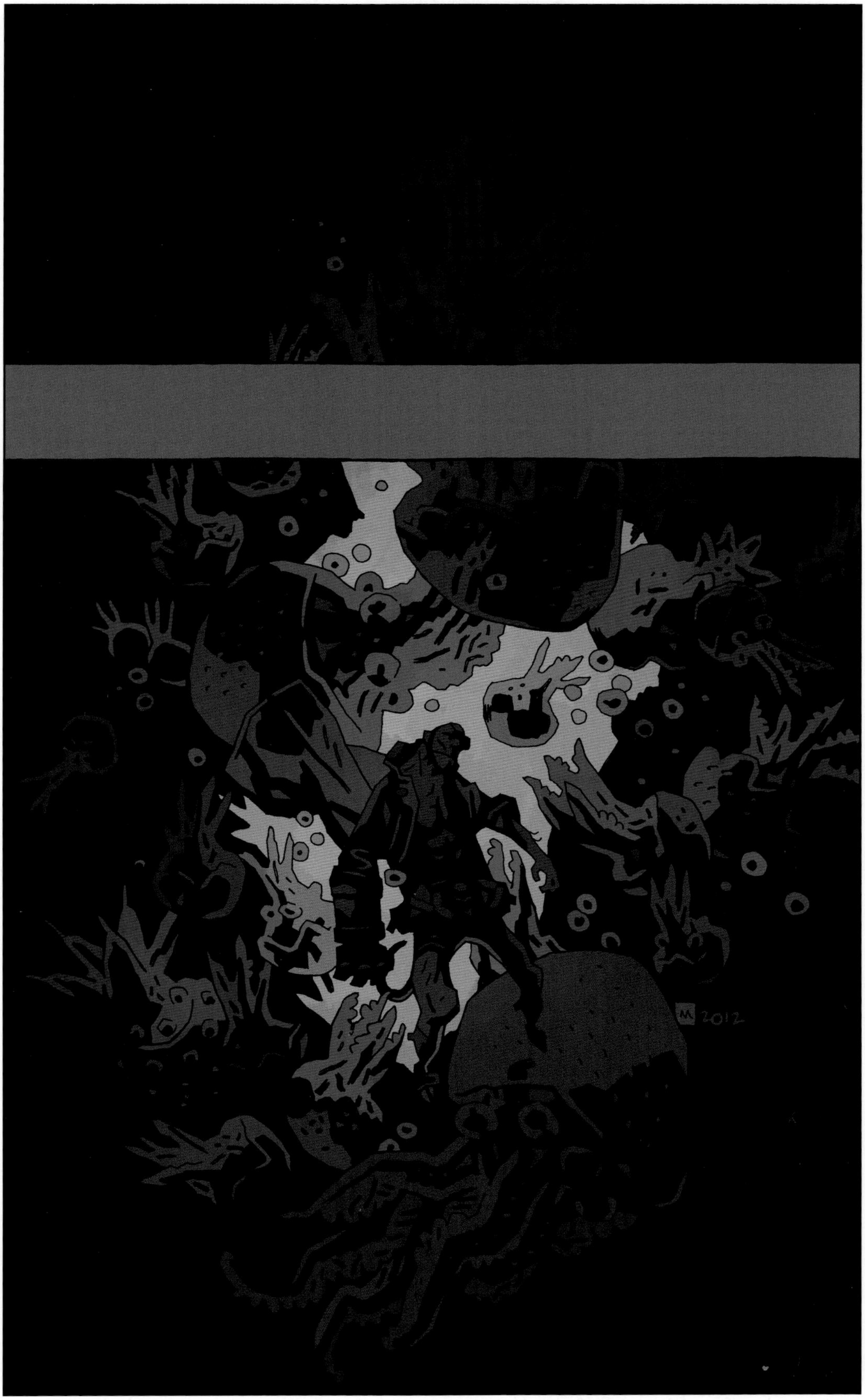
M 2012

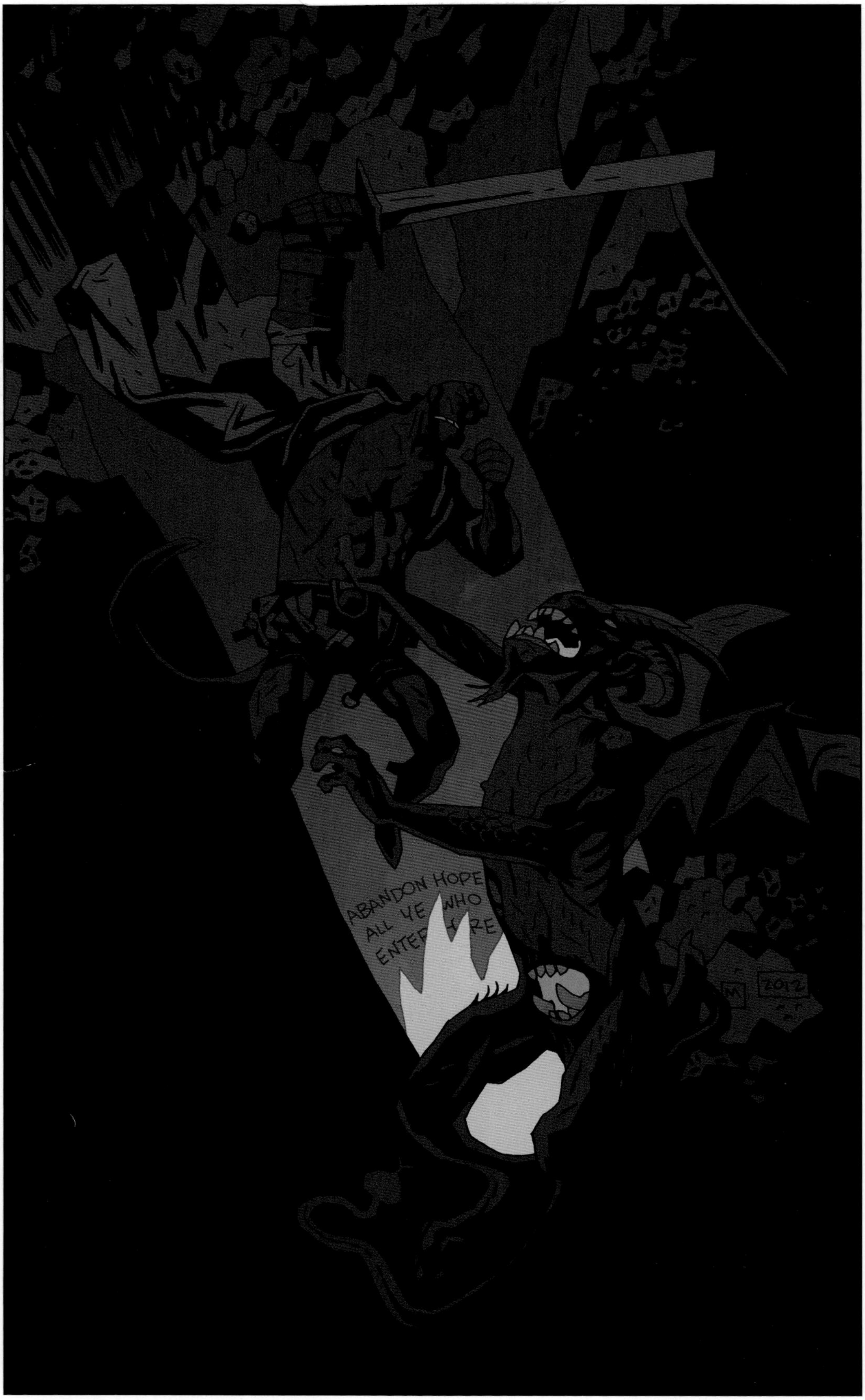
ABANDON HOPE
ALL YE WHO
ENTER HERE
M 2012